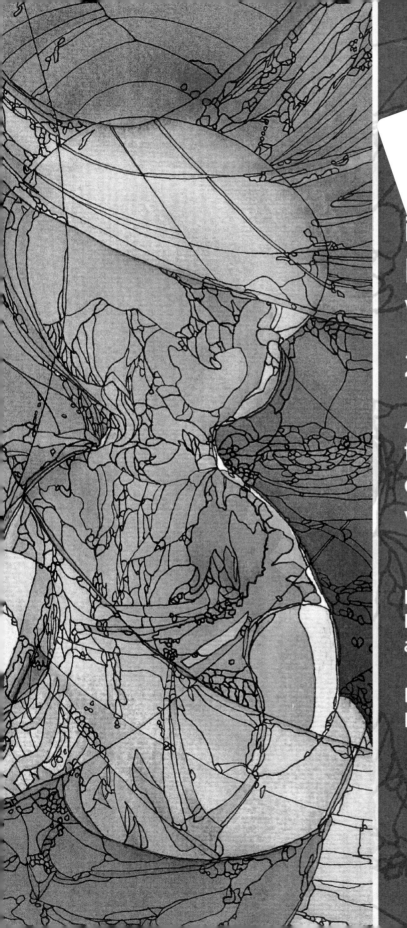

...arding
in a Public
Protection
World:

2nd Edition

A handbook
for protecting
children and
vulnerable adults

By
Russell Wate QPM
and Nigel Boulton

Foreword by
Lord Laming

Pavilion

Multi-agency Safeguarding, 2nd Edition
A handbook for protecting children and vulnerable adults

Published by:
Pavilion Publishing and Media Ltd
Blue Sky Offices, Cecil Pashley Way,
Shoreham by Sea, West Sussex
BN43 5FF
Tel: 01273 434 943
Email: info@pavpub.com

Published 2019

ISBN: 978-1-912755-38-7

Pavilion Publishing and Media is a leading publisher of books, training materials and digital content in mental health, social care and allied fields. Pavilion and its imprints offer must-have knowledge and innovative learning solutions underpinned by sound research and professional values.

Authors: Dr Russell Wate & Nigel Boulton
Production editor: Mike Benge, Pavilion Publishing and Media Ltd.
Cover design: Emma Dawe, Pavilion Publishing and Media Ltd.
Page layout and typesetting: Phil Morash, Pavilion Publishing and Media Ltd.
Printing: Ashford Press

The authors have kindly offered to donate all royalties from the sale of this book to two charities close to their hearts that work to safeguard vulnerable children: Embrace and Winston's Wish.

In aid of

Contents

Foreword

By Lord Laming, reproduced from the first edition of this book.

I am very pleased to make a small contribution to this important book. Its importance is due to the seriousness of the subject and reflected in the vast experience of the authors, Russell Wate and Nigel Boulton. The failure to consistently provide protection for the most vulnerable of children and adults is a scar on our society. This is all the more so because the legislation is both clear and comprehensive. From this sound basis it ought to be possible to identify early those who are potentially at great risk, and to intervene in ways that secure their well-being. The authors have drawn upon lessons from tragic events in the past, but it is encouraging that they have highlighted good practice and have demonstrated that the work can be both successful and a source of real professional satisfaction. This book is a practical guide to identifying tell-tale signs of danger and measures of intervention, along with risk assessment, multi-agency working and how successful law enforcement can work. The good news is that with the right vision, appropriate training, professional confidence and good leadership, it is possible to operate high-quality protection services.

Society has a responsibility to secure the safety and proper development of those who are in danger of exploitation, neglect or abuse. Each of the key public services has its own unique set of responsibilities. They cannot act as substitutes for the other. That is why inter-agency work is so essential. It is not enough for any agency to operate in isolation. Unless practitioners have the skill and confidence to work comfortably across organisational boundaries they are not suited to this work. The frontline professional in each of the agencies deserves our full support. The work not only demands professional knowledge and skills, but it can be emotionally challenging. Witnessing the exploitation and deliberate harm of a vulnerable child or adult can be most distressing. This is especially so when their relative weakness is being exploited by those who are in a position to provide care, support and guidance. Make no mistake, this is work that demands commitment, competence and personal toughness. But, when done well, it is also remarkably rewarding.

This book should be read by everyone involved in this work, be they on the frontline or in senior management. The authors have devoted many hours to its production. Their qualities are clearly demonstrated by their decision to devote their proceeds to charity, Embrace Child Victims of Crime and Winston's Wish. I do hope that others will respond by putting into day-to-day practice the sound instruction and guidance they have put before us. It gives me great pleasure to have this opportunity to warmly commend this book.

The Lord Laming

About the charities

The authors Russell Wate and Nigel Boulton and the contributors Marisa De Jager, Aelfwynn Sampson, Helen Murphy, Jody Watts, John Hodge, Duncan Sheppard, Sally Lester, Amy McKee and Paul Rollinson, have kindly agreed to donate all of their royalties equally to the two charities detailed below.

In aid of

Winston's Wish is a national childhood bereavement charity, supporting children, young people and their families – as well as the professionals supporting them – after the death of a parent or sibling. Founded in 1992, Winston's Wish was the first childhood bereavement charity to be established in the UK, and today continues to lead the way in providing professional guidance, information and practical support to bereaved children, their families and professionals, through its Freephone National Helpline, online support, face-to-face support, publications and training.

The charity gives parents, carers and professionals the tools to talk to children about what is happening and how they may be feeling when someone close to them is dying or has died, so that – over time – they may be able to make sense of it and learn to live with their loss.

Embrace Child Victims of Crime (CVOC) is a national children's charity solely focused on delivering emotional, practical and cheer-up support to children and young people, and immediate families, affected by serious crime including homicide in all its forms, violent crime and sexual abuse.

The charity offers a range of support for children and their immediate families to help them cope, recover and move on from life-changing trauma. Their support falls into four distinct areas:

Emotional: Embrace's young victim support officers provide a personal and dedicated service to children and families, working with them to identify the right package of care and keeping them informed and involved throughout.

Therapy: Their talking and listening therapy is delivered by an extensive network of specialist children's counsellors and they are developing a family-focused approach in this area and can also sometimes offer specialist therapies.

Practical: For households on low income, the charity can help fund items that will assist in the child's recovery such as household items, clothing or leisure pursuits, or equipment for schooling.

Well-being: Building confidence and happy memories through funded activities including theme park tickets, Euro Disney peer group support breaks and Christmas gifts that would otherwise be unobtainable.

With the right intervention, children impacted by crime can fulfil their potential and go on to lead healthy and happy lives. Visit the website today for more details www.embracecvoc.org.uk

About the authors

Dr Russell Wate QPM MSc

Russell has been an Independent Chair of various Safeguarding Children and Adult Boards for the last nine years. He has strong operational and strategic understanding of public protection having worked in the field for over 25 years; the first five of these were working jointly in operational settings with social care and other partners.

While working for central government he was a member of the team that produced the 2010 version of *Working Together*[1]. He was also a key member for the whole of Professor Munro's review of child protection in 2011.

He has recently been a member of the UEA and Warwick Universities team that produced, on behalf of Department for Education in 2019, *Complexity and Challenge: A triennial analysis of serious case reviews 2014-2017*. He was also a key member of Baroness Kennedy's working group that produced updated guidance in 2016 relating to the investigation of infant deaths. He has carried out numerous SCRs and DHRs all around the country and is a member of the national pool of SCR authors.

He is retired police officer who for the last six years of his service was the Detective Chief Superintendent for the Cambridgeshire Constabulary.

Prior to his promotion to Chief Superintendent he was responsible for the investigation into the recovery of the bodies of Holly Wells and Jessica Chapman, and was subsequently fully involved in the Bichard Inquiry. He has received 14 commendations from judges and senior officers for investigations he has led. He worked at a national level for government and the Association of Chief Police Officers (ACPO) in relation to policy and standards issues concerning the safeguarding of children, in particular as the national police lead for the investigation of child deaths.

In the 2008 Birthday Honours List he was given the honour by the Queen of the Queen's Police Medal for his work nationally, both as a detective and in safeguarding. He has a doctorate with his thesis on investigating child deaths.

---

1   www.gov.uk/government/publications/working-together-to-safeguard-children--2

Nigel Boulton MA

Nigel served as a police officer for 31 years. He spent most of his career as a Detective serving for 11 years as a Detective Superintendent leading and managing the investigation of Homicide and Serious and Organised Crime enquiries. He worked extensively in the UK and abroad. He spent the final three years of his service as the Head of Crime and Operations for a police command area spanning two local authorities.

It was during this period that he designed and delivered the original concept of Multi Agency Safeguarding Hubs, or MASH as it is widely known, the true design of which draws on his experiences dealing with risk assessment and decision making in relation to extremely sensitive intelligence. The model and concept is now used widely in the UK and in various locations across the world.

Since finishing service, he has run his own consulting company and associates network specialising in the design and delivery of true Multi Agency Safeguarding Hubs, which together with his social work partner he has continued to develop and evolve.

He is also partner in a safeguarding company that provides safeguarding expertise across the social work, policing and health sectors including the provision of social work practice improvement through a unique 'live learning' model. The organisation also works alongside the internationally renowned inclusive theatre company Chicken Shed, to raise the voice of the child by way of performing and creative art. This has allowed the child's voice and the lived experiences of children to be researched, which has in turn influenced national policy considerations for social work practice.

During his policing service he worked at the national level in relation to investigative interviewing, and during this time he created the 'Significant Witness' interview strategy and led the development of the interview advisor role.

As well as providing consulting services through his company and the partnership, he has supported the Local Government Association peer review process as a specialist peer in relation to safeguarding.

Lead contributor, social work consultant and chapter author

Marisa De Jager

Marisa is a practicing social worker with statutory operational and strategic management experience. She is passionate about effective social work practice, has a deep commitment to continuing professional development, investment in practice and building on transformational strength-based and reflective practice models that ensure prevention, diversion and intervention opportunities making a difference to children and young people's lives.

Marisa trained in South Africa, coming to the UK in 2003. While working in South Africa she experienced at first hand the need for innovation and community-based solutions to social work and societal issues.

Marisa provides specialist, experience-based social work and safeguarding consulting and is a partner in the safeguarding organisation Nib SharedVision. She has strong experience working with stakeholders, including service users, carers, families and communities to deliver change and quality improvements across systems.

Marisa designed and now leads the social work and safeguarding improvement programmes delivered by her organisation across the public sector. She regularly undertakes safeguarding reviews for the private, public, charity and museum sectors. She leads, motivates and inspires social workers and others across organisations ensuring the services provided are effective and responsive. Marisa is the main architect of the national and international #voc #childsvoice (Voice of the Child) campaign on social media platforms, and works in partnership with the theatre and dance company Chickenshed, ensuring inclusive child participation through the use of performing and creative arts intending to use children's voices to inform service design and evolution as well as social work practice improvement.

Marisa has presented at several national and international conferences including BAPSCAN in the UK and ISPCAN in Canada and The Hague.

Acknowledgements

Our thanks and recognition

We could not have produced this book without the help, support and guidance of family, friends and professional colleagues. We are hugely indebted to those who, with great enthusiasm and energy, penned individual chapters or were involved in their writing. We feel it appropriate because of their commitment to our project to identify them together with personal biographies.

Additional chapter authors

Aelfwynn Sampson (Chapter 6: Sexual violence, refreshed and additional content)

Aelfwynn Sampson is a DCI in Northumbria Police having previously served up to Detective Inspector in Durham Constabulary and has 20 years' policing experience, latterly specialising in Safeguarding and Serious Crime. In Northumbria Police she is lead for Child Protection and Child Death and is an accredited Senior Investigating Officer. Aelfwynn has been SIO for a number of high-profile cases including non-recent abuse by a female school teacher on young male pupils, sexual assault by a premiership footballer and a 'no body' homicide.

Helen Murphy (Chapter 6: Sexual violence, original content)

Helen Murphy is the Business Intelligence Manager for Northumbria Police, leading on performance management, academic research and evidenced based policing, and victim and community insight. Previously to this she worked in Durham Constabulary for over 10 years in a variety of roles. She was a Safeguarding Manager for four years, managing the Durham MASH, the ERASE (Educate and Raise Awareness of Sexual Exploitation) team who also problem solved repeat missing children and the preventative response to safeguarding. She was the strategic co-ordinator for domestic and sexual abuse ensuring the domestic and sexual violence action plans were implemented and co-ordinated across two community safety partnerships. She also held varied analytical roles including strategic analysis around safeguarding issues.

After graduating Sheffield University with a BSc Hons in biochemistry and an MA in biotechnology law, Helen worked as an analyst and analytical manager in the private sector before joining Durham Police in 2007 as a community analyst.

Jody Watts (Chapter 7: Internet safeguarding, refreshed and additional content)

Jody Watts first started working for Peterborough City Council in 2010 before joining the Peterborough Safeguarding Children Board in 2011, providing support in all areas of the Board's work including co-ordinating Serious Case Reviews, designing the Multi-Agency Performance Report and development of its website.

In 2015, Jody became the Communications and E-safety Lead for the Peterborough Safeguarding Children and Adults Boards where he developed and updated a range of communication resources. In 2016, Jody undertook an online safety survey with over 2,000 local children and young people, which sought to gain their views on what they are using online. In 2017, Jody became chair of the Cambridgeshire and Peterborough's Online Safeguarding Group and helped develop the Multi-Agency Online Safeguarding Strategy and guidance. Jody continues to offer expert advice to local professionals on the subject of online safety, and is currently working on a multi-agency training programme.

John Hodge (Chapter 7: Internet safeguarding, original content)

John Hodge joined Devon and Cornwall Constabulary in 1988 having served 11 years in the Royal Navy. He became a Detective in 1991 and was employed in a wide variety of investigative work, including Serious and Organised Crime, Human Trafficking and Drugs Importation.

In 2001, due to a recreational interest in computers and the internet, he was a founder member of Devon and Cornwall's Hi-Tech Crime Unit, tasked with investigating computer and internet facilitated criminality. During the following six years, he carried out investigations into child sexual abuse, fraud, hacking, race hate crime and cyber-attacks.

In 2007 he was seconded to the Child Exploitation and Online Protection Centre, where he was part of the Victim Identification Team, taking part in the successful identification worldwide of a total of 107 victims of child sexual abuse whose images had been located on the internet. John has carried out investigations and training on behalf of Interpol, Europol, the EU and other national and international law enforcement and judicial organisations.

He retired from the police service in July 2011 and joined the British Recorded Music Industry as Head of Internet Investigations. This combined his professional and recreational interest in computer technology with his love of modern music.

Duncan Sheppard (Chapter 8: Multi Agency Public Protection Arrangements (MAPPA))

Duncan has 30 years' experience as a Suffolk Police Officer, and has spent the last three years working as the National Police lead for the Multi Agency Public Protection Arrangements (MAPPA), which is responsible for strategic policy, expert advice and quality assurance of serious case reviews and the implementation of the new national police risk framework, known as ARMS. He has 15 years' experience working in multi-agency safeguarding specialising in child abuse investigations, child sexual exploitation and sex offender management.

In 2016 he set up Sheppard Associates Ltd and has become a national and international multi-agency trainer in safeguarding, sex offender management, interviewing skills and risk assessments. He has conducted reviews for police forces and other countries into their procedures and operations to do with MAPPA, child sexual exploitation and information exchange, including serious case reviews in the UK. He has worked with a number of large charities improving their safeguarding structures, policy and procedures.

Sally Lester (Chapter 8: Multi Agency Public Protection Arrangements (MAPPA))

Sally Lester qualified as a probation officer in 1981 and worked in field teams, a probation hostel and a young offender's institution before undertaking a range of management roles, latterly as Assistant Chief Officer in North Yorkshire. She has worked for HMI Probation since 2004, and from 2011 as HM Assistant Chief Inspector, leading the inspection of work with adult offenders, and most recently as head of inspection of the National Probation Service.

Sally has had a long-standing interest in public protection and learning the lessons from serious incidents. In her role in HMIP she has reviewed cases where serious further offences have been committed.

In 2014, Sally was seconded to NOMS for a year as joint head of the MAPPA team and NOMS lead on ViSOR. For the last 15 years she has also been involved in development work with other jurisdictions where probation services are being introduced, including Turkey, Bulgaria, Croatia, Albania, Georgia, Macedonia and the Ukraine.

Sally is currently a member of the Greater Manchester independent police ethics committee.

Dr Amy McKee (Chapter 11: Channel: safeguarding individuals vulnerable to radicalisation)

Amy McKee is a clinical psychologist based in the North West of England providing risk assessments, management advice and consultancy and treatment interventions. She has extensive experience in working with offenders who present with complex forensic and mental health needs.

She provides training to specialist investigation and interviewing courses with a focus on understanding the offender. She has provided advice on media appeals, investigative interview strategies and downstream monitoring support to police forces throughout the UK on a number of major inquiries.

Amy has worked closely for a number of years with the Counter Terrorism Policing UK, providing consultation services, risk and threat assessments, interview advice and training and research.

Paul Rollinson (Chapter 11: Channel: safeguarding individuals vulnerable to radicalisation)

Paul Rollinson is a Detective Inspector working for Counter Terrorism Policing North West. His operational portfolio includes extensive experience in the investigation of serious and complex crime, the safeguarding of vulnerable children and adults and counter terrorism policing.

As a Detective Inspector for the Counter Terrorism Policing North West he has worked on the implementation of 'Channel', a Home Office initiative aimed at reducing the risk of radicalisation among vulnerable individuals.

Through effective multi-agency working with strategic partners across Greater Manchester's 10 local authority areas, this agenda has been successfully mainstreamed into local safeguarding practices for children and adults.

While studying for his MA in Police Science and Management, he completed his dissertation on Channel, specifically looking at its effectiveness in reducing the risk of radicalisation. This work was nationally recognised and he was awarded the National Imbert Prize.

Contributors to chapters

Estelle Thain

Estelle Thain is an advanced practitioner currently working in the sexual exploitation team in Peterborough. Estelle qualified as a social worker in July 2009, gaining a first-class BA Hons in social work at Northampton University. Estelle's first post as a social worker was in Cambridgeshire in the intake and assessment team and after almost two years, in July 2011, Estelle left Cambridgeshire to work in Peterborough.

She started in Peterborough in the family support team and in January 2012 was seconded into the child sexual exploitation team. In November 2012, Estelle was awarded 'Children's Social Worker' and 'Overall Social Worker of the Year', and in May 2014 Estelle received a safeguarding children's award from the LSCB for her work with young people who have been sexually exploited. Estelle is married and has five children, between 25 and six years of age, all of whom are very patient and supportive of her social work career.

Helen Foster

Helen Foster has been a practicing midwife since 1983. While working as a community midwife she developed a passion and intense interest in improving both the health and social outcomes for mothers and their babies. This led to a changing in the direction of her career from mainstream midwifery practice to undertaking a specialist midwifery role, caring for women with complex needs. On a personal level she underwent a very steep learning curve, having to gain extensive knowledge of public health agendas and safeguarding procedures.

In 2010 she was honoured to receive two awards for her work, first receiving a highly commended award in the National All Party Parliamentary Awards and an award from the Trust for Living the Values. Both were in recognition for her work with women with complex needs.

Joanne Early

Joanne Early is the Homicide Regional Manager for London at Victim Support and oversees a team of case workers who support people bereaved by homicide. She has extensive experience in supporting people through traumatic situations and previously had a 12-year career with the London Ambulance Service as a control service manager. She has been instrumental in not only making positive changes in support for bereaved families but also influencing change within other criminal justice departments. In 2018 she was commended by the Metropolitan Police Assistant Commissioner for her role in organising support for the bereaved after several terror attacks in London.

Joanne also provides multi-agency training to all professionals involved in the chain of child protection and criminal justice systems. She has worked with some of the top experts in the country including senior police officers, counter terrorist police, clinical psychologists, local authorities, safeguarding boards, hospitals and the media.

Sam Hunt

Sam Hunt has been a registered general nurse since 1992. During her time nursing, Sam has undertaken a multitude of roles including practice development, Ward Sister and Matron. In 2005, Sam took over as assistant general manager for maternity, children, neonates and safeguarding children. During this time she gathered a wealth of experience in both children and, specifically, safeguarding. Sam commenced her current role in 2011, which includes leading and managing a children and neonatal service within the Acute Trust. This role also includes the title of Named Nurse for Safeguarding Children. Sam undertakes safeguarding supervision, debriefing and training along with a clinical role.

Support to the book

We were also supported by and are very grateful to the following colleagues who either contributed sections and examples to the text, critically read parts of the manuscript from a professional perspective or helped identify documents and texts which may be of use to those who pick up the book with the intention of widening their knowledge of public protection.

David Marshall QPM, Dr Emilia Wawrzkowicz, Jody Watts, Angela Whitaker, Deidre Reed, Joanne Procter, Rachel Maloney, Kirstie White and Gwenton Sloley.

And finally…
We wish to thank our families for their patience and support, in particular Russell's wife Deborah, who has become his personal editor; Mary Boulton, for her patience and critical support to her husband; and Rebecca Boulton, for her amazing proofreading skills.

Introduction

By Nigel Boulton and Russell Wate

Public protection, like most things in professional life, is subject to change. Change in the context in which it must operate; change brought about by research; and change created through innovation, energy and commitment.

The first edition of this book gave practitioners of whatever profession an overview of the complex and very different areas of public protection practice. It translated the processes, guidelines and language used, to enable them to have a workable understanding of the varied areas of practice that may impact their own working lives. As well as exploring the law and guidance for each, it identified key learning points and case studies to assist practitioners to better understand the world of public protection in all its guises.

Any practitioner who begins work in the difficult and unique professional arena of public protection feels that they are entering a different world, made up of its own unique processes and guidelines, and which, on many occasions, appears to have a language all of its own.

This second edition builds on this successful and well-received format by not only updating the content in line with changes to legislation, statutory guidance and best practice, but also includes new content that identifies new ways of thinking and delivering safeguarding practice, which we believe are important and need to be considered by all safeguarding professionals. This book, as before, is intended to be useful to all professionals, regardless of their role, experience or status within the public, private and voluntary sectors, who may need a swift and important insight into a professional world that they may not be wholly conversant with.

The book aims to cover all the main safeguarding areas. These range from working with children, adults at risk and domestic abuse, as well as trying to understand safeguarding in relation to the internet. It introduces for the first time the subject areas of 'children living in special circumstances' and contextual safeguarding (risk beyond the family), as well as drawing greater focus on the importance of Early Help provision.

This revised edition, as before, looks at sexual violence and understanding processes that deal with both dangerous individuals and sex offenders. It considers issues of safeguarding where there may be the possibility of radicalisation, and it updates on the long-awaited changes to the law in relation to the 'Deprivation of Liberty: Authorisation of arrangements enabling care and treatment' of a cared-for person over 16 years of age. The chapter on 'intelligence led safeguarding', together with the Multi Agency Safeguarding Hub (MASH) model, has been revised to provide an understanding of how the concept has evolved to a needs analysis model that ensures all need, harm and risk is identified, enabling the most appropriate prevention, diversion and intervention strategies to be employed for children, families and adults at risk.

The authors and contributors are grateful to have the positive endorsement of Lord Laming, who kindly wrote the original foreword, and we make no apology for using it within this 2nd edition. He is held in the highest regard by safeguarding professionals and society in general for his work concerning the protection of children. He is regarded as a national authority and has proven to be a voice that needs to be listened to.

We sincerely hope this revised edition of Multi Agency Safeguarding in a Public Protection World supports and assists safeguarding professionals in their efforts to protect and support the most vulnerable in society.

Chapter 1: Safeguarding Children

By Russell Wate, Marisa de Jager and Nigel Boulton

Chapter overview

- The moral and statutory duty to safeguard children.
- Definitions of 'Safeguarding', 'Child Protection' and 'Child in Need'.
- Types of abuse.
- Supervision, reflection, reflective practice and critical reflection.
- Practice wisdom.
- Professional dangerousness.
- Thresholds and levels of activity to safeguard children and young people.
- Information sharing: an ethos and requirement.
- Multi-Agency Safeguarding Arrangements.
- Designated and named professionals.
- Meeting descriptions: Strategy and Child Protection conferences.
- Special Educational Needs and disabilities.
- Assessments: key indicators including the 10 safeguarding pitfalls.
- Resilience and Adverse Childhood Experiences (ACE).
- Evidence informed assessment tools.
- Achieving Best Evidence.
- Initial child protection conference.
- Written agreements.
- Legislation.
- Emergency and Police Protection Orders.
- The Public Law Outline (PLO) 2014.
- Pre-birth stage or newly born: Care and Supervision Proceedings.
- Voice of the Child, Lived Experience and Journey of the Child.

Safeguarding children is often seen as the key priority in public protection. Society is deeply concerned about protecting them, and there is usually a public outcry and extensive media reporting in cases of child abuse and, in particular, abusive child deaths. There have been a number of high-profile examples, such as the deaths of Victoria Climbié, Peter Connolly and Daniel Pelka, and more recently Poppy Worthington, which demonstrate the strength of feeling around these issues. A concern for many professionals who work in this area of public protection is that media reports are often very accusatory about their work and can look for individual scapegoats.

Nelson Mandela, as shown by the following quotes, has highlighted what he believes is the responsibility that societies have to safeguard and promote the welfare of children:

'History will judge us by the difference we make in the everyday lives of children.'

'Our children are our greatest treasure. They are our future. Those who abuse them tear at the fabric of our society and weaken our nation.'

'The true character of a society is revealed in how it treats its children.'

(Nepaul, 2013)

These comments hopefully resonate with everyone and echo a moral duty that we all feel to protect and safeguard children. For professionals working in this area, however, there are also statutory obligations and duties on them to protect children.

Almost 25 years ago, the United Nations formally introduced the Convention for the Rights of Children (CRC), which the UK ratified in 1991. The four main principles that form the core of the convention are:

1. Non-discrimination (article 2): All children have rights, regardless of race, colour, sex, language, religion, political or other opinion, national, ethnic or social origin, property, disability, birth or other status.
2. Best interests (article 3): The child's best interests must be a primary consideration in all decisions affecting her or him.
3. Life, survival and development (article 6): All children have a right to life, and to survive and develop – physically, mentally, spiritually, morally, psychologically and socially – to their full potential.
4. Respect for the views of the child (article 12): Children have the right to express themselves freely on matters that affect them, and to have their views taken seriously.

The death of Jasmine Beckford in the mid-1980s helped to bring about some changes to practice. This case involved three-year-old Jasmine and her younger sister being assaulted numerous times by their step father, Maurice Beckford, ultimately resulting in Jasmine's death. Both Jasmine and her younger sister were on the then 'child at risk register', and professionals from all agencies visited the home on over 70 occasions, however they only once saw Jasmine and never saw her alone.

There were also a number of other high-profile child deaths at this time, including a public inquiry into the allegations of widespread child abuse in Cleveland. As a result of all of these, the Children Act (1989) was introduced. This act has 10 principles, the key ones for professionals to know are:

- Paramountcy – the child's welfare should be of paramount concern.

- Individuality – all children should be treated as individuals. Their opinions should be listened to and all decisions should take account of their wishes.

- Consultation/co-operation and co-ordination – central to the Children's Act and crucial to the success of child protection work is the principle that all departments of the local authority and the other relevant agencies (including police, health and voluntary organisations) should consult, co-operate and co-ordinate their activities so as to achieve the best result for the child and/or his or her family.

These principles are still in place today, as are key sections of the act, which are described in detail later in this chapter. The key for all professionals is to treat the welfare of the child as paramount and to place the child at the centre of their thinking.

A child is anyone who is not yet 18 years old. Even if a 16-year-old is living on their own or is in further education, in the armed services or a young offender's institution, this does not alter the fact that they are a child or affect their entitlement to protection under the Children Act (1989).

After this act, the government issued guidance in the form of an updated version of *Working Together to Safeguard Children*. The current version of the guidance came into practice in July 2018 and many of the definitions that are used in this chapter are the official government definitions and come from the various *Working Together to Safeguard Childrens* guidance. The current guidance that professionals need to be familiar with is available at: https://assets.publishing.service.gov.uk/government/uploads/system/uploads/attachment_data/file/729914/Working_Together_to_Safeguard_Children-2018.pdf (accessed August 2019).

After the tragic death of Victoria Climbié in 2000, a public inquiry was established, led by Lord Laming. Victoria was severely beaten by her great aunt and her boyfriend, so much so that she had 128 separate injuries all over her body of different ages and severity. Victoria seemed invisible to agencies and, in this case, language difficulties also emerged. Lord Laming made a series of recommendations, one of which resulted in the Children Act (2004) to supplement the 1989 act with the intention of bolstering and supporting the protection of children. The 2004 act made *Working Together to Safeguard Children* statutory guidance, and that new version was produced in 2006, which included Local Safeguarding Children Boards. (The Children and Social Work Act (2017) abolished these Boards and replaced them with Multi-Agency Safeguarding arrangements, which will be discussed later in this Chapter.)

The most important and fundamental section that applies to all those who work in a public service, whether it is their primary role working with children or not, is Section 11 of the act, which states [emphasis added]:

'Each person and body to whom this section applies must make arrangements for ensuring that –

> e. *Their functions are discharged having regard to the need to* **safeguard and promote the welfare of children**; *and*

> f. *Any services provided by another person pursuant to arrangements made by the person or body in the discharge of their functions are provided having regard to that need.'*

So, in essence, whether someone works for the local authority, health services, probation, police, education or a voluntary sector provider supplying services to one of those public bodies, their organisation, and they personally, have a duty to safeguard and protect the welfare of children. Safeguarding children is everybody's responsibility where the child should be at the centre of all enquiries. Safeguarding is sometimes like a jigsaw puzzle, and in order to complete this jigsaw all agencies may have different pieces and need to work together.

Key learning

- United Nations CRC:
  - The child's best interests are the primary concern.
  - Children have the right to have their views taken seriously.

- Children Act (1989):
  - The child's welfare should be of paramount concern.
- All decisions should take account of the wishes of the child.
- Children Act (2004): Section 11
  Statutory organisations and individuals have a duty to safeguard and promote the welfare of children.
- *Working Together to Safeguard Children* (2018) is the key guidance for all professionals.

Key definitions

A child-centred approach is fundamental for all multi-agency professionals. It is often asked what 'safeguarding' actually means and what is the difference between this term and the term 'child protection'?

Safeguarding

Safeguarding needs to be considered in a far wider context than just preventing abuse.

The Oxford Dictionary online (Feb 2015) definition is helpful to consider:

'Protect from harm or damage with an appropriate measure (verb) or

a measure taken to protect someone or something or to prevent something undesirable (noun).'

There are three key responses to issues of need, harm and risk concerning a child – these are activities to prevent, divert from, or intervene to stop the harm or risk.

Safeguarding professions will widely acknowledge the following four descriptors, or aims of safeguarding, but practitioners need to keep a completely open mind when considering whether safeguarding is required:

- Protecting children from maltreatment.
- Preventing impairment of children's health or development.

- Ensuring that children are growing up in circumstances consistent with the provision of safe and effective care.

- Taking action to enable all children to have the best outcomes.

There are different actions or steps that professionals will take as result of whether they are safeguarding or protecting children. *Working Together* describes them as follows:

Child protection

Child protection is part of safeguarding and promoting welfare. It refers to the activity that is undertaken to protect specific children who are suffering, or are likely to suffer, significant harm.

The key difference is that safeguarding is the activity in its widest sense, preventing children suffering any need, harm or risk and being able to grow up being kept safe. Child protection is the action of protecting an individual child who is suffering or who you strongly believe could suffer significant harm unless action is taken.

Child in need

A child in need is defined under the Children Act (1989) as a child who is unlikely to achieve or maintain a reasonable level of health or development, or whose health and development is likely to be significantly or further impaired, without the provision of services; or a child who is disabled. Children in need may be assessed under section 17 of the Children Act (1989) by a social worker. The critical factors to be taken into account in deciding whether a child is in need under section 17 are:

- what will happen to a child's health or development without services being provided

- the likely effect the services will have on the child's standard of health and development.

Generally, it is the local authority children services departments who will decide if a child is 'in need' or not, but it could also be the local voluntary services. Other terms sometimes used here are 'team around the child' (TAC) or 'team around the family' (TAF), which is where local multi-agency partners seek to have a plan of local services to try and fill the perceived need gap for that child or for the family. They will hold meetings that involve all professionals who are engaged with that child and family, ensuring they bring relevant information to share. Actions arising from these meetings form a plan to safeguard the 'child in need'.

Child protection activity

The Children Act (1989) introduced the concept of significant harm as the threshold that justifies compulsory intervention in family life, in the best interests of children. It gives local authorities a duty under section 47 to make enquiries when they have *reasonable cause to suspect that a child who lives or is found in their area is suffering, or likely to suffer, significant harm,* to enable them to decide whether they should take action to safeguard or promote that child's welfare. If it is decided the case is a section 47 enquiry, there would usually be a joint agency visit with children's social care and the police working together.

Although significant harm is the threshold at which a local authority has a duty to intervene, there is no strict definition and it is not described in detail anywhere.

There are two key principles that apply to child protection activity:

- Safeguarding is everyone's responsibility: for services to be effective each professional and organisation should play their full part.
- A child-centred approach is vital: for services to be effective they should be based on a clear understanding of the needs and views of children.

Types of abuse

Working Together to Safeguard Children (DFE, 2018) describes four main types of abuse that children suffer, and they may suffer more than one of these at any one time. *Working Together* firstly describes what it means by abuse.

Somebody may abuse or neglect a child by inflicting harm, or by failing to act to prevent harm. Children may be abused in a family or in an institutional or community setting by those known to them or, more rarely, by others. Abuse can take place wholly online, or technology may be used to facilitate offline abuse. Children may be abused by an adult or adults, or another child or children.

The four types of abuse are:

- physical, including fabricated or induced illness
- emotional

- sexual
- neglect.

Physical abuse

Physical abuse may involve hitting, shaking, throwing, poisoning, burning, scalding, drowning, suffocating or otherwise causing physical harm to a child. A parent or carer may also cause physical harm by fabricating the symptoms of illness or deliberately inducing illness in a child.

Emotional abuse

Emotional abuse is the persistent emotional maltreatment of a child such as to cause severe and persistent adverse effects on the child's emotional development:

- It may involve communicating to children that they are worthless, unloved or inadequate, or that they are valued only because they meet the needs of another person.
- It may feature expectations being imposed on children that are inappropriate to their age or level of development.
- It may include interactions beyond a child's developmental capability.
- It may involve over-protection, limitation of exploration and learning opportunities or preventing a child from participating in normal social interaction.
- It may involve witnessing the ill-treatment of another, serious bullying that causes children to feel frightened or in danger, or the exploitation or corruption of children.
- Some level of emotional abuse is involved in all types of maltreatment, though it may occur alone.

Sexual abuse

Sexual abuse involves forcing or enticing a child or young person to take part in sexual activities, not necessarily involving a high level of violence, including prostitution, whether or not they are aware of what is happening:

- It may involve physical contact including penetrative (eg. rape, either anal, vaginal or oral) or non-penetrative acts.

- It may include non-contact activities such as looking at or producing pornographic material, watching sexual acts or encouraging children to behave in sexually inappropriate ways.

- Sexual abuse may be perpetrated by men, women or other children.

Neglect

Neglect is the persistent failure to meet a child's basic physical and psychological needs.

It is likely to result in the serious impairment of the child's health or development.

It may occur during pregnancy as a result of maternal substance abuse.

Once a child is born, neglect may involve:

- failing to provide adequate food, clothing and shelter, including exclusion from home or abandonment

- failing to protect a child from physical and emotional harm or danger

- failing to ensure adequate supervision including the use of inadequate carers

- failing to provide access to appropriate medical care or treatment

- neglect of, or unresponsiveness to, a child's basic emotional needs.

A child living in poverty can be regarded as being neglected, however this is not always the case and both poverty and neglect should be viewed as separate risks to that child.

Key learning

Safeguarding – the activity to prevent, divert from, or intervene in, all need, harm and risk concerning children in general.

Child protection – protecting individual children identified as either suffering, or likely to suffer, significant harm as a result of abuse. Often under Section 47 of the Children Act (1989).

Child in need – under section 17 of the Children Act (1989), those children whose vulnerability is such that they are unlikely to reach or maintain a satisfactory level of health or development.

Types of abuse – physical, emotional, sexual, neglect.

Supervision of all staff working in safeguarding

The need to ensure that supervision occurs has been described in numerous reports as a crucial part of child protection work, not just in children's social care but across all agencies.

Serious case reviews also highlight this as key to keeping children safe and to support practitioners. In his report that followed the death of 'Baby P', titled *The Protection of Children in England: A progress report*, Lord Laming encapsulated what the purpose of supervision is:

'Regular, high-quality, organised supervision is critical, as are routine opportunities for peer learning and discussion. Currently, not enough time is dedicated to this and individuals are carrying too much personal responsibility, with no outlet for the sometimes severe emotional and psychological stresses that staff involved in child protection often face. Supervision should be open and supportive, focusing on the quality of decisions, good risk analysis, and improving outcomes for children rather than meeting targets.'
(2009)

Supervision in social work, health and numerous other professions needs to be recognised as fundamentally different to management oversight or where the term is used to describe case management activity.

The British Association of Social Work promotes the following definition, derived from research on supervision within social work and particularly within multi-agency teams:

'Supervision must enable and support workers to build effective professional relationships, develop good practice, and exercise both professional judgement and discretion in decision-making. For supervision to be effective it needs to combine a performance management approach with a dynamic, empowering and enabling supervisory relationship. Supervision should improve the quality of practice, support the development of integrated working and ensure continuing professional development. Supervision should contribute to the development of a learning culture by promoting an approach that develops the confidence and competence of managers in their supervision skills. It is therefore at the core of individual and group continuing professional development.'
(For more information, visit www.basw.co.uk/system/files/resources/basw_13955-1_0.pdf (accessed August 2019))

Reflection, reflective practice and critical reflection

Reflection, reflective practice and critical reflection underpin good practice when working with children and families. Good quality reflective practice enables professionals to navigate a way through any *'analysis paralysis'* and to develop practice knowledge, skills and wisdom. The concept of reflection, reflective practice and critical reflection has been discussed since the early 1990s.

In professional practice, reflective practice is helpful in many of the safeguarding professions as a way of ensuring ongoing scrutiny, improved practice skills, learning from experience and creating practice theory together with its meaning as a form of accountability or supervision.

It ensures a greater understanding of the need for professional values, the demands on professionals who are involved and effectiveness in uncertainty. Reflective practice ensures a professional 'owns' their cases and is responsible for them.

The Fook and Gardner approach to critical reflection, for example, encourages deconstruction and analysis of personal or professional experience to understand the different assumptions, relationships and influences embedded within it and how it affects our practice.

As new understandings emerge, the individual can reconstruct an incident and develop new techniques to deal with similar in the future. The model provides a practical, meaningful and structured approach that speaks to workplace demands.

As practitioners we learn from experience and therefore improve practice by learning directly from our own practice experience.

The role of 'practice wisdom'

Child protection and safeguarding practice and decision making is complex. In everyday practice, professionals use their own experience-based learning, or 'practice wisdom', by combining their individual objective, procedural and experiential knowledge. Intuition, or 'gut feeling', has a key role in the use and development of practice wisdom.

Academics have sought to articulate their understanding of practice wisdom over the years with two clear and differing thoughts emerging:

1. Some have described it as an intellectual capacity within the professional that enables them to combine and integrate knowledge, belief, thoughts, emotion, actions etc. to support and strengthen decisions and proposed activity (O'Sullivan, 2005).

2. This ability has been described as being akin to a vehicle integrating both subjective and objective information in the development of knowledge (Klein & Bloom, 1995).

These descriptions of practice wisdom feel as if they differ with a view that practice wisdom is a form of knowledge in and of itself.

In the Social Work Dictionary, Barker (1999: 370) defines practice wisdom as, *'the accumulation of information, assumptions, ideologies and judgement that have been particularly useful in fulfilling the expectations of the job'.*

The suggestion is that practice wisdom is the application of practice knowledge and is acquired automatically through experience.

It is obvious that the levels of practice wisdom acquired by any professional will be extremely variable and even those who can be said, and accept, to have acquired a sufficient level may not on all occasions utilise it to the best advantage.

Accepting the differing academic views concerning practice wisdom, it is incontrovertible that professionals amass knowledge, experience and beliefs that can all be drawn upon to enable the challenging of individual hypotheses and support practice-based decision making and activity.

Professional dangerousness

In his report to Parliament, Lord Laming said, *'Please keep me safe!'* (2009). This simple but profoundly important message is the very minimum upon which every child and young person should be able to depend when professionals work with families.

Professional dangerousness essentially refers to poor working practice that can leave a child in danger, and can be caused by professionals being over optimistic in their thinking, as well failing to be as professionally curious as they should be. Many serious case reviews identify it an ongoing concern within the safeguarding professions.

Professional dangerousness often occurs as a direct response to the actions of families where there are childcare concerns, as a result of our discomfort within our role, or when workers who are responsible for child protection leave the child at risk of significant harm as a result of their assumptions, attitudes or behaviour.

It can occur within the practices of individual workers, within teams of professionals, within entire departments or between agencies.

Professional dangerousness can also be attributed to a range of biases that can be present in a myriad of ways and should always be guarded against.

Multi-agency Safeguarding Arrangements

Multi-agency boards have been in place for many years and were originally called Area Review Committees and Area Child Protection Committees. However, after the death of Victoria Climbié and Lord Laming's subsequent report, it was decided they needed a statutory footing to ensure that all partners worked with each other to safeguard and promote the welfare of children. The act that created Local Safeguarding Children Boards (LSCBs) is the Children Act (2004).

HM Government commissioned a review of safeguarding arrangements. This review, called the Wood Review after its author, Alan Wood, recommended the abolition of LSCBs. As a result of this, The Children and Social Work Act (2017) abolished the functions of LSCBS and inserted new Multi-agency Safeguarding Arrangements.

These new arrangements, highlighted below, detail who the safeguarding partners are:

'Safeguarding partners
A safeguarding partner in relation to a local authority area in England is defined under the Children Act 2004 (as amended by the Children and Social Work Act, 2017) as:
(a) the local authority
(b) a clinical commissioning group for an area any part of which falls within the local authority area
(c) the chief officer of police for an area any part of which falls within the local authority area.'

The purpose of these local arrangements is to support and enable local organisations and agencies to work together. To fulfil this role, the three safeguarding partners must set out how they will work together and how they will work with any relevant agencies. Relevant agencies are those organisations and agencies whose involvement the safeguarding partners consider may be required to safeguard and promote the welfare of children locally, such as other health providers and schools.

To be effective, these arrangements should link to other strategic partnership work happening locally to support children and families. This will include other public boards including health and wellbeing boards, Adult Safeguarding Boards, Channel Panels, Improvement Boards, Community Safety Partnerships, the Local Family Justice Board and MAPPAs.

The local safeguarding arrangements must be published and must include:

- arrangements for the safeguarding partners to work together to identify and respond to the needs of children in the area

- arrangements for commissioning and publishing local child safeguarding practice reviews (more detail on this is in Chapter 3)

- the process for undertaking local child safeguarding practice reviews, setting out the arrangements for embedding learning across organisations and agencies

- arrangements for independent scrutiny of the effectiveness of the arrangements

- geographical boundaries (especially if the arrangements operate across more than one local authority area)

- how all early years settings, schools (including independent schools, academies and free schools) and other educational establishments will be included in the safeguarding arrangements

- how the safeguarding partners will use data and intelligence to assess the effectiveness of the help being provided to children and families, including early help

- how inter-agency training will be commissioned, delivered and monitored for impact, and how they will undertake any multi-agency and inter-agency audits

- how the arrangements will include the voices of children and families

- how the threshold document setting out the local criteria for action aligns with the arrangements.

Thresholds

It is vital that multi-agency safeguarding partners should have in place procedures to identify where children and families are in need of help to resolve their problems and issues, and to stop these deteriorating as children get older. All of those working with children and their families must understand what their role is in identifying early concerns, how they can highlight them and with whom, and how to share information with other professionals to enable early identification and assessment.

The safeguarding partners should publish this as a threshold document, which sets out the local criteria for action in a way that is transparent, accessible and easily understood. This should include:

- the process for the early help assessment and the type and level of early help services to be provided
- the criteria, including the level of need, for when a case should be referred to local authority children's social care for assessment and for statutory services under:
  - section 17 of the Children Act (1989) (children in need)
  - section 47 of the Children Act (1989) (reasonable cause to suspect a child is suffering or likely to suffer significant harm).

An important part of this is obtaining early help, which is normally done by a practitioner through the completion of an early help assessment. This should happen when:

- a practitioner is worried about how well a child or young person is progressing (eg. concerns about their health, development, welfare, behaviour, progress in learning or any other aspect of their well-being)
- a child or young person, or their parent/carer, raises a concern with a practitioner
- a child's or young person's needs are unclear, or broader than the practitioner's service can address.

The process is entirely voluntary and informed consent is mandatory. Families do not have to engage, and if they do they can choose what information they want to share. Children and families should not feel stigmatised by the use of an early help assessment, and indeed they can ask for this early help assessment to be initiated. It is not a 'referral' process but a 'request for services'. The practitioner assesses needs using the assessment template. This is not a full and in-depth risk assessment, however if a child or young person reveals they are at risk, the practitioner should follow the local safeguarding referral process immediately. If the family do not consent to this early help assessment, practitioners may need to consider if there is any risk that needs a formal assessment.

Whether it is this early help assessment or another process that is in place, for early help to be effective local agencies need to work together, often through a local Early Help hub, in order to:

- identify children and families who would benefit from early help

- undertake an assessment of the need for early help

- provide targeted early help services to address the assessed needs of a child and their family, which focuses on activity to significantly improve the outcomes for the child.

Munro (2011) states:

'Services offering early help are not aimed just at preventing abuse or neglect but at improving the life chances of children and young people in general. The arguments for early help are three-fold. First there is the moral argument for minimising adverse experiences for children and young people. This is endorsed by the UNCRC and the Children Act (1989). Secondly, there is the argument of 'now or never' arising from the evidence of how difficult it is to reverse damage to children and young people's development. The third argument is that it is cost effective when current expenditure is compared with estimated expenditure if serious problems develop later.'

All local multi-agency safeguarding arrangements either have in place, or should have in place, this threshold policy to ensure there is a consistent approach to referring and accessing services across the local authority area, so that children get the right help at the most appropriate time. It still requires professional judgement, and needs to be evidence based regarding the level of concern about either the child or young person suffering significant harm or identifying children that need additional support.

Highlighted below are three different models that are being used around the country (although there will be more in use). Multi-agency professionals may recognise one of these as the one used in their area, but it is worth viewing the others to help them get a different and wider perspective of how thresholds operate.

Figure 1.1: Effective Support Windscreen

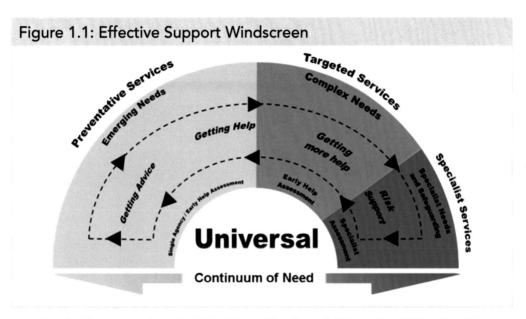

(Reproduced with permission from Cambridgeshire and Peterborough Safeguarding Children Board, from their document *Effective Support for Children and Families in Peterborough and Cambridgeshire* ©2018)

Figure 1.2: The windscreen model

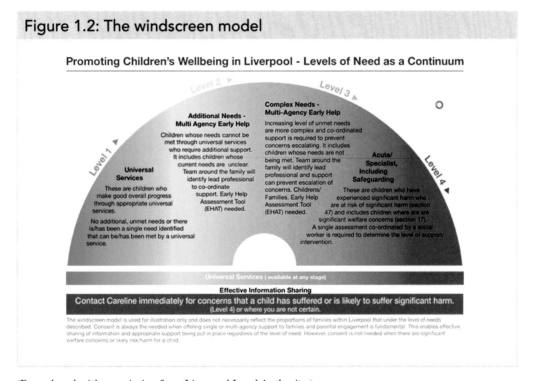

(Reproduced with permission from Liverpool Local Authority.)

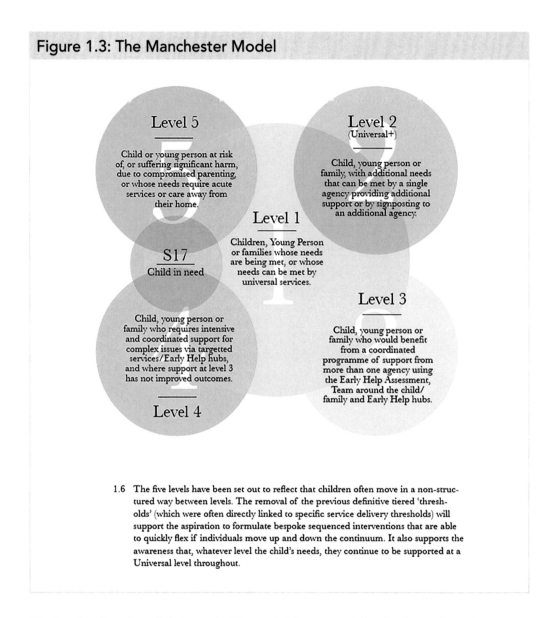

Figure 1.3: The Manchester Model

1.6 The five levels have been set out to reflect that children often move in a non-structured way between levels. The removal of the previous definitive tiered 'thresholds' (which were often directly linked to specific service delivery thresholds) will support the aspiration to formulate bespoke sequenced interventions that are able to quickly flex if individuals move up and down the continuum. It also supports the awareness that, whatever level the child's needs, they continue to be supported at a Universal level throughout.

The levels of need model shown in Figure 1.2 is a way of developing a shared understanding and explaining the approach across all the services and partnerships, ensuring a consistent response is applied by all, in a particular local authority area.

In this model, all services and interventions seek to work openly with the family (or with young people on their own where appropriate) in order to support them to address identified needs at the right level of intervention. It is recognised that this is never a static process and situations change, and as a result so does the level of need and risk. This means that children and young people may 'step up' and need more specialist intervention, or 'step down' as interventions have an impact and their needs and risks change as a consequence.

There are four or five areas in a Windscreen, or the Manchester Model (Figure 1.3), and these are also known as levels. Universal services are level 1, where there are no additional needs, only generic services or support are required. Level 2 is where targeted support is required and additional needs have to be met, but they are low. An Early Help Assessment may be filled in at this stage.

Level 3 is where further support is required from multi-agency partners. This could involve a child-in-need meeting and plan – in essence, a section 17 enquiry.

Levels 4 or 5 in Figure 1.3 cover those children who are in need of immediate care and protection. A comprehensive statutory assessment under Section 17 of the Children Act could also be required. Intervention under Section 47 of the Children Act may be required for those children who are at immediate risk of significant harm and legal action may need to be taken or the local authority may need to accommodate the child in order to ensure their protection.

Figures 1.4 and 1.5, adapted from *Working Together* (DFE, 2018), outline the process that should be taken in relation to safeguarding referrals. Particular note should be taken of Figure 1.5 where there are immediate concerns in relation to safeguarding a child.

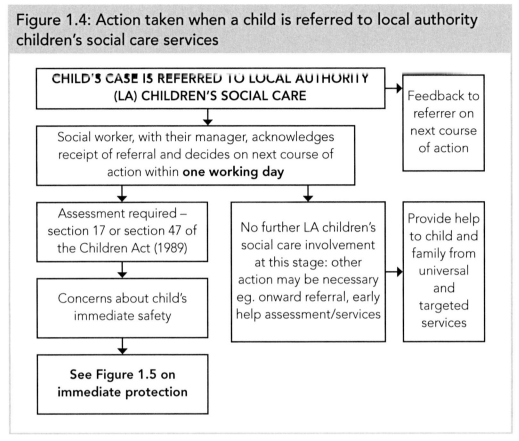

Figure 1.4: Action taken when a child is referred to local authority children's social care services

CHILD'S CASE IS REFERRED TO LOCAL AUTHORITY (LA) CHILDREN'S SOCIAL CARE

Feedback to referrer on next course of action

Social worker, with their manager, acknowledges receipt of referral and decides on next course of action within **one working day**

Assessment required – section 17 or section 47 of the Children Act (1989)

No further LA children's social care involvement at this stage: other action may be necessary eg. onward referral, early help assessment/services

Provide help to child and family from universal and targeted services

Concerns about child's immediate safety

See Figure 1.5 on immediate protection

(© Crown Copyright)

Figure 1.5: Immediate protection

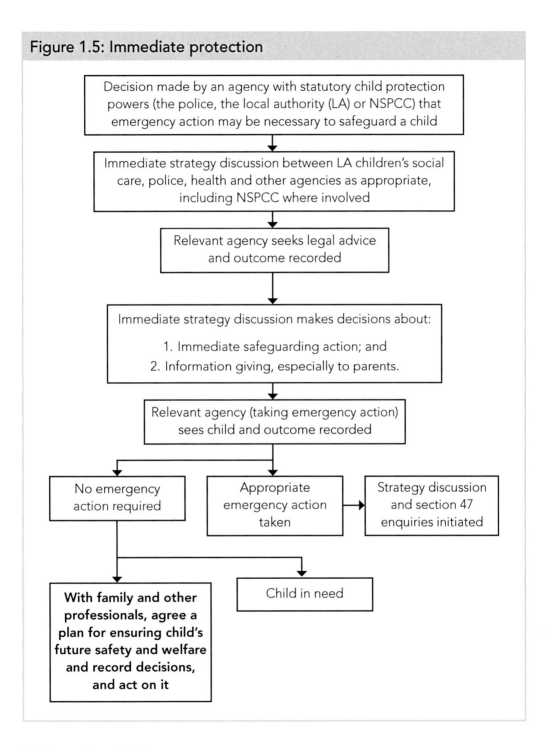

(© Crown Copyright)

MASH

Many local authorities have a Multi-Agency Safeguarding Hub (MASH) or similar partnership model in place (see Chapter 9 for more details). MASH models are usually managed by a social work manager and have a variety of safeguarding partners co-located to facilitate legal, efficient and effective sharing of information, when it is appropriate.

MASH is a consent-based model but professionals can override consent if they believe a child is at risk or suffering significant harm. MASH receives referrals from various professionals, notifications from the police and concerns from members of the public. Decisions are made as to whether any appropriate prevention, diversion or intervention activity is required.

All referrals and notifications from professionals need to be evidence informed and the referrer has to be accountable for the content and timeliness of all referrals to a local authority. Consent should always be considered at the time of referral and not considered as a task for social work.

Referrals

In *How Safe Are Our Children?* (NSPCC, 2018), the NSPCC states that during the year 2016/17 there were 646,120 referrals made to children's social care in England. The sheer volume of these referrals is a good demonstration of the extreme pressure that not only social workers are under, but all other professionals working in child protection. Furthermore, it is a problem that is increasing year on year – for comparison, in 2008/09 there were 547,000 referrals.

All practitioners must be aware that if they believe that a child is suffering or likely to suffer significant harm, they should refer this information at the earliest opportunity to children's social care.

Practitioners should also be aware that referrals are not always accepted, and they should be ready to challenge this decision if they feel it is not the right one. All multi-agency safeguarding partnerships should also have in place an escalation policy or, as named in some areas, a 'professional disagreement policy', to ensure that any challenge not accepted has a resolution pathway.

Information sharing

Information sharing within safeguarding practice is protected and regulated by way of the Data Protection Act (2018) and the European Union's General Data Protection

Regulation (GDPR). Local authority children services and all safeguarding partners have incorporated a GDPR statement as part of day-to-day practice.

When children and families are engaged with the local authority children's service, a discussion is held regarding consent and the use of data on information systems. These discussions are with parents who hold Parental Responsibility or those granted as carers by the court.

By providing consent, the parents/carers agree for the safeguarding practitioner to speak with other professionals and share personal information/data in order to assist with making the right decisions at the earliest opportunity unless the child is deemed to be at risk of significant harm, in which case more urgent action is required.

The processing of data must be fair and comply with all data protection principles including privacy notices. Information sharing will be covered in greater detail in Chapter 9, however it is worth highlighting here that the policy of sharing information in child protection cases stems from the Children Acts of 1989 and 2004. This legislation means that the default position is that professionals will share information with social care, and not doing so may be legally indefensible. Fears about sharing information must not be allowed to stand in the way of the need to protect the safety and promote the welfare of children, which must always be the paramount concern.

To ensure effective safeguarding arrangements, all organisations and agencies should have arrangements in place that set out clearly the processes and the principles for sharing information. The arrangement should cover how information will be shared within their own organisation/agency, and with others who may be involved in a child's life. Current government guidance is available at www.gov.uk/government/publications/safeguarding-practitioners-information-sharing-advice (accessed August 2019).

Designated and named professionals

Good places for professionals to seek advice are 'named' and 'designated professionals', posts that every area should have in place. Their role is described as follows:

'… *a designated professional lead (or, for health provider organisations, named professionals) for safeguarding. Their role is to support other professionals in their agencies to recognise the needs of children, including rescue from possible abuse or neglect. Designated professional roles should always be explicitly defined in job descriptions. Professionals should be given sufficient time, funding, supervision and support to fulfil their child welfare and safeguarding responsibilities effectively.'*

These designated and named health professionals are extremely knowledgeable in their field of expertise. It is not only health professionals that should seek out their advice, but professionals from other agencies would benefit from their help and support when necessary.

Keeping Children Safe in Education (2019) states that 'Governing bodies, proprietors and management committees should ensure an appropriate senior member of staff, from the school or college leadership team, is appointed to the role of designated safeguarding lead'.

The designated safeguarding lead should take lead responsibility for safeguarding and child protection (including online safety). This should be explicit in the role holder's job description. This person should have the appropriate status and authority within the school to carry out the duties of the post. They should be given the time, funding, training, resources and support to provide advice and support to other staff on child welfare and child protection matters, to take part in strategy discussions and inter-agency meetings, and/or to support other staff to do so, and to contribute to the assessment of children.

It is a matter for individual schools and colleges as to whether they choose to have one or more deputy designated safeguarding leads. Any deputies should be trained to the same standard as the designated safeguarding lead and the role should be explicit in their job description. While the activities of the designated safeguarding lead can be delegated to appropriately trained deputies, the ultimate lead responsibility for child protection, as set out above, remains with the designated safeguarding lead; this lead responsibility should not be delegated.

If an area has a Multi-Agency Safeguarding Hub (MASH), there will be specialist agency advisors working within the hub, with whom practitioners can consult. In a number of areas, they have both designated doctor (paediatrician) and designated nurse roles. These roles are not only essential to individual agencies, but also to the safeguarding partnership for specialist advice and support.

Strategy discussion

A strategy discussion will take place if it is believed that a child or young person is suffering or likely to suffer significant harm. *Working Together* (DFE, 2018) describes this meeting as:

'Whenever there is reasonable cause to suspect that a child is suffering, or is likely to suffer, significant harm there should be a strategy discussion involving local authority children's social care, the police, health and other bodies such as the referring agency. This might take the form of a multi-agency meeting or phone calls and more than one discussion may be necessary. A strategy discussion can take place following a referral or at any other time, including during the assessment process.'

It is the children's social care department that should convene a strategy discussion, with the purpose of determining the child's welfare and to plan rapid future action if there is reasonable cause to suspect the child is suffering or is likely to suffer significant harm. The minimum representatives from their agencies involved in this strategy discussion should be a local authority social worker, health practitioners and a police representative. Other relevant practitioners will depend on the nature of the individual case.

As a result of this strategy discussion, which is recorded (and the records disseminated as soon as possible), a decision will be made as to whether a single agency will attend and assess – normally children's social care – or a joint enquiry under section 47 will take place, involving mostly children's social care and the police. Serious case reviews into why a child has died and where abuse or neglect is suspected have highlighted over a number of years a lack of challenges made by practitioners and agencies, and, as already mentioned, it is important that if professionals do not agree with the suggested course of action, they challenge it and, if necessary, use the multi-agency safeguarding partnership escalation procedures.

Once a decision has been made, the single or joint agency visit will take place to assess the case and it is essential that the child or young person is seen, preferably alone, and that their views and feelings are taken into consideration. Telephone conversations may take place in order to plan any safeguarding activity that is to take place, however they should be recorded.

A strategy discussion should not be considered as a one-off event at the start – ongoing strategy discussions by professionals when appropriate are needed to progress a safeguarding plan. Some strategy discussions do take place in a MASH, however this is discussed in more detail in Chapter 9.

A complex strategy meeting could also take place if the allegations concern a professional or someone else who works with children and young people, whether employed or voluntary. These meetings are called by the designated officer from the local authority, which every local authority should have, or a team that deals with these allegations.

'County level and unitary local authorities should ensure that allegations against people who work with children are not dealt with in isolation. Any action necessary to address corresponding welfare concerns in relation to the child or children involved should be taken without delay and in a coordinated manner. Local authorities should, in addition, have designated a particular officer, or team of officers (either as part of multi-agency arrangements or otherwise), to be involved in the management and oversight of allegations against people who work with children. Any such officer, or team of officers, should be sufficiently qualified and experienced to be able to fulfil this role effectively, for example qualified social workers. Any new appointments to such a role, other than current or former designated officers moving between local authorities, should be qualified social workers. Arrangements should be put in place to ensure that any allegations about those who work with children are passed to the designated officer, or team of officers, without delay.' (DFE, 2018).

Figure 1.6 from *Working Together to Safeguard Children* highlights the pathway that should be used in strategy discussions.

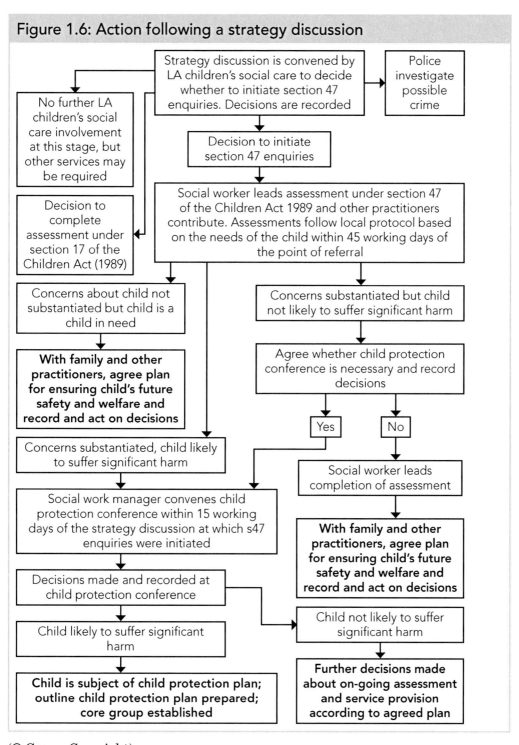

Figure 1.6: Action following a strategy discussion

(© Crown Copyright)

Special Educational Needs and disabilities

Professionals should be aware of the risks posed to disabled children, who are over three times more likely to be abused or neglected than non-disabled children. One study, conducted in 2000, found that:

- 31% of disabled children had been abused, compared with nine per cent among the non-disabled child population.

- Disabled children were 3.4 times more likely to be abused or neglected than non-disabled children. They were:
    - 3.8 times more likely to be neglected
    - 3.8 times more likely to be physically abused
    - 3.1 times more likely to be sexually abused
    - 3.9 times more likely to be emotionally abused.

(Sullivan & Knutson, 2000)

Specific consideration should be given by all professionals to the specific needs of disabled children, who should be given sufficient recognition and priority in the assessment process.

The Children and Families Act (2014) takes forward the reform programme set out in *Support and Aspiration: A New Approach to Special Educational Needs and Disability: Progress and Next Steps* by:

- Extending the Special Educational Needs (SEN) system from birth to 25 and giving children, young people and their parents greater control and choice in decision-making.

- Replacing Statements of Special Educational Needs and learning difficulty assessments with birth-to-25 Education, Health and Care Plans.

- Offering families Personal Budgets. Young people and parents of children who have Education, Health and Care Plans have the right to request a Personal Budget, which may contain elements of education, social care and health funding.

- Creating a duty for joint commissioning, which requires local authorities and health bodies to work in partnership when arranging provision for children and young people with Special Educational Needs.

- Requiring local authorities to involve children, young people and parents in reviewing and developing provision for those with Special Educational Needs and to publish a Local Offer of services.

- Extending the entitlement to an assessment to all young carers under the age of 18, regardless of who they care for or the type and frequency of this care.

- Giving Parent Carers the right to a stand-alone assessment.

Local authorities should adopt a key working approach, which provides children, young people and parents with a single point of contact to help ensure the holistic provision and co-ordination of services and support.

The local authority must engage other partners it thinks appropriate to support young people with Special Educational Needs and disabilities. This might include voluntary organisations, CAMHS, local therapists, Jobcentre Plus and their employment support advisers, housing associations, careers advisers, leisure and play services.

The local authority must consult with children and young people with SEN or disabilities and their parents. Joint commissioning arrangements must consider the needs of children and young people with Special Educational Needs and disabilities.

Local authorities and Clinical Commissioning Groups (CCGs) should consider the role that private, voluntary and community sector providers can play in delivering services.

Local authorities must review the special educational provision and social care provision in their areas for children and young people who have SEN or disabilities and the provision made for local children and young people who are educated out of the area, working with the partners to their joint commissioning arrangements.

Many children and young people with Special Educational Needs or disabilities will have their needs met within local mainstream education provision. This is known as SEN Support. Mainstream educational settings must use their best endeavours to make sure that a child with SEN gets the support they need. This means doing everything they can to meet children and young people's SEN, including providing any necessary support that is 'additional to' and 'different from' what is available for all pupils, and they must do this as part of the cycle of assessing, planning and teaching. This support must be reviewed on a regular basis.

Educational settings should record details about the additional or different provision they make to meet a child or young person's special educational needs in an individual learning plan, such as a School Focused or SEN Support Plan. Where necessary and agreed by the family and the educational setting, it should also involve bringing in additional support from other professionals such as educational psychologists, therapists, or other schools.

Both the Children and Families Act (2014) and the Care Act (2015) impose upon local authorities a duty to provide children and young people with information, advice and support relating to their SEN or disability, and transition, including matters relating to health and social care. It must include information, advice and support on the take-up and management of Personal Budgets.

Children and young people should be involved in the design or commissioning of services providing information, advice and support. This information, advice and support should be provided through a dedicated and easily identifiable service. Information, advice and support services should be impartial, confidential and accessible and should have the capacity to handle face-to-face, telephone and electronic enquiries. Local authorities must take steps to make these services known to children and young people and their parents in their area as well as head teachers, proprietors and principals of schools and post-16 institutions in their area, and others where appropriate.

Advocacy services must be available to young people through the transition phase.

The local offer of services must include details of how information, advice and support related to SEN and disabilities can be accessed and how it is resourced. It must also include a short breaks duty statement giving details of the local range of services and how they can be accessed, including any eligibility criteria in accordance with the Breaks for Carers of Disabled Children Regulations (2011).

Requesting an Education, Health and Care Needs Assessment

An Education, Health and Care Needs Assessment is an assessment undertaken by a local authority of the education, health and care needs of a child or young person aged 0 to 25 with SEN or disabilities to determine whether it is necessary to make provision for those needs in accordance with an Education Health and Care Plan.

The following people have a specific right to ask a local authority to conduct an Education, Health and Care Needs Assessment:

- A child's parent.
- A young person over the age of 16 but under the age of 25.

■ A person acting on behalf of a school or post-16 institution (this should be with the knowledge and agreement of the parent or young person where possible).

In addition, anyone can bring a child or young person who has (or may have) SEN to the attention of the local authority, e.g. foster carers, health and social care professionals, education staff, youth offending teams or probation providers, or a family friend.

Following a request or a child having been brought to its attention, the local authority must (unless it has already undertaken such an assessment during the previous six months) determine whether an Education, Health and Care Needs Assessment is necessary, and communicate that decision within six weeks. It must give its reasons where it decides not to proceed.

Where the local authority considers that special educational provision may need to be made in accordance with an Education, Health and Care Plan and is considering whether an Education, Health and Care Needs Assessment is necessary, it must notify:

■ the young person/parent, and must inform them of their right to express written or oral views and submit evidence

■ the health service (the relevant Clinical Commissioning Group (CCG) or NHS England where it has responsibility for a child or young person)

■ local authority officers responsible for social care for young people with SEN

■ the principal (or equivalent) of any education establishment the child attends.

In considering whether an Education, Health and Care Needs Assessment is necessary, the local authority should consider whether there is evidence that they have not made the expected progress, despite the education establishment having taken relevant and purposeful action to identify, assess and meet the special educational needs of the child or young person.

Local authorities must consult the child or young person and parent throughout the process of assessment and production of an Education, Health and Care Plan.

Education, Health and Care Needs Assessments should be combined with other social care assessments where appropriate. As far as possible, there should be a 'tell us once' approach to sharing information during the assessment and planning process so that families and young people do not have to repeat the same information to different agencies, or different practitioners and services within each agency.

It must be discussed with the child, young person and parents what information they are happy for the local authority to share with other agencies. A record should be made of what information can be shared and with whom.

Where particular services are assessed as being needed, their provision should be delivered and should not be delayed until the Education, Health and Care Plan is complete.

Following the completion of an Education, Health and Care Needs Assessment, if the local authority decides that an Education, Health and Care Plan is not necessary, it must notify the child, young person or parent, the education and the health service and give the reasons for its decision. This notification must take place as soon as practicable and at the latest within 16 weeks of the initial request or of the child or young person having otherwise been brought to the local authority's attention. The local authority must also inform the child, young person or parent of their right to appeal the decision and the time limit for doing so. They will also be advised of the requirement for them to consider mediation should they wish to appeal, the availability of information, advice, support and how to access disagreement resolution services.

Key learning

- Every multi-safeguarding partnership arrangement will have in place a threshold document – this policy helps practitioners to consider where their concerns fit in the multi-agency partnership.

- Information sharing to safeguard children is both lawful and vital.

- Supervision and reflective practice are key to good safeguarding practice.

- Practice wisdom enables practitioners to integrate types of knowledge, modes of thinking, emotions and action in ways that facilitate sound judgment.

- Professional dangerousness and bias need to be constantly guarded against.

- Strategy discussions – sharing of information in order to plan the way to safeguard a child or young person.

- The designated officer from the local authority gives support and advice on allegations against professionals.

- The Special Educational Needs (SEN) system covers from birth to 25 years.

- Children, young people and their parents have greater control and choice in decision-making within the SEN system.

- SEN families are entitled to manage a personal budget.

Assessments

Professionals have to try and understand the information they are being presented with and how to assess the level of risk to children. The next few pages are both a guide to help professionals with these assessments and also where they can go to gain further information.

The local authority and its social workers have specific roles and responsibilities to lead the statutory assessment of children in need (section 17, Children Act (1989)) and to lead child protection enquiries (section 47, Children Act (1989)). *Working Together* (DfE, 2018) says that:

'Assessment should be a dynamic process, which analyses and responds to the changing nature and level of need and / or risk faced by the child from within and outside their family. It is important that the impact of what is happening to a child is clearly identified and that information is gathered, recorded and checked systematically, and discussed with the child and their parents / carers where appropriate.'

As part of their safeguarding training in 2013, the Royal College of General Practitioners issued a handout with checklists titled *Signs and Indicators of Abuse*. These checklists are based on materials developed by the NSPCC and the Community Education Development Centre in Coventry, plus others including Reder *et al* (1993). The following tables are taken from these checklists.

Signs that may indicate physical abuse

Physical indicators	Behaviour indicators
■ Unexplained injuries or burns, particularly if they are recurrent. ■ Untreated injuries or lingering injuries not attended to. ■ Bruises and abrasions around the face, particularly if they are recurring damage or injury around the mouth. ■ Bilateral injuries such as two bruised eyes. ■ Bruising to soft areas of the face eg. cheeks. ■ Bite marks. ■ Burns or scalds (note the pattern and spread of the injury eg. cigarette burns). ■ Weals suggesting beatings.	■ Improbable excuses given to explain injuries. ■ Refusal to discuss injuries. ■ Admission of punishment that appears excessive. ■ Shrinks from physical contact. ■ Refusal/avoiding getting undressed for gym – keeps arms and legs covered in hot weather. ■ Fears medical help. ■ Self-harming behaviours. ■ Aggression towards others. ■ Over-compliant behaviour or a 'watchful' attitude. ■ Deterioration in school work. ■ Unexplained pattern of absences, which may serve to hide bruises or other physical injuries. ■ Fears or is reluctant to return home or to have parents contacted.

(© Royal College of General Practitioners)

Signs that may indicate emotional abuse

Physical indicators	Behaviour indicators
■ Delays in physical development eg. milestones delayed or underweight, lethargic (there may be medical reasons for this, however, and medical advice is essential). ■ Self-mutilation.	■ Delays in intellectual development. ■ Over-reaction to mistakes. ■ Continual self-depreciation. ■ Sudden speech disorders. ■ Social isolation – does not join in and has few friends. ■ Extremes of compliance, passivity and/or aggression/provocativeness. ■ Compulsive stealing eg. other children's packed lunches. ■ Rocking, thumb sucking, hair twisting, etc. ■ Drug, alcohol or solvent abuse. ■ Fear of parents being contacted.

(© Royal College of General Practitioners)

Signs that may indicate neglect

Physical indicators	Behaviour indicators
■ Constant hunger. ■ Poor personal hygiene. ■ Constant tiredness. ■ Inadequate clothing. ■ Untreated medical problems.	■ Social isolation – does not join in and has few friends. ■ Low self-esteem. ■ Frequent lateness or non-attendance at school. ■ Destructive tendencies. ■ Poor relationships with peers. ■ Compulsive stealing and scavenging. ■ Rocking, hair twisting and thumb sucking etc.

(© Royal College of General Practitioners)

Signs that may indicate sexual abuse

Physical indicators	Behaviour indicators
■ 'Love bites'. ■ Other bite marks. ■ Signs of self-harming (eg. deep scratches/cuts on arms). ■ Tiredness, lethargy. ■ Pregnancy or sexually transmitted infections.	■ Sudden changes in behaviour and school performance. ■ Sexual awareness inappropriate to the child's age – shown for example in drawings, vocabulary, games etc. ■ Provocative sexual behaviour. ■ Frequent public masturbation. ■ Fear of undressing for games or activities. ■ Tendency to cry easily. ■ Regression to younger behaviour eg. thumb sucking, playing with discarded toys, acting like a baby. ■ Depression and withdrawal.

(© Royal College of General Practitioners)

The Cardiff Child Protection Systematic Reviews and the NSPCC have produced a series of excellent leaflets that, to date, focus on the recognition and investigation of suspected abuse/maltreatment, which can be accessed at: www.core-info.cardiff.ac.uk/?s=leaflets (accessed August 2019).

Current leaflets that are available to download are:

- *Head and Spinal Injuries in Children.*
- *Emotional Neglect and Emotional Abuse in Pre-school Children.*
- *Bruises on Children.*
- *Fractures in Children.*
- *Oral Injuries and Bites on Children.*
- *Thermal Injuries on Children.*

Further information in relation to stages of development has been produced by Research in Practice, which, although only covering up to 11 years of age, shows appropriate development stages for age groups and is geared towards frontline practitioners. (For more information, see www.rip.org.uk/frontline).

Working Together to Safeguard Children (DfE, 2018) uses the Assessment Framework Triangle to help practitioners assess children and families.

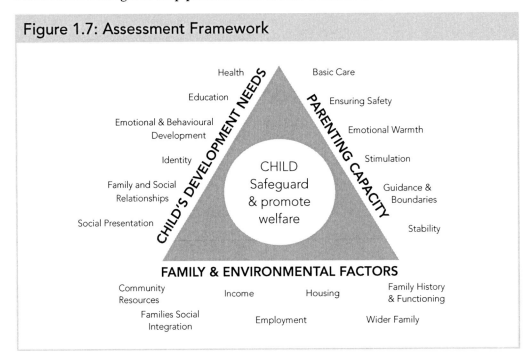

Figure 1.7: Assessment Framework

(Taken from *Working Together to Safeguard Children* © Crown copyright, 2018)

One of the sides of the assessment triangle looks at parenting capacity. In this area it is important that professionals are aware of the 'toxic trio' (Brandon *et al*, 2009), which consists of domestic violence, mental ill-health and substance misuse, that have been identified as common features in families where harm to children occurs. In nearly three-quarters of the serious case reviews examined by Brandon *et al* (2009), the children lived in an environment where parents and carers were struggling with mental ill-health and/or domestic violence and/or substance misuse and/or poverty.

An article written by a number of highly respected professionals in the field of safeguarding children was published by the NSPCC in 2010 (Broadhurst *et al*), which looked at assessments and what pitfalls to avoid. All professionals should heed their advice, as listed in the key learning points overleaf. This guidance provides practitioners with a concise and accessible summary of research findings relevant to all stages of decision making and assessment when working with children and families.

The evidence-informed learning identifies 10 individual and systemic issues that may occur in the initial assessment of children living at home. For each of these pitfalls, key research messages are summarised, followed by a list of critical questions for the reader. The guidance offers advice to all practitioners tasked to make robust, evidence-based judgements relating to child welfare when considering prevention, diversion and intervention concerning all need, harm and risk.

The publication was written primarily for local authority children social workers undertaking statutory assessments under sections 17 or 47 of the Children Act (1989), but nowadays is also useful to all professionals working within an Early Help setting providing diversion or preventative service, or in a MASH assisting with need, harm and risk identification as well as informed defensible decision making.

Key learning

10 pitfalls

1. An initial hypothesis is formulated on the basis of incomplete information, and is assessed and accepted too quickly. Practitioners become committed to this hypothesis and do not seek out information that may disconfirm or refute it.

2. Information taken at the first enquiry is not adequately recorded, facts are not checked and there is a failure to feedback the outcome to the referrer.

3. Attention is focused on the most visible or pressing problems; case history and less 'obvious' details are insufficiently explored.

4. Insufficient weight is given to information from family, friends and neighbours.

5. Insufficient attention is paid to what children say, how they look and how they behave.

6. There is insufficient engagement with parents (mothers/fathers/other family carers) to assess risk.

7. Initial decisions that are overly focused on age categories of children can result in older children being left in situations of unacceptable risk.

8. There is insufficient support/supervision to enable practitioners to work effectively with service users who are uncooperative, ambivalent, confrontational, avoidant or aggressive.

9. Throughout the initial assessment process, professionals do not clearly check that others have understood their communication. There is an assumption that information shared is information understood.

10. Case responsibility is diluted in the context of multi-agency working, impacting both on referrals and response. The local authority may inappropriately signpost families to other agencies, with no follow up.

Figure 1.8 is taken from the Scottish government's *A Guide to Getting it Right for Every Child* (2012), and is an effective visual way of ensuring that professionals maintain focus and keep the child at the centre of all assessments.

Figure 1.8: My world triangle

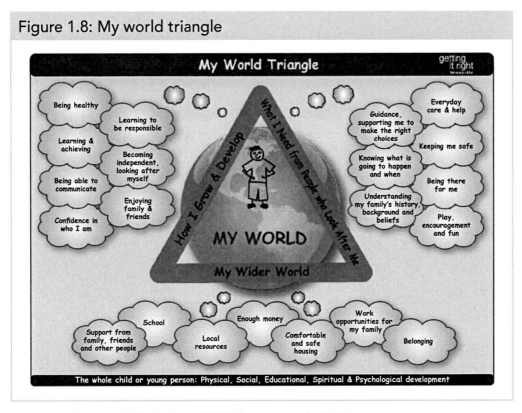

(Taken from *Getting it Right for Every Child* © Crown copyright, 2012)

Resilience and Adverse Childhood Experiences (ACE)

Research shows that chronic, severe stressors in childhood can cause toxic, traumatic biological responses to the developing brain, often with long-term consequences for health and emotional well-being. This research also tells us that responsive relationships with caregivers and strong community supports can buffer the effects of Adverse Childhood Experiences (ACEs), allowing children to develop to their potential. (See Chapter 3 for further information in relation to ACE.)

Recognising that children and adults have and continue to experience trauma, many safeguarding partnerships now aim to become better informed on its effects. The use of trauma informed practice in their work is really important.

They can adopt measures to strengthen the resilience of the children and young people they serve, thereby helping to improve outcomes for children from early childhood education, to schools, to foster care and the youth offending system. (See chapter 2 for more information.)

Key learning

- The child should be at the centre of any assessment by a professional.

- Assessments of children need to include them, their environment and their family.

- The toxic trio is domestic abuse, substance misuse (which includes drugs and alcohol) and parental mental health.

- Adverse Childhood Experiences.

Assessment tools: evidence informed

There are a number of assessment tools available, and different agencies and local authorities use ones they feel most suitable to their local context. A number of the more commonly used ones are highlighted below.

The Anchor Principles of Assessment

Anchor principles can be used as a framework for analytical thinking in assessment and by safeguarding professionals who work with children and their families. A sound analytical assessment will:

- provide a picture of the child, their parent(s) and their story

- provide an understanding of why the assessment is being done and what you will get out of it

- be specific about the individual child's needs

- be clear about the seriousness of the needs and the likely consequences/harm/ risk should needs not be met/addressed

- state what is going to happen next as a result of the assessment

- show an understanding of family history and context – context is key

- identify what we don't yet know and need to find out – assessment is an ongoing process

- show an understanding of the emotional implications of what has been observed for the family

- adopt an open and questioning mind – is this the only way of understanding this? Uncertainty is acceptable.

There are five anchor principles

1. What is the assessment for? Good planning prior to completing an assessment is crucial to success. Clarity about the purpose of the assessment from the beginning allows practitioners to identify key issues and identify and collect knowledge that will be relevant for the individual case including research, practice experience and observation of the family.

2. What is the story? Any young person or parent should be able to read and understand their assessment. Parents are the experts on their family story but it may be different from the child's narrative so may need to be challenged; parents need to be aware of the social worker's narrative of the story as presented in the assessment. When the worker is with the child and family they need to continuously ask, 'what is the impact of the parental behaviour on the child?' and be specific about the needs of the child and family.

3. What does the story mean? The point of analysing the assessment is to understand what the story means to the family and child and the impact on the child. Analyse the relationship between information (what you read or are told) and experiences (what you see and hear) to inform your judgement of the key issues and required intervention.

4. What needs to happen? The whole purpose of assessment is to identify the impact of past and current circumstances on the child and family and to agree what needs to happen. Links need to be made between the story, the meaning of the story and what needs to happen next, otherwise we won't be focused and effective.

5. How will we know we are making progress? The purpose of assessment is to decide the best way to address need, so it is essential to measure and review progress. If the outcome is achieved you can move to the next action, where the outcome is not achieved, we need to ask more questions and develop a new understanding of what the story means. People's circumstances can change for a variety of reasons and new information can come to light at any point. This can make old information appear in a different light or new information can arise as time passes. Either of these circumstances may lead you to revise your understanding of the case and reframe old needs or identify new ones. This in turn will require new outcomes to be identified and new interventions decided.

Principles one and two should be used in allocation supervision. Principles three, four and five should be used in subsequent supervisions to aid analysis of the assessment, formulate the plan and agree on the measures that will demonstrate whether progress is being made or not.

The Anchor Principles of Assessment can be used alongside any assessment tool depending on circumstances and what changes need to be effected to reach the best possible outcome for the child and their family.

Assessment tools

Selection of key assessment tools often used around the country

- Signs of Safety and Strengthening Families
- Neglect risk assessment tool – Graded Care profile
- Assessing Sexual Abuse – Brook light system
- Discrepancy matrix
- ECOMAP
- 3 Stage Theory Framework – Theory Circle (Collingwood, 1999)
- EVOLUTION prompts – Identification of need, harm and risk

Signs of Safety and Strengthening Families

One widely used risk assessment in current use in the UK is the 'Signs of Safety' model, helping practitioners with risk assessments and safety planning for non-statutory and statutory cases.

Signs of Safety is a systemic way of working with families at all levels of need which identifies strengths, reduces risks to children and enables solutions to family problems to be found as early as possible to prevent family breakdown and dysfunction. It contributes to the Strengthening Families approach (see below).

The Signs of Safety model is intended to help practitioners across different disciplines to work collaboratively and in partnership with families and children while undertaking risk assessments and safety planning. The tool allows risk assessments to be produced and directly link these to the creation of action plans for increasing safety, and to reduce risk and danger by identifying areas that need change while focusing on strengths, resources and networks that the family have.

The principles and practice of the Signs of Safety model have been formulated as a response to a number of the systemic challenges identified in child and family systems, of which many were critiqued in the Munro review (2011). Signs of Safety requires collaborative work across all agencies and multi-agency practitioners and encourages family participation through listening to the contributions of the child, the parents and all the relevant personal and professional links to a family's network.

Its approach to managing risk and safety encourages transparency and rigour in professional judgement when identifying risks and strengths, and provides a coherent framework for planning future interventions.

Created by Andrew Turnell and Steve Edwards in Western Australia during the 1990s, Signs of Safety is now used in at least 12 different countries across Australasia, North America and Europe.

For more information, see www.signsofsafety.net/signs-of-safety/ (accessed August 2019).

Strengthening Families

The Strengthening Families approach was developed out of the Signs of Safety model. In 2000, the model was further developed by Rob Sawyer and Suzanne Lohrbach who developed a family case planning conference (FCPC) that built upon the ideas of Andrew Turnell as well as the general principles of restorative practice and the Family Group Conference process.

In the UK, Signs of Safety tends to be used for triage, to inform risk analysis and case supervision, while the Strengthening Families approach is used in social care as an inclusive approach to risk assessment and planning in child protection conferences. It is designed to create a shared focus between professionals and family members that promotes the safety of the child.

The approach is aimed at helping families to participate more fully, assisting all participants to assess the risk to children more accurately, assisting all participants to be more engaged in the development and implementation of a child protection plan. It requires professionals to be clear and concise in the way they gather and present information and contribute to the conference.

The overall aim is to ensure that parents, children and professionals are all working positively together to ensure that the main aim is achieved – the safety of children.

Neglect risk assessment tool – Graded Care profile

In neglect cases, a number of areas around the country make use of the Graded Care Profile, or a variation of it, to helm them to risk-assess neglect. This Graded Care Profile was created by consultant paediatrician Dr Srivastava. He worked with the NSPCC to update the original tool and developed a more user-friendly and comprehensive version called Graded Care Profile 2 (GCP2).

The tool helps professionals measure the quality of care being given to children where there are concerns that they might be being neglected. Professionals use GCP2 to 'grade' aspects of family life on a scale of 1 to 5. The assessment helps identify the support needed to improve the level of care children receive.
The evaluation carried out by the NSPCC of the original GCP tool found that it helped practitioners:

- focus on the child
- build relationships with families
- improve the recording and reporting of neglect.

Assessing Sexual Abuse – Brook light system

Professionals who work with children and young people often struggle to identify which sexual behaviours are potentially harmful and which represent healthy sexual development. The Brook sexual behaviours traffic light tool supports professionals working with children and young people by helping them to identify and respond appropriately to sexual behaviours.

The traffic light system categorises the sexual behaviours of young people and is designed to help professionals:

- make decisions about safeguarding children and young people
- assess and respond appropriately to sexual behaviour in children and young people

■ understand healthy sexual development and distinguish it from harmful behaviour

By categorising sexual behaviours as green, amber or red, professionals across different agencies can work to the same standardised criteria when making decisions and can protect children and young people with a unified approach.

More information on the Brook traffic light tool is available at www.brook.org.uk/brook_tools/traffic/Brook_Traffic_Light_Tool.pdf (accessed August 2019)

Discrepancy Matrix

The Discrepancy Matrix encourages practitioners to explore any discrepancies they see within evidence that has been taken from different and multiple sources. This visual tool considers there to be a distinction between how evidence can be interpreted and weighted by practitioners. This is shown within the four different stages of the matrix; ambiguous, missing, assumption-led and firm ground.

The tool encourages the practitioner to consider the quality and relevance of the information gathered. The benefit of this tool is that it enables practitioners to consciously and critically reflect upon their decision making and what is informing their judgement when undertaking assessments.

More information, see:
Mainstone F (2014) *Mastering Whole Family Assessment in Social Worker: Balancing the needs of children, adults and their families*. London: Jessica Kingsley Publishers.

Wonnacott J (2012) *Mastering Social Work Supervision*. London: Jessica Kingsley Publishers.

Morrison T (2009) *The role of the scholar-facilitator in generating practice knowledge to inform and enhance the quality of relationship-based social work practice with children and families*. Doctoral thesis. University of Huddersfield.

ECOMAP

An ecomap is a flow diagram that maps family and community systems and the relationships between the different elements. It was developed as a visual tool for social workers in the 1970s by Dr Ann Hartman, when she applied the concept of an ecosystem to human communities to 'focus on the complex ecological system that includes the family and the total environment'.

Ecomaps graphically present family-environment interactions and changes at a given point in time. This visual aid enables the worker to see the connections of children and families with those around them in both family and their wider community. It highlights their support and frailties, as well as tensions, needs and risks.

An ecomap is often completed in conjunction with genograms, which provide a specific picture of a family with links across and between generations.

Ecomaps demonstrate the family's relationships and connections to the external world. They can primarily be used in two contexts:

- By the professional (and/or network) to develop a clear picture of the family situation from the professional's perspective.

- As a direct work tool with families which is done with families and/or young people.

Ecomaps therefore provide a visual picture of the family within in their current social context together with the contextual issues affecting them.

3 Stage Theory Framework (Theory Circle) (Collingwood, 1999)

The 3 Stage Theory Framework is a visual and interactive tool that can be used independently by practitioners as well as collaboratively in a group setting. This model is very child centred and draws upon a range of perspectives including sociological, psychological and ecological. It comprises the three progressive stages of applying theory to practice.

Stage one is focused on the service user profile, all referral information and the reasons for involvement.

At this stage it is important that practitioners consider significant information relating to the service user including age, gender, family composition, friends and key life events. The aim is for the practitioner to become acquainted with the world of the child. Stage one should involve planned direct work with a child or young person and redacted (and service user agreed) versions can be shared with other practitioners for their own records.

Stage two is the 'theory circle' that is made up of two distinct halves. The two halves identify the relevance and links between different child centric academic theories to explore what may be occurring in a child's or young person's world.

The left half of the 'Theory Circle' encourages the practitioner to consider the environment the child or young person is inhabiting and apply theoretical perspectives that inform this. These may include attachment, development and systems theory. The right-hand side of the circle considers the theoretical methods of intervention, which could include task-centred, crisis intervention, psychodynamic etc.

Stage three requires the practitioner to consider their own practice theory and wisdom in the context of their work with the child/young person. This is broken down into three categories: knowledge, skills and values.

- *Knowledge* allows the practitioner to explore their organisational influences such as policy and procedures, the legislative framework within which they work and the resources available to them.

- *Skills* requires the practitioner to consider what skills they would need to possess to apply the interventions and to effect the necessary change.

- *Values* ensures that the practitioner considers their own value base and any ethical conflicts and dilemmas that may occur or may be found when intervening with the child/young person. This could include considering issues such as choice and consent. The aim in this stage is that the practitioner becomes more self-aware of the power they hold within their role, they understand their position in promoting change with the service user and can practice in an anti-discriminatory manner.

More information is available from Whiting and Birch (2005) Integrating theory and practice: The Three-Stage Theory Framework. *Journal of Practice Teaching* **6** (1) p6-23.

EVOLUTION prompts – Identification of need, harm and risk

EVOLUTION is a 'prompt' tool for professionals to enhance dynamic and efficient delivery of safeguarding activity.

Professionals tend to use different risk assessments to identify threat, risk or concern. This has meant, on occasions, that the language of need, harm and risk has often been inconsistent, and has led to misunderstandings and partners not articulating in the same safeguarding language.

EVOLUTION 'prompts' provide an early-warning system and ensure holistic thinking.

EVOLUTION is a mnemonic and the 'prompts' ensure that professionals are able to consider and articulate what they have seen and heard (evidenced) following attendance at a household and when interacting with members of the public in any setting. The prompts ensure that nothing is missed inadvertently and that practitioners are considering the known triggers of need, harm and risk in all situations, even when the individual has a multitude of other tasks to consider. It was designed to be easy to use by all partners.

EVOLUTION forms part of a whole-system approach within a safeguarding partnership as it will prompt practitioners to highlight immediately those who need help and support, or even challenge their own behaviours, not just the behaviours of those who are subject of the assessment.

It encourages and supports frontline staff to collect and articulate evidence to support decision-making and assessment by using their professional judgement, curiosity and discretion. It is an aide to professional practice, and it allows concerns or gaps in information to be identified and analysed even when professionals cannot fully identify an area of need, harm and risk, but their professional experience and knowledge is making them suspect things are not as they should be within a given 'prompt' area.

EVOLUTION 'prompts' and the information gathered starts the understanding within the partnership of need, harm and risk picture. The 'prompts' add value in a fuller partnership picture.

This enables all services to target interventions at those in need, suffering harm or at risk. It also ensures that help is provided at the earliest opportunity to children, adults and families. EVOLUTION enhances assessments and it is a professional's way of obtaining a service for children, vulnerable adults and families.

Achieving best evidence

In certain circumstances, if it is suspected that a criminal offence may have occurred, the police and children's social care will carry out an Achieving Best Evidence (ABE) interview. Updated guidance on how best to do this was issued in 2011 (Ministry of Justice, 2011). The purpose of this guidance is to assist those responsible for conducting video-recorded interviews with vulnerable, intimidated and significant witnesses, as well as those tasked with preparing and supporting witnesses during the criminal justice process. The guidance incorporates best practice from local areas and the expertise of practitioners, charities and voluntary groups who support victims and witnesses at a local level.

The consent of parents is normally required in order to conduct an interview, and in cases where an adult with parental responsibility refuses to allow a child to be interviewed, whether that interview was to have been video recorded or not, and the child is not competent to consent of their own accord, the interview cannot take place.

In terms of competence to consent, a child under 16 years *can* consent themselves if it can be demonstrated that they have sufficient understanding and intelligence to understand fully what is being proposed (Lord Fraser, Gillick v West Norfolk and Wisbech AHA [1986] 1AC 112). This used to be called 'Gillick competence', but is now known as the Fraser guidelines as he was the presiding judge in the case.

Depending on the criminal allegation, it may be appropriate for the child or young person to have a paediatric examination, normally with consent from the parents or carers in order to do this.

Initial child protection conference

Once an assessment has been completed, an Initial Child Protection Conference (ICPC) will be held (within 15 days of the strategy discussion) if it is felt that there are still concerns that there is a likelihood of significant harm, which will look at actions to keep that individual child or children safe.

Working Together to Safeguard Children (DFE, 2018) describes this conference as follows:

'Following section 47 enquiries, an initial child protection conference brings together family members (and the child where appropriate), with the supporters, advocates and professionals most involved with the child and family, to make decisions about the child's future safety, health and development. If concerns relate to an unborn child, consideration should be given as to whether to hold a child protection conference prior to the child's birth.'

The conference is chaired by an independent chair, although they are answerable to the Director of Children Services, and parents are invited to attend as are all agencies that are involved with the child (as well as other statutory bodies) and that have a role and duty to keep the child or young person safe.

As a multi-agency group, they need to review and analyse all relevant information and plan how best to safeguard and promote the welfare of the child. If an agency has some confidential information that they wish to share but do not want the parents to be party to, the chair can exclude them from certain sections of the conference. The social worker allocated to the case should, however, have shared their report with the chair before the conference commences.

The conference will make recommendations about whether the child will be placed on the child protection register and form a plan as to how agencies can keep the child safe in the future, setting up a core group to do this.

The criteria for holding an initial child protection conference may not have been met or the conference may make a decision to step a child down from being on the register to a child in need. Most areas have in place child-in-need procedures and a series of meetings will be held to follow these procedures.

Key learning

- The recording of children's accounts for evidence has to comply with Achieving Best Evidence guidelines (Ministry of Justice, 2011).

- The competence of the child must be taken into account.

- Initial child protection conferences are where a decision can be made to place a child on a child protection register.

Case study: Emma

Emma is 20 and lives alone in a supportive housing project. She is not in a relationship with the father of her baby but she is part of a large family who offer intermittent support. Emma presented to maternity services with her first pregnancy, and during discussion she disclosed that she had some learning needs, having received a level of special education. Information gathering and assessing of her individual parenting capacity by the midwifery service over the following weeks revealed that Emma presented with a chaotic lifestyle, struggling to manage finances and unable to achieve some basic self-care.

Following discussion with Emma, and with her consent, it was felt that her unborn baby should be referred to children's services where assessments could be undertaken relating to Emma's parenting ability. The outcome of the children's social care assessment was that the unborn baby should be considered as a child in need, and these procedures needed to be in place. →

An incident then occurred where a child who was temporarily in Emma's care received significant injuries. These injuries were not believed to have been purposefully caused, but very poor judgement on Emma's behalf had been identified as a key factor, including her failure to recognise the need to seek immediate medical advice.

The case remained classified as a child in need, and midwifery concerns were brought to the attention of the safeguarding lead during supervision. This led to the implementation of escalation procedures to raise their concerns with children's services. As a result of this, a plan was agreed that the social worker was to undertake a risk assessment, and then the findings would be reviewed. Following the completion of the risk assessment, midwifery concerns remained high and so the case was highlighted to the team manager. A strategy discussion took place and the outcome was that the case was to progress to a section 47 enquiry.

A further multi-agency strategy discussion was undertaken and then an initial child protection conference was convened. The decision of the conference was that the baby should, at birth, be placed on a child protection plan under the category of neglect.

The plan at this stage was that, following transfer from hospital, Emma and her baby would reside at her mother's who had agreed to support her daughter with the care of her baby. Emma delivered a healthy baby girl and when both mother and baby were fit for transfer home, a discharge planning meeting was arranged. Concerns were raised as Emma's mother stated that she could not attend the discharge planning meeting as she had other commitments. This raised questions about Emma's mother's understanding of the full implications of her commitment as she was seen as a pivotal part of the plan to safeguard this baby. A plan was agreed that Emma and her baby would remain in hospital to facilitate the monitoring of their interactions, and for children's services to undertake further assessment.

The outcome of this assessment was that Emma required a residential assessment. Emma and her baby were transferred from hospital to a residential unit. After this further assessment it became clear that the baby should be put up for adoption through the Family Court.

Written agreements

These are often used by social workers when they work with families to ensure that they lay out what parents and families need to do to ensure they keep their children safe from harm. This happens rather than a move to more formal legal proceedings.

Emma Schooling from Ofsted gives some useful advice to professionals in relation to written agreements which can be found at: https://socialcareinspection.blog.gov.uk/2018/01/23/effective-written-agreements/ (accessed August 2019).

'Learning from inspection and from SCRs has given us some helpful guidance on how written agreements can be used more effectively. Here are some of the key ingredients:

- *Written agreements should be specific and have clear expectations. Professionals need to be assured that parents genuinely understand the agreement.*

- *Agreements should be underpinned by thorough assessment that is clear about risk and protective factors of all relevant adults and family members.*

- *They should be produced with parents who are equally committed to changing their behaviour.*

- *There must be clarity on how the written agreement will be monitored and reviewed in accordance with multi-agency plans and how this will inform the assessment of risk and action taken.*

- *A clear focus should be on the work undertaken with family members to effectively manage risk and protect children – in particular work to change the behaviour of the perpetrator.*

- *The limitations of these agreements should be made clear.'*

Legislation

Key topics covered

- Children Act (1989)
- Police Protection
- Emergency Protection
- Section 8 Orders
  - Residence
  - Contact
  - Prohibited Steps
  - Special Issue Orders

- Section 20 Agreements
- Special Guardianship Orders
- Public Law Outline 2014
- Section 31 Orders
- Care and Supervision Proceedings at pre-birth stage or when a child is newly born
- Flexible powers of the court
- Interim Care and supervision orders
- Care Order
- Good Practice Steps

What are the general principles of the Children Act (1989)?

Section 1 of the Children Act (1989) sets out three general principles:

- The welfare of the child is paramount.
- Delay is likely to prejudice the welfare of the child.
- A court shall not make an order unless to do so would be better for the child than making no order (the 'no order' principle). The 'no order' principle is that 'the court … shall not make the order or any of the orders unless it considers that doing so would be better for the child than making no order at all'. In applying the welfare principle, the court will consider a checklist of factors set out in the Children Act (1989), including:
- The child's wishes and feelings – the older the child, the greater the weight given to them.
- Their physical, emotional and educational needs.
- The likely effect on the child of any change in their circumstances.
- The age, sex, background and characteristics of the child that the court thinks is relevant.
- Any harm the child has suffered or is at risk of suffering.

The 'welfare principle'

The welfare principle under Section 1 is the overarching principle which applies to all proceedings under the Children Act (1989). The Act states that:

'When a court determines any question with respect to the upbringing of a child; or the administration of a child's property or the application of any income arising from it, the child's welfare shall be the court's paramount consideration.'

Avoiding delay is important in relation to the welfare principle. The Children Act (1989) states that *'the court shall have regard to the general principle that any delay in determining the question is likely to prejudice the welfare of the child'*.

Police protection powers

Under section 46 of the Children Act (1989), where a police officer has reasonable cause to believe that a child is likely to suffer significant harm, they may remove the child to suitable accommodation or take reasonable steps to ensure that the child's removal from any hospital or other place in which they are then being accommodated is prevented. No child may be kept in police protection for more than 72 hours.

As well as the above orders, a family court may either award an interim care order or full care order to a local authority in order to ensure the child is safeguarded.

Emergency protection powers

The court may make an emergency protection order under section 44 of the Children Act (1989) if it is satisfied that there is reasonable cause to believe that a child is likely to suffer significant harm if they are not removed to different accommodation provided by the applicant, or does not remain in the place in which the child is then being accommodated.

Where the applicant is the local authority, an emergency protection order may also be made if enquires (for example, made under section 47) are being frustrated by access to the child being unreasonably refused to a person authorised to seek access, and the applicant has reasonable cause to believe that access is needed as a matter of urgency.

An emergency protection order gives authority to remove a child and place them under the protection of the applicant, almost always the local authority.

Section 8 orders

Section 8 of the Children Act (1989) sets out a range of orders which a court can make. These are:

- residence orders
- contact orders
- prohibited steps orders
- specific issue orders.

These orders are designed to deal with disputes between private individuals, usually parents, family members or others with an interest in the child or children. They also need to be concerned with the upbringing of the child or children.

A court can make any of these orders regardless of any specific order requested to be made by the parent or others in an application by them.

Residence orders

A residence order under Section 8 of the Children Act (1989) settles the arrangements to be made as to the person with whom a child is to live. Residence orders normally last until the child reaches 18 years of age.

If an order is made in favour of an unmarried father without parental responsibility, the court will also make an order giving him parental responsibility.

In situations where a residence order is made in favour of a person who is not the parent or guardian of the child, such as a grandparent, that person will have parental responsibility for the child for the duration of the order.

Contact orders

A contact order sets out visitation rights of a party with whom the child is not resident. It will set out the contact (direct or indirect) the child can have with the other parent, such as when they can stay and for how long, where they can meet, how and when phone and Skype contact is to be made, and other types of indirect contact.

The court can also attach conditions to a contact order. For instance, if contact is obstructed by the other party, a fine can be imposed.

In deciding whether to make a contact order, the court's approach is that a child should have contact with the other parent unless there are good reasons not to allow it, such as a real risk of physical or emotional harm. It is the normal presumption that a child would benefit from continued contact with a natural parent.

Prohibited Steps Orders

Under the Children Act (1989), the court can make an order preventing a parent from doing something that they would normally be legally permitted to do by virtue of their parental responsibility.

Prohibited steps orders last until the child reaches the age of 16 except in 'exceptional circumstances'.

Specific Issue Orders

Conversely, a Specific Issues Order is an order directing a parent to take specific action, or course of action. For example, registering a child at a specific school, what religion the child should be brought up in, and so on. A Specific Issue Order lasts until the child reaches the age of 16 except in exceptional circumstances.

Section 20 Children Act (1989) Agreements

Section 20 of the Children Act (1989) sets out how a local authority can provide accommodation for a child within their area if that child is in need of it, due to being lost/abandoned or there being no person with parental responsibility for that child. Anyone with parental responsibility can voluntarily allow the local authority to accommodate their child under section 20.

Section 20 is 'voluntary accommodation', although parents can often be left with no alternative but to give their agreement when requested to do so. The voluntary accommodation can either be with formal local authority foster carers or, alternatively, with a family member who has been approved by the local authority (often a grandparent).

Sometimes section 20 voluntary accommodation can work very well and be to the advantage of the children, parents and the local authority. However, often this is not the case and parents will find that the voluntary accommodation continues for far longer than they originally anticipated or intended. What begins as a short-term agreement can quite easily end up spanning several months while the local authority continue assessments at a pace of its own choosing. Unless they are able to pay privately, parents will very often not have access to a solicitor during this time leaving them at a real disadvantage when considering timescales for assessment or the identity of an expert to be instructed.

The 26-week timescale for court care proceedings does not start until the case is issued and therefore time spent in voluntary section 20 accommodation pre-proceedings does not count towards this. This simply extends the time the children will be accommodated and living away from their parents. Once a case is in proceedings, parents have the advantage of challenging local authority decisions knowing they will be open to judicial scrutiny.

Special Guardianship Orders

Special Guardianship is a formal court order which places a child or young person with someone permanently and gives this person parental responsibility for the child. This could be a grandparent, close relative or a family friend. They need to apply to the court, which will consider their suitability and the child's needs based on a report from the local authority. Special Guardianship means that the child lives with carers who have parental responsibility for them until they are grown up. If the child was looked after before the Special Guardianship Order was granted, they will no longer be the responsibility of the local authority. The order usually lasts until the child is 18 years old.

A person can apply for a Special Guardianship Order if:

- they are a local authority foster carer and the child has lived with them for at least one year preceding the application.

- the child has lived with the person for three of the last five years (and the child has not stopped living with them more than three months before the application)

- they are the guardian of the child (they do not need to be related to the child)

- they have the consent of those who have parental responsibility for the child

- they have the consent of the local authority if the child is looked after

- they have a Child Arrangements Order or a Residence Order in respect of the child and they have the consent of the person in whose favour the Order was made

- they have permission from the court to make the application.

The person must also be over 18 and must not be the child's birth parent. A person can apply jointly with one or more people, and joint applicants do not need to be married.

A Special Guardianship Order has several potentially positive effects: it gives a child the security of a long-term placement, the child's birth parents retain shared parental responsibility, and it gives the Special Guardian day-to-day control (jointly, if there are several Special Guardians). Unlike adoption, a Special

Guardianship Order will not remove parental responsibility from the child's birth parents. This means that the Special Guardian will have responsibility for the day-to-day decisions as well as all the important decisions about the child or young person, but will need to consult the birth parents at times where key decisions are being made such as changing their name, moving overseas or agreeing adoption.

The Public Law Outline (PLO) 2014

When a social worker is very concerned about the welfare of a child, they may wish to consider taking the case to court so they can make Court Orders to protect the child.

Public Law Outline 2014, more commonly referred to as PLO, is a Ministry of Justice legal framework for children's care and supervision proceedings which identifies how social workers are required to deal with these sorts of cases. It should always be read in conjunction with the Children Act (1989) and other statutory guidance.

This framework should be followed when considering whether to initiate proceedings for a care or supervision order.

The Public Law Outline sets out streamlined case management procedures for dealing with children's public law cases. The aim is to avoid care proceedings if possible and, for those cases where proceedings are necessary, identify and focus on the key issues for the child, with the aim of making the best decisions for the child within a timetable set by a court. They are designed to avoid the need for unnecessary hearings.

As well as the court timetable, the case management tools within the PLO identify the documentation to be filed by the local authority and other parties, including case summaries and a schedule of proposed findings, advocates' discussions and meetings.

In the revised Public Law Outline (2014), both the filing and service of documents is more focused, with a concentration on what is relevant, central and key, rather than what is peripheral or historical.

Local authority materials are expected to be much shorter than previously, and they should be more focused on analysis than on history and narrative. Even if there has been local authority involvement with the family extending over many years, both the social work chronology and the summary of the background circumstances as set out in the social work statement must be kept appropriately short, focusing on the key significant historical events and concerns and rigorously avoiding all unnecessary detail.

When social workers are considering an application to the court to consider orders to protect the child, they will in the majority of circumstances invite parents to a Public Law Outline Meeting (PLO) or a pre-proceedings meeting.

The safety and welfare of the child should never be put in jeopardy by delaying issuing proceedings (whether because of lack of documentation or otherwise), and immediate action such as an application for an Emergency Protection Order (EPO) should be taken where necessary. Depending on the circumstances, the court may require a statement of evidence of significant harm, and care plan for an EPO application.

Section 31 of the Children Act (1989)

A local authority can start 'care proceedings' if they're very concerned about a child's welfare. They can apply for a 'care order' under Section 31 of the Children Act (1989), which means the local authority will have parental responsibility for the child and can determine where they live, and who with. The court may also grant a supervision order that enables the local authority to gain access to the family home for the purposes of assessment. Conditions can also be attached in some cases, when appropriate. It may require a child to live in a specified place, do certain activities and report to a particular place at a set time.

Supervision orders impose a duty on the local authority to 'advise, assist and befriend' the child.

The biggest difference between a care and a supervision order is that a care order grants the local authority parental responsibility for the child, meaning that it can take decisions for the child and override the wishes of the parents. Under Section 31 of the Children Act (1989), a court may make a Care or Supervision Order only if it is satisfied that the threshold criteria for significant harm has been met.

Under the Public Law Outline (2014) and the Children and Families Act (2014), there is a 26-week time limit for the completion of care and supervision proceedings. This places an increased emphasis on pre-proceedings work and the quality of assessments. Information from other partner agencies is essential within both pre-proceedings work and assessments to fully inform the historic and current picture concerning the child before proceedings are commenced. Proceedings, however, are not delayed if there is a need to protect the child.

Where adoption is the permanent plan for the child and no care order has been made, combined care and placement order applications are made so that decisions can be reached swiftly. Where there are on-going Care Proceedings, the Placement Order application is submitted as soon as the decision has been made. The court may make both orders, which would ensure that the child remains protected should the Placement Order be revoked (as the Care Order would automatically be reactivated).

Placement Order applications are not subject to the 26-week time limit, but an early application will ensure best use of court time and help keep to a minimum the overall length of the process. The application must clearly state why the parents cannot parent the child.

Care and Supervision Proceedings at pre-birth stage or when a child is newly born

When a local authority becomes aware of an unborn child and there are concerns for their welfare or safety, they will carry out a pre-birth assessment to ensure they are aware of all the circumstances surrounding the child, which in turn will inform any legal action they may need to take before or after the birth.

The pre-birth assessment informs a pre-birth conference, which is normally held eight weeks before the due date for the birth of the child. Here, decisions are made as to the type of any intervention that may be required or legal processes to be instigated from that date. The pre-birth conference is a partnership meeting.

Local procedures within each safeguarding partnership lay out the procedures and timescales for pre-birth considerations and should always be consulted.

A High Court judgment (Nottingham City Council v LW & Ors [2016] EWHC 11(Fam) (19 February 2016)) has sought to provide 'good practice steps' with respect to public law proceedings regarding newly born children and particularly where children's services are aware at a relatively early stage of the pregnancy.

From previous judgments it is established that, 'At an interim stage the removal of children from their parents is not to be sanctioned unless the child's safety requires interim protection'.

It is important to ensure that, for both the child and the parent(s):

- any hearing should be considered a 'fair hearing' commensurate with Article 6 of the Human Rights Act (the right to a fair trial)
- the fact that a hospital is prepared to keep a new born baby is not a reason to delay making an application for an ICO.

A hospital may not detain a baby against the wishes of a parent with parental responsibility, and the capability of a maternity unit to accommodate a healthy child can change within hours and is dependent upon demand.

Where a Pre-birth Plan recommends an application for an ICO to be made on the day of the birth, 'it is essential and best practice for this to occur'.

Once it has been determined that there is sufficient evidence to make an application for an ICO and removal of a child, any additional evidence (e.g. from the maternity unit) must not delay the issuing of proceedings.

Flexible powers of the court

Although the Public Law Outline sets out a prescribed set of stages, it also provides for flexibility at any stage of the proceedings. Steps, which the court will ordinarily take at the various stages of the proceedings, may be taken at another stage if the circumstances of the case so merit.

The flexible powers of the court include the ability for the court to cancel or repeat a particular hearing, to give directions without a hearing including setting a date for the final hearing (or a period within which the final hearing will take place), or to take oral evidence at a hearing.

Where it is anticipated that oral evidence may be required at a Case Management Hearing (CMH), Further Case Management Hearing (FCMH) or Issues Resolution Hearing (IRH), the court must be notified well in advance and directions sought for the conduct of the hearing.

Interim care and supervision orders

At the start of care proceedings, a local authority under Section 38 of the Children Act (1989) may ask the family court to make a temporary court order, called an 'interim care order'. If the court agrees, the council can take the child into care on a temporary basis. This can initially be for up to eight weeks. It can take up to 26 weeks for a court to decide what should happen to the child. Some complex cases can take longer.

During this time a social worker, an officer from the Children and Family Court Advisory and Support Service (Cafcass) and other professionals will try to understand the reasons why the child may be at risk. They will also look at what can be done to keep them safe.

They will talk to the parents and the child. They may talk to other family members or friends about looking after the child if they can't safely live at home.

Care Order

The local authority can seek a full care order under section 31 of the Children Act (1989). This grants the local authority parental responsibility for the child, meaning that it can take decisions for the child and override the wishes of the parents.

If it is a full Care Order, the local authority is responsible for:

- making sure that an appropriate standard of care is provided
- making sure only suitable people are employed to look after the child
- providing proper training and support to staff and foster carers
- listening to the child's views and parents' views about care arrangements and taking their religion, race, culture and background into account
- making sure the child has someone independent to talk to and knows how to complain if necessary. They will be appointed an Independent Reviewing Officer who is the person who ensures that children looked after by the local authority have regular reviews to consider the care plan and placement. It is the role of the Independent Reviewing Officer to ensure that a child's views are taken into consideration and that the local authority is fulfilling its duties and functions.

The child may be placed with either:

- another relative
- a foster carer
- a children's home.

Good practice steps

In all but the most exceptional and unusual circumstances, local authorities must make applications for public law proceedings in respect of newborn babies in the most-timely fashion, and especially where the circumstances arguably require the removal of the child from its parent, within no more than five days of the child's birth.

The Pre-birth Plan should be rigorously adhered to by social work practitioners, managers and legal departments and informed by partnership information.

The voice of the child, lived experience and the journey of the child

First, let's consider what we mean by 'the child's voice'. The child's voice not only refers to what children say directly, but to many other aspects of their presentation. It means seeing their experiences from their point of view. When working with children or young people it is essential to gain a clear picture of their wishes, thoughts and feelings. It is good practice to ask the child or young person which practitioner they would like to gather this information from them.

The right of a child or young person to be heard is identified in Articles 12 and 13 of the UN Convention on the Rights of the Child:

Article 12:
'The state shall assure to the child who is capable of forming his or her own views the right to express those views freely in all matters affecting the child, the views of the child being given due weight in accordance with the age and maturity of the child. For this purpose, the child shall in particular be provided the opportunity to be heard in any judicial and administrative proceedings affecting the child, either directly, or through a representative or an appropriate body, in a manner consistent with the procedural rules of national law.'

Article 13:
'The child shall have the right to freedom of expression; this right shall include freedom to seek, receive and impart information and ideas of all kinds, regardless of frontiers, either orally, in writing or in print, in the form of art, or through any other media of the child's choice.

The exercise of this right may be subject to certain restrictions, but these shall only be such as are provided by law and are necessary:
(a) For respect of the rights or reputations of others; or
(b) For the protection of national security or of public order (ordre public), or of public health or morals.'

Section 53 of the Children's Act (2004) makes it a statutory duty to ascertain the child's wishes and feelings as part of any assessment, regarding the provision of service and any action to be taken in relation to them by a local authority. The importance of gathering the wishes and feelings of a child or young person has been consistently highlighted in lessons learned from serious case reviews.

In too many cases local and national reviews have found:

- a child was not seen frequently enough by the professionals involved, nor were they asked about their wishes or feelings
- agencies did not listen to adults who tried to speak on behalf of the child and who had important information to contribute
- parents and carers prevented practitioners from seeing and listening to the child
- practitioners focused too much on the needs of the parents or adults, especially vulnerable adults, and overlooked the implications for the child
- agencies did not interpret their findings well enough to protect the child: the child's voice was not heard.

The UK Government ratified the United Nations Convention on the Rights of the Child in 1991, recognising in UK law children's rights to expression and to receiving information.

These rights are reinforced by the Human Rights Act (1998), Article 10, Freedom of Expression.

The lived experience of the Child

The 'lived experience of the child' includes what a child sees, hears, thinks and experiences every day that impacts on their development and welfare whether that be physically or emotionally.

As practitioners we need to put ourselves in the child's shoes and think what is life like for this child right now in the context he or she is living in?

A child centred approach

Professor Eileen Munro stated that:

'Everyone involved in child protection should pursue an ethos of child-centred working and recognise children and young people as individuals with rights, including their right to participation in decisions about them in line with their age and maturity'.

In other words, *'the system* [child protection] *should be child-centred'.*

The 'journey of the child' is considered from the time a child is identified as needing support to when they receive it. This journey, which will include the child's wishes and feelings, must be articulated by all practitioners within a child's record with an expectation that a child may at any time in their life wish to request access to the record.

They may well read what has been written about them and the reasons for decisions which directly affected their lives. Accurate and thorough recording is therefore essential as well as being incredibly important to the child.

Key learning

- There are numerous and varied assessment tools available for practitioners.

- The recording of children's accounts for evidence must comply with Achieving Best Evidence guidelines (Ministry of Justice, 2011).

- Written agreements can sometimes be used rather than legal intervention by social workers.

- The 'Welfare Principle' is the paramount overarching aim of the Children Act (1989).

- The age and competence of the child must be given due weight.

- Multiple orders can be sought by social workers under the Children Act (1989).

- Emergency and police protection.

- Public Law Outline (PLO): streamlined case management procedures.

- Care and Supervision orders under the Children Act (1989).

- Voice of the Child, lived experience and Journey of the Child: Articles 11 &12 of the UN's Convention on the Rights of the Child.

Further reading

The Department for Education's *Working Together to Safeguard Children* guidance. These are available online:

2010 version: http://webarchive.nationalarchives.gov.uk/20130401151715/https://www.education.gov.uk/publications/standard/publicationdetail/page1/dcsf-00305-2010 (accessed August 2019).

2018 version: https://assets.publishing.service.gov.uk/government/uploads/system/uploads/attachment_data/file/729914/Working_Together_to_Safeguard_Children-2018.pdf (accessed August 2019).

Lord Laming's *The Victoria Climbié Inquiry*, is available online at: https://www.gov.uk/government/uploads/system/uploads/attachment_data/file/273183/5730.pdf (accessed August 2019).

The Munro Review of Child Protection: Final report – a child-centred system is available online at: https://www.gov.uk/government/publications/munro-review-of-child-protection-final-report-a-child-centred-system (accessed August 2019).

The United Nations Convention on the Rights of the Child 1989 is available at: http://www.unicef.org/crc/

References

Barker L (1999) *The Social Work Dictionary*. Washington DC: National Association of Social Workers Press.

Brandon M, Bailey S, Belderson P, Gardner R, Sidebotham P, Dodsworth J, Warren C & Black J (2009) *Understanding Serious Case Reviews and Their Impact: A biennial analysis of serious case reviews* 2005-07. London: Department for Children, Schools and Families.

Brearley P (1982) *Risk and Social Work*. Routledge, Kegan Paul.

Broadhurst K, White S, Fish S, Munro E, Fletcher K & Lincoln H (2010) *Ten Pitfalls and How to Avoid Them* [online]. London: NSPCC. Available at: http://www.nspcc.org.uk/globalassets/documents/research-reports/10-pitfalls-initial-assessments-report.pdf (accessed August 2019).

Cambridgeshire and Peterborough Safeguarding Children Board (2018) *Effective Support for Children and Families in Peterborough and Cambridgeshire* [online]. Peterborough: www.safeguardingcambspeterborough.org.uk/wp-content/uploads/2018/11/Effective-Support-for-Children-and-Families-Thresholds-Document.pdf (accessed August 2019).

Collingwood P (2005) Integrating theory and practice: the Three Stage Theory Framework. *The Journal of Practice Teaching* **6** (1) 6-23.

Department for Education (2010) *Working Together to Safeguard Children*. London: DfE.

Department for Education (2018) *Working Together to Safeguard Children*. London: DfE.

Department for Education (2019) *Keeping Children Safe in Education*.

Deroos Y (1990) The development of practice wisdom through human problem-solving process. *Social Service Review* **64** 276–287.

Fook J & Gardner F (2007) *Practising Critical Reflection*. Maidenhead: Open University Press.

Fook J & Gardner F (eds) (2013) *Critical Reflection in Context*. London: Routledge.

Kitchner KS and Brenner HG (1990) Wisdom and reflective judgment: knowing in the face of uncertainty. In: RJ Sternberg (ed) *Wisdom: Its nature, origins and development*. Cambridge: Cambridge University Press.

Klein WC and Bloom M (1995) Practice wisdom. *Social Work* **40** (6) 799–807.

Lord Laming (2009) *The Protection of Children in England: A progress report* [online]. London: TSO. Available at: http://webarchive.nationalarchives.gov.uk/20130401151715/http://www.education.gov.uk/publications/eOrderingDownload/HC-330.pdf (accessed August 2019).

Ministry of Justice (2011) *Achieving Best Evidence in Criminal Proceedings: Guidance on interviewing victims and witnesses, and guidance on using special measures*. London: Ministry of Justice.

Munro E (2011) *The Munro Review of Child Protection: Final report – a child-centred system*. London: TSO.

Nepaul V (2013) *Nelson Mandela on Children* [online]. Huffington Post. Available at: www.huffpost.com/entry/nelson-mandela-on-childre_b_4394706

NSPCC (2018) *How Safe Are Our Children?* London: NSPCC.

O'Sullivan T (2005) Some theoretical propositions on the nature of practice wisdom. *Journal of Social Work* **5** (2) 221–242.

Reder P, Duncan S & Gray M (1993) *Beyond Blame: Abuse tragedies revisited*. London: Routledge.

Royal College of General Practitioners (2013) *Signs and Indicators of Abuse*. London: RCGP.

Scottish Government (2012) *A Guide to Getting it Right for Every Child* [online]. Available at: http://www.scotland.gov.uk/Resource/0045/00458341.pdf (accessed August 2019).

Smith E, Johnson R and Andersson T (2018) *Implementation evaluation of the Scale-up of Graded Care Profile 2*. London: NSPCC

Sullivan PM and Knutson JF (2000) Maltreatment and disabilities: a population-based epidemiological study. *Child Abuse and Neglect* **24** (10) 1257–1273.

Chapter 2: Children living in special circumstances: understanding need, harm and risk

By Marisa de Jager and Nigel Boulton

Chapter overview

- Understanding need, harm and risk.
- Young carers.
- Private fostering.
- Bullying.
- Relinquished children.
- Children living with domestic abuse, parental mental ill health, substance or alcohol misuse.
- Unaccompanied minors and asylum-seeking children.
- Contextual safeguarding.
- Criminal exploitation.
- Partnership prevention, diversion and intervention.
- County lines.

Introduction

The term 'children living in special circumstances' does not describe a tightly defined group and features a range of contexts, needs and behaviours. Children living in special circumstances are widely defined as those who are at risk of achieving poorer outcomes than their peers, have a particular need of good quality, accessible services to promote their health and well-being, yet may be least likely to receive them.

This chapter covers some groups who may have unrecognised and unmet needs and would potentially benefit from a holistic, multi-agency response. It is widely acknowledged that the only way to deliver an appropriate response or a prevention strategy to help these children is to have a highly co-ordinated multi-agency, whole family approach addressing the needs of the child, recognising the importance of links between child and adult services and the value of targeted support. Local partnerships need to be aware of local issues and trends, and be curious at a strategic and operational level about what is happening.

Children need professionals who are well trained, skilled and persistent and who recognise need, harm and risk factors. The behaviours that children present with, such as offending or violence, may result from exploitation outside the home and/or from abuse at home. Any interventions need to consider all need, harm and risk in the context of other vulnerabilities such as criminal and sexual exploitation.

Preventing and responding to issues of need, harm and risk that affect children and young people creates a huge challenge for all safeguarding partnerships nationally and locally. For professionals to respond and support appropriately they must ensure that they have the building blocks in place to work effectively and quickly. Agencies need to understand the context of the child's behaviour as well as the impact, for example trauma, post-traumatic stress disorder (PTSD), mental health issues or substance misuse.

Everyone involved must understand local issues so that responses can be carefully co-ordinated to meet local need. Partnerships need to not only identify and respond to the presenting need, harm or risk factor, but must work with children, parents and local communities to understand and drive prevention and diversion opportunities and raise awareness.

When a child presents, for example, as an unaccompanied minor, has offending or other concerning behaviour or is a young carer, professionals need to be curious and compassionate and ask:

- what is the exposure to need, harm or risk and impact on the child's development
  and

- what is happening in this child's life that is causing them to behave this way?

Young carers

Background and definition

The Children and Families Act (2014) amended the Children Act (1989) to make it easier for young carers to obtain an assessment of their needs by introducing the 'whole family' approach to assessment and support.

Local authorities must offer a Young Carer's Needs Assessment under the Children and Families Act (2014) where it appears that a child is involved in providing care for a family member and requires support. A similar provision was introduced in the Care Act (2014), requiring local authorities to consider the needs of young carers if, during the assessment of an adult carer or adult with care needs, it appears that a child is providing, or intends to provide, care.

Under the Children and Families Act (2014), a young carer is defined as:

'A person under 18 who provides, or intends to provide, care for another person. The concept of 'care' includes practical or emotional support, and 'another person' means anyone within the same family be they adult or child.'

Young carers undertake a wide range of caring roles and responsibilities in the family home including providing emotional support and personal care, undertaking housework and budgeting. The duty on local authorities to identify and assess the support needs of young carers applies regardless of the type of support they are providing.

The Children and Families Act (2014) definition excludes children providing care as part of contracted work or as voluntary work unless the local authority consider that the relationship between the person cared for and the child is such that it would be appropriate for them to be regarded as a young carer.

Identifying young carers

Local authorities are expected to take 'reasonable steps' to identify children in their area who are young carers. The local authority must offer to carry out an assessment if it appears that the young carer may have needs for support and, if so, should identify what those needs are. The duty to assess applies where there is an appearance of need. There does not have to be a specific 'request'.

Identifying young carers is not always easy. Research has found that a significant proportion of young carers do not disclose their caring responsibilities to their school, and that often young people (and their families) do not recognise themselves as 'young carers'. Furthermore, parents and carers can be reluctant to disclose information about caring responsibilities for fear of repercussions, including children's social care involvement and potential family separations.

Adopting a whole family approach is recommended as the best way to identify young people who are caring for a family member. This means that whenever an adult is receiving social care or support, any assessments undertaken should always include discussions about children in the household to identify if they have caring responsibilities and may, therefore, require support as a young carer.

Providing the right care to adult family members at the right time is vital and helps to ensure that children do not take on inappropriate caring tasks. The need for children to provide care is increased when services for ill or disabled adults (or other family members) are inadequate, inappropriate or missing, and when family-based interventions are not provided.

Schools also have a vital role to play in identifying and supporting young people who are helping to care for family members.

Assessing need and providing support

A Young Carer's Needs Assessment must consider whether the care being provided by the child is excessive or inappropriate, and how the child's caring responsibilities affect their well-being, education and development. Clear communication between professionals and families at the start of the assessment process is important to allay any concerns parents and young people may have about the assessment and its likely consequences.

Local authority adults' and children's services should work together to offer young carers and their families an effective service that avoids the need for multiple assessments. The assessment should be carried out in a manner which is appropriate and proportionate to the needs and circumstances of the young carer to whom it relates.

Assessments of young carers and the people they care for are intrinsically linked, and the regulations allow local authorities to combine assessments. Whoever carries out the assessment must:

■ be appropriately trained

■ have sufficient knowledge and skill to be able to carry out the assessment

■ be an appropriate person to carry out the assessment having regard to the young carer's circumstances, in particular the young carer's age, sex and understanding.

Ideally, assessments should be carried out promptly following identification or disclosure of a young person's caring responsibilities. In carrying out the assessment, the local authority must consider:

■ the young carer's age, understanding and family circumstances

■ the wishes, feelings and preferences of the young carer

■ any differences of opinion between the young carer, the young carer's parents and the person cared for, with respect to the care which the young carer provides (or intends to provide)

■ the outcomes the young carer seeks from the assessment.

The local authority must consult with people with expertise and knowledge in relation to the young carer as part of the assessment process, including teachers, health workers and other relevant adults. It is important to speak to the child alone, wherever possible, and to observe how they relate with their parents and siblings.

Transition

Sections 63 and 64 of the Care Act (2014) introduced duties for local authorities in respect of young carers making the transition to adulthood. The Act under Section 63(1) requires local authorities to seek the consent of the young carer to undertake a Young Carers Assessment, widely known in practice as Transition Assessments, if they are likely to have needs for support when they reach 18, and if the timing of the assessment offers 'significant benefit'. The timing of any assessment should be discussed with the young carer and their family. Much of the information necessary to complete a Transition Assessment may have already been collected as part of the Young Carer's Needs Assessment. Transition Assessments for young carers must also specifically consider whether the carer is able to care now, and whether they are prepared and willing to continue to be a carer after they reach adulthood at 18.

Privately fostered children

The Children (Private Arrangements for Fostering) Regulations (2005) and the amended Section 67, Children Act (1989), provide the statutory regulatory framework for private fostering. Private fostering is an arrangement whereby a child under the age of 16 (or 18 if the child has a disability) is placed for 28 days continuously (but can include occasional short breaks) or more in the care of someone who is not the child's parent, a person with parental responsibility or a relative in their own home.

It is a requirement that the local authority is notified if there is an intention to place a child in a private fostering arrangement. This duty encompasses the person who proposes to foster the child, any person involved in the arrangements or a parent or person with parental responsibility who is not involved with the arrangement but is aware of the intention.

The notification must be made at least six weeks before the arrangement is to begin, or immediately if the arrangement is to begin within this time period.

Private foster carers are often relatives from the extended family. A 'relative' is defined under Section 105 of the Children Act (1989) as:

'… a grandparent, brother, sister, uncle or aunt (whether full blood or half blood or by marriage or civil partnership) or step-parent.'

The local authority has a duty to visit the premises where the child is to be fostered within seven days of the notification, speak with the proposed carer and the child (alone, unless deemed inappropriate) in order to satisfy themselves that the placement is suitable and the child is safe.

A local authority is required to visit the child at least every six weeks within the first year and at least every 12 weeks for all subsequent years

Victims of bullying

Bullying is a form of abuse and can be defined as *'any unsolicited or unwelcome act that humiliates, intimidates or undermines the individual involved and includes cyber-bullying'* (DfE, 2018). Bullying is deliberately hurtful behaviour, usually repeated over a period of time, where it is difficult for the victims to defend themselves.

The damage inflicted by bullying is often underestimated. It can cause considerable distress to children and young people, to the extent that it affects their health and development and can be a source of significant harm, including self-harm and suicide. Victims of bullying might suffer emotional distress, social isolation, accidents, illness, non-participation, poor self-esteem and morale, and low levels of functioning in the different areas of their lives.

Bullying can lead to exploitation in its different forms, including financial, social and sexual exploitation, scapegoating and ostracism. Harassment, which can take many different forms including stalking, is also a form of bullying.

'Virtual' bullying via mobile phone or online (e.g. text messaging, email, social networks and instant messaging services) can occur in or outside school and at all times of the day or night, with a potentially bigger audience, which can be increased easily by individuals forwarding messages and data through social media with ease, uncontrolled and unseen.

The main types of bullying are:

- Physical abuse (e.g. hitting, kicking, stabbing and setting alight), including filming with mobile telephone, and theft, commonly of mobile telephones.

- Verbal, mobile telephone or online (internet) message abuse (e.g. racist, sexist or homophobic name-calling or threats). This type of non-physical bullying may include sexual harassment.

- Mobile telephone or online (internet) visual image abuse. These can include real or manipulated images.

- Emotional abuse (e.g. isolating an individual from the group or emotional blackmail).

Consequences of bullying

Children who are bullied are often afraid to go to school and may make up health problems to stay at home. Many, however, develop actual health problems due to the stress and there may be a decline in school attainment.

All forms of bullying can cause serious emotional distress, which often leads to anxiety, fear, low self-esteem, feelings of worthlessness and depression. Research reveals that bullied children are also more likely to think about committing suicide. It has been suggested that 44% of suicides by young people in the UK are linked to bullying.

Relinquished children

The term 'relinquished child' is used to describe a child, usually a baby or at pre-birth stage, whose parents are making the choice of adoption for the child.

All local authorities have a statutory duty to respond to a request from a parent or guardian for their child to be placed for adoption, and a separate process to progress this, at least in the initial stages, outside of any care proceedings process, is established in Part 3 of the Adoption and Children Act (2002). For more information, see: www.legislation.gov.uk/ukpga/2002/38/part/1/chapter/3 (accessed August 2019).

Working with a request for a child to be relinquished will be challenging for many practitioners because most children's best interests is served by being with their parent and it will be important to ascertain the reasons why the mother sees adoption as the best course of action, and to offer challenges to this through a counselling process.

Counselling should be undertaken as promptly as possible following the referral, by an experienced practitioner who has knowledge and skills in adoption, and include a discussion about the issue's adoption brings for both the parent or guardian and the child.

Involving the birth father without Parental Responsibility

There is no duty on a local authority to make enquiries of a father without Parental Responsibility, or his family, when a child is being relinquished by the mother, unless this is considered to be in the best interests of the child.

If the identity of the birth father becomes known advice can be given for them to obtain a Parental Responsibility Order under section 4 (1) of the Children Act (1989) or a Child Arrangements Order under the Children's and Families Act (2014).

In making this decision, the practitioner must balance:

- the principle that the welfare of the child is paramount
- the nature of the child's relationship with the father
- the nature and extent of the father's relationship with the child's mother and any siblings of the child
- whether it would be contrary to Article 8 of the Human Rights Act (1998) (Right to respect for private and family life) to prevent disclosure of the birth of a child to its father
- the mother's wishes for the child
- the mother's right to confidentiality
- the avoidance of unnecessary delay.

Where a birth father acquires Parental Responsibility and the mother has already consented to adoption, and the child has been placed for adoption, Section 19 of the Adoption and Children Act (2002) considers that the father has also consented to the placement for adoption. However, the birth father can then withdraw his consent, provided he does so before an application has been made to court for an Adoption Order. For more information, see: www.legislation.gov.uk/ukpga/2002/38/section/19 (accessed August 2019).

However, where the local authority wishes to continue with the adoptive placement, a placement order application must be applied for. Where the application is before the court, there is no obligation for the local authority to return the child to either parent.

Consent and competency

The local authority as the adoption agency must be sure that the parent or the guardian is competent to give consent. During the counselling sessions, care should be given to identifying whether the parent(s) are capable of giving consent, especially if there is evidence of:

- learning disabilities
- mental health issues
- cultural, ethnic or faith issues
- consent being given conditionally, etc.

Where there is concern as to the parent's understanding, an additional and specialist assessment should be sought from another professional, preferably someone who already knows the parent such as an approved mental health social worker, a disabilities social worker, GP, midwife or health visitor, psychiatrist, psychologist or someone who can offer a faith or cultural perspective.

If it is known that there is an issue of competency at the point of referral or at an early stage in the process, then the local authority should not ask the Children and Family Court Advisory and Support Service (CAFCASS) to witness consent until any such issues are resolved. Where a parent is under 18 years (i.e. considered to be a 'child' themselves within the meaning of the Children Act (1989)), they can be considered to give valid consent if assessed as competent by the counselling practitioner.

The High Court in Re S (Child as parent: Adoption: Consent) [2017] EWHC 2729 made clear that parental capacity to consent to a child being accommodated under section 20 of the Children Act (1989) does not equate to their capacity to consent to an adoption order in respect of the child. The capacity to consent is decision-specific. (The case concerned a 'child parent' (i.e. below 18 years of age) with learning disabilities.) The principles in this case, however, will be of relevance in considering parental capacity, irrespective of their age.

The court set out the salient or 'sufficient' information that is required to be understood by a parent regarding extra-familial adoption:

■ The child will have new legal parents, and will no longer be their son or daughter, in law.

■ Adoption is final and non-reversible.

■ During the process, other people (including social workers from the adoption agency) will be making decisions for the child, including who can see the child, and with whom the child will live.

■ Parents may wish to obtain legal advice if they wish before taking the decision.

■ The child will live with a different family forever; the parent will (probably) not be able to choose the adopters.

■ Parents will have no right to see the child or have contact with the child; it is highly likely that direct contact with the child will cease, and any indirect contact will be limited.

■ The child may later trace the parent, but contact will only be re-established if the child wants this.

- There are generally two stages to adoption: the child being placed with another family for adoption, and being formally adopted.

- For a limited period of time the parent may change their mind, however once placed for adoption, their right to change their mind is limited, and is lost when an adoption order is made.

When determining the competence of a parent in these circumstances, 'all practicable steps' must be taken to help them to make the decision, for example using simple language, visual aids or other means. A parent will be treated as understanding the information relevant to a decision if they are able to understand an explanation of it given to them in a way which is appropriate to their circumstances.

The decision to consent to adoption is significant and life-changing. Before exercising their decision, the parent should freely and fully understand the information set out on the consent forms, which should be conveyed and explained to them in an appropriate way. There is no expectation that the parent would be able to understand the precise language of the consent forms.

If there is any doubt about the competence of a parent to give consent to adoption or placement for adoption, the issue should be referred to a court.

Where it is considered that the parent is not capable of giving informed consent but the local authority decide to place the child for adoption following their counselling and assessment, an application for a Placement Order must be made.

The parent(s) can withdraw their consent to the child's placement for adoption at any stage prior to the prospective adopters issuing an adoption application in relation to the child in writing. On receiving the Notice of Withdrawal, the local authority (as the agency) will lose the authority to place and there should be an immediate review of the child's plan for adoption. Following legal advice, the local authority may decide to apply for a Placement Order.

Throughout this process it will remain important:

- That the child's welfare and best interests remains paramount.

- To ensure there is minimal delay in securing the child's permanent future plan, and therefore referrals to CAFCASS, the Adoption Team and, if required a Placements Application Order, together with completion of all necessary documentation, are made in a timely way.

- That effective counselling is offered to the parent(s) with regard to the decision, and clear consideration is given to the parent(s) competency to make the decision.

- The parent(s) are fully aware of their rights and options throughout the process with regard to the child.

- That the practitioner remains in contact with the parent for as long as possible to 'get to know' the parent(s) so as to be able to provide information for the child later in their life.

Children's Social Services should seek to ensure that, following a request for a child to be relinquished, the matter should be transferred to the appropriate team best able to work with the parent/guardian and progress the child's plan as soon as possible. For more information, see www.proceduresonline.com (accessed August 2019).

Children living with domestic abuse, parental mental ill health, substance/alcohol misuse

The term 'toxic trio' is used to describe the issues of domestic abuse, mental ill health and substance/alcohol misuse. These have all been identified as common features of families where harm to women and children occurs. They are now viewed as key indicators of increased risk of harm to children and young people.

In an analysis of 139 serious case reviews between 2009-2011 (Brandon *et al*, 2012), investigations showed that in over three quarters of incidents (86%) where children were seriously harmed or died one or more of the toxic trio played a significant part.

While most commonly associated with violence perpetrated by men against women, domestic violence and abuse can also be perpetrated by women on men, can occur within same sex relationships, to or from a child, or can be perpetrated by a carer against someone they are looking after.

Domestic violence and abuse may be exacerbated by other factors e.g. mental illness, substance misuse (including alcohol), homelessness and housing need, pregnancy, new birth and separation.

Section 120 of the Adoption and Children Act (2002) extended the definition of 'harm', as stated in the Children Act (1989) to include *'impairment suffered from seeing or hearing the ill treatment of another'*. Prolonged or regular exposure to domestic violence can have a serious impact on a child's development and emotional well-being, despite the best efforts of the victim parent to protect the child. The harm is caused by the person who causes the child to see or hear the ill treatment, which is the perpetrator of the violence or abuse. It is not acceptable for perpetrators or others to describe this as unintentional or to hold the victim responsible for the child witnessing the abuse. For more information, see www.legislation.gov.uk/ukpga/1989/41/contents (accessed August 2019).

The impact will be exacerbated when violence is combined with any form of substance misuse.

These issues are discussed further in Chapter 4: Domestic violence and abuse.

Unaccompanied minors and asylum-seeking children

Definitions

The cohort of unaccompanied migrant children and child victims of modern slavery includes a wide range of children in a variety of circumstances that a local authority will need to be aware of in order to ensure that they receive appropriate legal advice and support.

There are a wide range of status possibilities for migrant children. Some will have been trafficked or persecuted and may have witnessed or been subject to horrific acts of violence. Other migrant children may have been sent in search of a better life, or may have been brought to the UK for private fostering and subsequently been exploited or abandoned when the arrangement fails.

In brief, the following categories regarding status are the most likely to be encountered. However, this list is not exhaustive and legal advice should be sought wherever there is uncertainty about a migrant child's status.

Categories of unaccompanied children include:

- **Unaccompanied asylum-seeking children**. Children who are claiming asylum in their own right, who are separated from both parents, and who are not being cared for by an adult who, in law or by custom, has responsibility to do so. Some will not qualify for asylum but may require 'humanitarian protection', where an individual is found not to be a refugee under the Refugee Convention but they are nevertheless at risk of serious harm on return to their country of origin. Others may not qualify for any leave to remain in the UK. Their status will be determined by the Home Office.

- **Unaccompanied migrant child not seeking asylum**. A child who is not seeking asylum because their reasons for being here are not connected to seeking protection, or who may be undocumented, or is not seeking asylum because they have not been advised of the need to do so. The child may be separated from both parents and is not being cared for by an adult who, in law or by custom, has responsibility to do so

- **Unaccompanied EEA national child**. A child who is a national of a European Economic Area country and who has entered the UK with a family member and has been separated from them or has entered independently. They have a right to reside in the UK for an initial period of three months. After this time, an EEA national child will only have a right to reside in the UK if they are exercising their free movement rights or they are the family member of an EEA national exercising free movement rights in the UK.

- **Asylum seeking child**. A child who is in the UK with family members and may have been transferred to the UK under the Dublin III Regulation to join a close family member and have their claim for asylum processed here.

Responsibilities of the local authority

Where it is established that a referral concerns a young unaccompanied child migrant, regardless of the category, this will always satisfy the criteria for services to a Child in Need under Section 17 of the Children Act (1989).

An unaccompanied child will become looked after by the local authority after having been accommodated by the local authority under Section 20(1) of the Children Act (1989) for 24 hours. Once accommodated, they will be subject to the appropriate regulations and the same provision as any other Looked After Child.

The local authority should have procedures in place to monitor their policies and performance and should record any modern slavery concerns on the child's care plan. As part of the general duty to assess and meet the needs of an unaccompanied asylum-seeking child, the local authority should ensure that the child has access to a legal representative. Unaccompanied children are highly likely to require specialist support from a variety of organisations and agencies.

Age assessment

Where the age of the child is uncertain and there are reasons to believe they are a child, the person will be presumed to be a child in order to receive immediate assistance, support and protection in accordance with Section 51 of the Modern Slavery Act (2015).

Assessments must be undertaken in accordance with standards established in case law and should only be carried out where there is reason to doubt that the individual is the age they claim.

A partnership approaches

All professionals involved in the care of unaccompanied children and child victims of modern slavery should be able to recognise indicators of trafficking, slavery, servitude and forced or compulsory labour, and should have an understanding of the particular issues likely to be faced by these children. This is a highly complex area of work and professionals will need to have available to them a solid understanding of the asylum process or colleagues or other professionals with such expertise.

The kinds of issues that may need to be negotiated include:

- an understanding of the Welfare Interview, Statement of Evidence Form

- the purpose of the asylum case review

- the importance of the substantive asylum interview

- the different possible outcomes of a child's asylum claim and how that impacts on pathway planning.

Social workers should also have a broad understanding of the immigration system, for example the immigration application process, different types of leave, making further leave to remain applications and the appeals process. Social workers should also have an understanding of the trafficking referral process and the wider child protection system around child victims of modern slavery, including how and when to refer a child to the National Referral Mechanism.

Legal advice can only be provided by a registered immigration advisor, ideally one with expertise in working with children. Legal Aid is available for asylum cases and Looked After Children will generally be eligible.

Unaccompanied minors reaching adulthood

Planning the transition to adulthood for unaccompanied children is a particularly complex process that needs to address their developing care needs in the context of their immigration status. Former unaccompanied children who qualify as care leavers and who have been granted leave to remain in the UK, or who have an outstanding asylum or other human rights claim or appeal, are entitled to the same level of care and support from the local authority as any other care leaver.

The extent of any support for former unaccompanied children who have turned 18, exhausted their appeal rights, established no lawful basis to remain in the UK and who should return to their home country, is subject to a Human Rights Assessment by the local authority. This is set out under the restrictions on local authority support for adults without immigration status.

For former unaccompanied children whose long-term future is in the UK, transition planning will need to consider the same challenges and issues facing any care leaver, such as education or preparing for independent living. Planning for children and young adults who have been granted refugee status or humanitarian protection should also consider when they may be required to make a further application for leave to remain. Where an unaccompanied child or child victim of modern slavery qualifies for local authority care leaving support, a personal adviser must be appointed to support them.

Planning may have to be based around short-term achievable goals while entitlement to remain in the UK is being determined. For the majority of unaccompanied children who do not have permanent immigration status, transition planning should initially take a dual or triple planning perspective, which, over time, should be refined as the young person's immigration status is resolved. Planning cannot pre-empt the outcome of any immigration decision but the following should be prepared:

- A transitional plan during the period of uncertainty when the care leaver is in the UK but without permanent immigration status.

- A longer-term plan should the care leaver be granted long-term permission to stay in the UK (for example through the granting of Refugee Status).

- A plan for their return to their country of origin at any appropriate point or at the end of the immigration consideration process, should that be necessary because the care leaver decides to leave the UK or because they are required to do so.

Assistance should be given in advance of their 18th birthday with the necessary applications for housing, Housing Benefit and any other relevant benefits. The social worker must ensure that the young person has accommodation ready to move to on his or her 18th birthday.

Access to public funds

Financial support for care leavers who are former unaccompanied child migrants should reflect their needs and their immigration status. Financial policies should highlight any entitlements and how their immigration status may affect these. Pathway plans should address employment opportunities and funding arrangements for education and training, taking account of the young person's immigration status.

If a young person has no recourse to public funds, they will be unable to access a number of welfare benefits and social housing. Subject to the Human Rights Assessment by the local authority[2] the provision of accommodation may form part of the leaving care support provided to a young person who has no recourse to public funds. Having 'no recourse to public funds' does not prevent a person from accessing other publicly funded services, but many of these will have eligibility criteria based on immigration status, which will need to be considered.

Asylum process – possible outcomes

There are four main possible outcomes of the asylum process for an unaccompanied child, which will determine what the long-term solution might be:

- **Granted refugee status** (i.e. granted asylum), with limited leave to remain for five years, after which time they can normally apply for settlement (i.e. indefinite leave to remain).

- **Refused asylum but granted humanitarian protection**, with limited leave to remain for five years, after which time they can normally apply for settlement (i.e. indefinite leave to remain). This is most commonly granted where the person is at risk of a form of 'ill treatment' in their country of origin but which does not meet the criteria of the Refugee Convention.
  As it is very likely that those granted refugee status or humanitarian protection will qualify for indefinite leave to remain, their care and pathway planning should primarily focus on their long-term future in the UK, in the same way as for any other care leaver.

---

2   Under Schedule 3 of the Nationality, Immigration and Asylum Act (2002) (as amended).

- **Refused asylum but granted Unaccompanied Asylum-Seeking Child (UASC) Leave**. This is normally for 30 months or until the age of 17½, whichever is the shorter period. This form of leave is granted to unaccompanied children who do not qualify for refugee status or humanitarian protection, but where the Home Office cannot return them to their home country because it is not satisfied that safe and adequate reception arrangements are in place in that country.

  It is a form of temporary leave to remain and is not a route to settlement. It is important to note that this decision is a refusal of the child's asylum claim and there is a right of appeal. The child should be assisted to obtain legal advice on appealing against such a refusal. Before the child's UASC Leave expires, they can submit an application for further leave to remain and/or a fresh claim for asylum, which will be considered. It is essential that they are assisted to access legal advice and make any such further application or claim before their UASC Leave expires.

  In such cases, care and pathway planning should consider the possibility that the child may have to return to their home country once their UASC Leave expires or that they may become legally resident in the UK long-term (if a subsequent application or appeal is successful). Planning should also cover the possibility that they reach the age of 18 with an outstanding application or appeal and are entitled to remain in the UK until its outcome is known.

- **Refused asylum and granted no leave to remain**. In this case the unaccompanied child is expected to return to their home country and their care plan should address the relevant actions and the support required. The Home Office will not return an unaccompanied child to their home country unless it is satisfied that safe and adequate reception arrangements are in place in that country. Any appeal or further application should be submitted where appropriate by the child's legal adviser.

Although the above are the four main outcomes for an unaccompanied child, there may be others. For example, a child may be granted discretionary leave depending on whether they meet other criteria such as needing to stay in the UK to help police with their enquires after being conclusively identified as a victim of trafficking. Other examples include:

- leave as a stateless person

- limited or discretionary leave for compassionate reasons

- limited leave on the basis of family or private life.

Contextual safeguarding

Contextual Safeguarding as a concept was developed by Carlene Firmin at the University of Bedfordshire to inform policy and practice approaches to safeguarding adolescents. It is an approach to understanding and responding to young people's experiences of significant harm caused from outside their families. It recognises that the different relationships that young people form in their neighbourhoods, schools and online, can feature violence and abuse. Parents and carers have little influence over these contexts, and young people's experiences of extra-familial abuse can undermine parent-child relationships.

Peer relationships become increasingly influential during adolescence, setting social norms which inform young people's experiences, behaviours and choices, and determine peer status. These relationships are in turn shaped by, and shape, the school, the neighbourhood and online contexts in which they develop. If young people socialise in safe and protective schools and community settings they will be supported to form safe and protective peer relationships. However, if they form friendships in contexts characterised by violence and/or harmful attitudes, these relationships too may be anti-social, unsafe or promote problematic social norms as a means of navigating or surviving in those spaces.

Contextual Safeguarding and child protection systems

The child protection system and the legislative and policy framework which underpins it was designed to protect children and young people from risks posed by their families and/or situations where families had reduced capacity to safeguard those in their care. Extra-familial risks can reduce or undermine the capacity of families and carers to safeguard young people. To this extent, extra-familial risks are accommodated by existing approaches.

However, in traditional systems extra-familial risk would be addressed by intervening with families to increase their capacity to safeguard the young people concerned from harm and/or relocating them away from harmful contexts.

A Contextual Safeguarding system, on the other hand, supports approaches that disrupt or change harmful extra-familial situations rather than move families or young people away from them. While parents and carers are not in a position to change the nature of extra-familial contexts, those who manage or deliver services in these spaces are, and they therefore become critical partners in the safeguarding agenda. This approach would extend the concept of 'capacity to safeguard' beyond families to those individuals and sectors who manage extra-familial settings in which young people encounter risk.

Criminal exploitation

For some of our children and young people today, grooming and threatening behaviour has become the norm and they might not recognise that they need help, support and protection. Criminal exploitation has received considerable media coverage and with a focus on the risks of 'county lines' and gang activity.

Child criminal exploitation occurs *'where an individual or group takes advantage of an imbalance of power to coerce, control, manipulate or deceive a child or young person under the age of 18. The victim may have been criminally exploited even if the activity appears consensual. Child Criminal Exploitation does not always involve physical contact; it can also occur through the use of technology. Criminal exploitation of children … includes for instance children forced to work on cannabis farms or to commit theft.'*
(Time to listen – a joined up response to child sexual exploitation and missing children; Ofsted, 2016; www.gov.uk/government/publications/joint-inspections-of-child-sexual-exploitation-and-missing-children)

Organised crime groups and gangs – 'County lines'

Organised crime groups and gangs, as defined by the Serious Crime Act (2015), is a group that:

- has as its purpose, or as one of its purposes, the carrying on of criminal activities

- consists of three or more persons who act, or agree to act, together to further that purpose.

Gang-related violence and drug dealing activity is defined as gang related if it occurs in the course of, or is otherwise related to, the activities of a group that:

- consists of at least three people

- has one or more characteristics that enable its members to be identified by others as a group.

In the UK we have seen a rise in criminal exploitation, especially when individuals or gangs use vulnerable children and adults to transport and sell Class A drugs, primarily from urban areas into market or coastal towns or rural areas in order to establish new drug markets or to take over existing ones. This has become known as 'County lines'. They also use children to transport and hide weapons and to secure dwellings of vulnerable people in the area, so that they can use them as a base from which to sell drugs.

County lines is used in the Serious Violence Strategy 2018 as a term to describe gangs and organised criminal networks involved in exporting illegal drugs into one or more importing areas within the UK, using dedicated mobile phone lines or other form of 'deal line'. They are likely to exploit children and vulnerable adults to move and store the drugs and money, and they will often use coercion, intimidation, violence (including sexual violence) and weapons.

Child criminal exploitation is defined in the same document as being: *'where an individual or group takes advantage of an imbalance of power to coerce, control, manipulate or deceive a child or young person under the age of 18 into any criminal activity (a) in exchange for something the victim needs or wants, and/or (b) for the financial or other advantage of the perpetrator or facilitator and/or (c) through violence or the threat of violence.'*

The victim may have been criminally exploited even if the activity appears consensual. Child criminal exploitation does not always involve physical contact; it can also occur through the use of technology.

County lines needs to be considered in respect of modern slavery, human trafficking and exploitation, alongside drug supply and violent crime. It is a highly lucrative illegal business model. Those who are running county lines can earn thousands of pounds per day. The adults running these networks are removed from the frontline activity of dealing. They exploit children who are put at high risk transporting and selling drugs, often many miles from home. There are high levels of violence and intimidation linked to this activity.

Children may be sent to another area of the country to live with a vulnerable adult whose home has been taken over by the gang in exchange for a continued supply of drugs. This is known as 'cuckooing'. While living in a vulnerable adult's home, far away from their own home, children may be required to set up or be part of a new drug market or expand an existing one.

This involves children putting themselves in extremely dangerous situations with vulnerable adults who are strangers who want to buy Class A drugs from them. Other dealers in the area may also target these children to prevent them taking over their 'patch'. Some children have been stabbed and killed by rival gangs or dealers. Often the first time that the police become aware of county lines activity in their area is as a result of a significant increase in knife crime and youth violence.

County lines may involve the commission of the offences of 'slavery, servitude and forced or compulsory labour' and 'human trafficking', as defined by the Modern Slavery Act (2015).

Children's travel may be 'arranged and facilitated by a person, with the view to them being exploited', which amounts to human trafficking as defined by section 2 of the Modern Slavery Act (2015). Children may then be forced to work for the drug dealer, often held in the vulnerable adult's home against their will and under the force of threat if they do not do as they are told. This meets the definition of 'slavery, servitude and forced or compulsory labour' within section 1 of the Modern Slavery Act (2015).

Tactics used by perpetrators include staging a fake robbery where the drugs and money concealed on the child are stolen by their own gang. In these cases, the child believes they have lost money, drugs or phone contacts that are valuable to those running the county lines and that they must work for free to repay the debt. Gangs might also threaten the safety of their family or parents, including directly at their homes. Younger siblings are often recruited through fear, violence and intimidation against the family of older exploited children.

All criminally exploited children are at risk of neglect, emotional harm, sexual exploitation and abuse, as well as substance misuse and extreme forms of violence. The trauma caused by intimidation, violence, witnessing drug use or overdoses and continued threats to themselves or to family members leads to significant mental and physical ill-health of exploited children.[3]

Recognising the signs of criminal exploitation is crucial. County lines activity is a problem across England. In a report from the National Crime Agency, 88% (of the 38 police forces that responded to a survey) reported county lines activity. The National Crime Agency recently assessed that there are more than 1,500 lines operating nationally, with evidence of increasing levels of violence. County lines activity affects many areas of the country, including market and seaside towns and areas of relative affluence that we might not naturally associate with organised crime.

While the term 'county lines' is becoming more widely recognised and used to describe situations where young people may be internally trafficked for the purpose of criminal exploitation, what is often less understood is the experiences a young person faces and the potential for them to be harmed through various forms of abuse and exploitation as a result.

There is currently no legal definition of county lines or criminal exploitation, and also very little guidance. Currently, the criminal exploitation of children and young

---

3   For more information, see *Criminal Exploitation of Children and Vulnerable Adults*, Home Office, 2018; www.gov.uk/government/publications/criminal-exploitation-of-children-and-vulnerable-adults-county-lines

people is often not fully understood by services working with young people, which can impact on the response that a child or young person receives.

Criminal exploitation interlinks with a number of multiple vulnerabilities and offences including the child being exposed to and or victim of physical and emotional violence, neglect, sexual abuse and exploitation, modern day slavery and human trafficking, domestic abuse and missing episodes.

The risk to a young person and their family and friends as a result of experiencing criminal exploitation can include but is not limited to:

- physical injuries: risk of serious violence and death

- emotional and psychological trauma

- sexual violence: sexual assault, rape, indecent images being taken and shared as part of initiation, revenge, punishment, internally inserting drugs

- debt bondage: a young person and family being in debt to the exploiters, which is used to control the young person

- neglect and basic needs not being met

- living in unclean, dangerous and or unhygienic environments

- tiredness and sleep deprivation: a child is expected to carry out criminal activities over long periods and through the night

- poor attendance and or attainment at a place of education.

Who is vulnerable to child criminal exploitation?

The national picture on child criminal exploitation continues to develop but there are recorded cases of:

- children as young as 12 years old being exploited by gangs to courier drugs out of their local area; 15-16 years is the most common age range

- both males and females being exploited

- white British children being targeted because gangs perceive that they are more likely to evade police detection

- social media being used to make initial contact with children and young people

- class A drug users being targeted so that gangs can take over their homes (known as 'cuckooing').

Gangs and groups are known to target vulnerable children and adults. Some factors that heighten a person's vulnerability include:

- having prior experience of neglect, physical and/or sexual abuse

- lack of a safe, stable home environment now or in the past (domestic abuse or parental substance misuse, mental health issues or criminality, for example)

- social isolation or social difficulties

- economic vulnerability

- homelessness or insecure accommodation status

- connections with other people involved in gangs

- having a physical or learning disability

- having mental health or substance misuse issues

- being in care (particularly those in residential care and those with interrupted care histories).

Partnership prevention, diversion and intervention

'Cumulative harm may be caused by an accumulation of a single adverse circumstance or event, or by multiple different circumstances and events. The unremitting daily impact of these experiences on the child can be profound and exponential, and diminish a child's sense of safety, stability and wellbeing.' (Bromfield & Miller, 2007)

Partnerships need to work together to better understand the need, harm and risk factors that quite often form part of a child or young person's daily life. It is only through combined efforts that safeguarding partnerships can set about the task of identifying vulnerability and children living in special circumstances, and responding in a responsible, flexible and optimistic way. An effective and efficient approach that considers the most appropriate prevention, diversion or intervention activity for the child or young person will ensure that a system is created that supports change and helps to create a safer and fairer environment for everyone.

This means that professionals need to work flexibly even when children, young people or their families are unwilling to engage. Many of the current systems to manage individual children or young people within the child protection system are based around risk in the family. It is vitally important that the safeguarding partnership focuses also on preventative and diversion opportunities before they escalate, and a child or young person is deemed to be at risk of significant harm.

There needs to be a multi-agency co-ordinated approach to awareness-raising with children, young people, parents and the wider local community, as well as disruption and prevention of those perpetrating exploitation. Multi-agency meetings must result in clear action planning, co-ordination of work across agencies and close monitoring of plans so that children and young people are protected and supported. Services need to be co-ordinated and easily accessible if children and young people, particularly those who have been exploited and may be reluctant to engage, are to use them and access help and support when needed.

Where assessment shows that it is safe and appropriate to do so, parents and families should be regarded as a part of the solution. It is crucial to work with them, not only to assess the need, harm or risk faced by the child or young person, but to help them understand what their lived experiences mean and how they can be supported and protected. The parents may need direct support and help to improve family relationships and keep their child safe.

With the growing use of technology and social media, all professionals need to adopt a much more sophisticated approach to their safeguarding responsibilities. To do this successfully, professionals need to recognise that children and young people do not use technology and social media in isolation. Their offline and online worlds converge, and both need to be understood when trying to identify the type of support that a child, young person and their family might need.

The importance of this increases whenever there are concerns about children and young people suffering or being likely to suffer significant harm. In such circumstances, it is essential that both the offline and online risks are accurately assessed and effectively mitigated.

Practitioners should maintain their relationships with children and young people, continue to exercise professional curiosity, and create safe spaces to build trust. Children and young people's needs and safety must always come first.

Further reading

Statutory Guidance on Adoption (July 2013)

ADCS, Good Practice Guidance for Adoption Agencies and CAFCASS: Children Relinquished for Adoption

Court Reports in Placement Order Applications and in Adoption/Special Guardianship Guidance

Section 22(1) Adoption and Children Act (2002)

References

Brandon M, Sidebotham P, Bailey S, Belderson P, Hawley C, Ellis C & Megson M (2012) *New Learning from Serious Case Reviews: A two year report for 2009-2011*. Department for Education

Bromfield L and Miller R (2007) *Specialist Practice Guide: Cumulative harm*. Melbourne, Victoria: Department of Human Services, State Government Victoria.

Daniel B, Wassell S and Gilligan R (2010) *Child Development for Child Care and Protection Workers* (2nd edition). London: Jessica Kingsley Publishers. (Particularly: Chapter 4 'Resilience and vulnerability' and Chapter 5 'Protective factors and adversity'.)

Department for Education (2018) *Keeping Children Safe in Education* [online]. Available at: www.gov.uk/government/publications/keeping-children-safe-in-education--2 (accessed September 2019).

Firmin C (2019) *Safeguarding Children and Young People from Sexual Exploitation and Associated Vulnerabilities: A briefing for inspectorates* [online]. University of Bedfordshire. Available at: https://contextualsafeguarding.org.uk/assets/documents/JTAI-briefing-update-FINAL.pdf (accessed September 2019).

Ofsted (2016) *Time to Listen: A joined up response to child sexual exploitation and missing children*. Available at: https://www.justiceinspectorates.gov.uk/hmicfrs/publications/response-to-child-exploitation-and-missing-children/ (accessed September 2019).

Nair P, Schuler ME, Black MM, Kettinger L and Harrington D (2003) Cumulative environmental risk in substance abusing women: early intervention, parenting stress, child abuse potential and child development. *Child Abuse and Neglect* **27** (9) 997–1017

Chapter 3: Complex child abuse

By Russell Wate

Chapter overview

There are a number of different forms of child abuse that make safeguarding more complex. This chapter highlights a selection of these and gives professionals a good perspective of what they involve and how to safeguard children who may be subjected to any of these complicated forms of child abuse. The issues explored in this chapter are:

- Contextual Safeguarding.
- Adverse Childhood Experiences (ACE).
- Child sexual exploitation.
- Female genital mutilation.
- Forced marriage.
- Fabricated and induced illness.
- Child death and child death reviews.
- Child Safeguarding Practice Reviews.

Contextual Safeguarding

As we have discovered in Chapter 1, the majority of harm that children suffer is inflicted on them by someone known to them. However this is not always the case, and harm can occur to them from outside of the family as the following the definition below, taken from *Working Together* (DfE, 2018), explains:

'As well as threats to the welfare of children from within their families, children may be vulnerable to abuse or exploitation from outside their families. These extra-

familial threats might arise at school and other educational establishments, from within peer groups, or more widely from within the wider community and / or online. These threats can take a variety of different forms and children can be vulnerable to multiple threats, including: exploitation by criminal gangs and organised crime groups such as county lines; trafficking, online abuse; sexual exploitation and the influences of extremism leading to radicalisation. Extremist groups make use of the internet to radicalise and recruit and to promote extremist materials. Any potential harmful effects to individuals identified as vulnerable to extremist ideologies or being drawn into terrorism should also be considered.'

This harm and risk is explored in much more detail in Chapter 2. which covers bullying, county lines, serious youth violence, prostitution, unaccompanied minors, modern day slavery and alcohol and substance misuse, often known as hidden harm.

Adverse Childhood Experiences (ACE)

Adverse Childhood Experiences (ACE) are traumatic experiences that occur before the age of 18 years and are remembered throughout adulthood. These experiences range from suffering verbal, mental, sexual and physical abuse, including neglect, to being raised in a household where domestic violence, alcohol abuse, parental separation or drug abuse is present. Evidence shows that children who experience stressful and poor-quality childhoods are more likely to develop health-harming and anti-social behaviours, perform poorly in school, be involved in crime and ultimately less likely to be a productive member of society.

The term was originally developed in the US for the Adverse Childhood Experiences survey, which found that as the number of ACEs increased in the population studied, so did the risk of experiencing a range of health conditions in adulthood. There have been numerous other studies which have found similar findings including in England and Wales. Preventing ACEs should be seen within the wider context of tackling societal inequalities. While ACEs are found across the population, there is more risk of experiencing ACEs in areas of higher deprivation. ACEs have been found to have lifelong impacts on health and behaviour and they are relevant to all sectors and involve all of us in society. We all have a part to play in preventing adversity and raising awareness of ACEs. Resilient communities have an important role in action on ACEs.

When children are exposed to adverse and stressful experiences, it can have a long-lasting impact on their ability to think, interact with others and learn. It is important that professionals do all they can to tackle these ACEs as soon as they can to prevent the consequences from continuing into adulthood.

Table 3.1, taken from the *Routine Enquiry for History of Adverse Childhood Experiences (ACEs) in the Adult Patient Population in a General Practice Setting: A pathfinder study* (Hardcastle & Bellis, 2018), outlines the prevalence of these negative experiences.

Table 3.1: Defining Adverse Childhood Experiences and their prevalence among adults in England		
ACE		Prevalence
Child maltreatment	Verbal abuse	17.3%
	Physical abuse	14.3%
	Sexual abuse	6.2%
Childhood household included	Parental separation	22.6%
	Domestic violence	12.1%
	Mental illness	12.1%
	Alcohol abuse	9.1%
	Drug abuse	3.9%
	Incarceration	4.1%

It is important for multi-agency practitioners to understand the impact of trauma and work in a trauma-informed way. In some areas in the country, authorities have totally changed their model of social work delivery to focus on this trauma informed practice.

Child sexual exploitation

Sexually abusing a child through exploitation is not a recent phenomenon. Child sexual exploitation (CSE) has always been present. In the past it was not properly acknowledged, and, to a certain extent, was hidden away, as the recent inquiries into cases such as Jimmy Savile, abuse in care homes, schools and within the church have revealed. Recent technological advances, such as instantly accessible social media, has enabled offenders to sophisticate their method of offending.

There has been a number of high-profile investigations recently, such as in Rotherham, Rochdale, Derby and Oxford, which have been widely reported in the media and which often give the impression that it is usually organised groups and gangs responsible for these abuses. This is not necessarily the case, however, and the abuse can be carried out by lone offenders with a number of victims. It is also important to note that, although most cases highlighted by the media involve girls, child sexual exploitation is also committed against boys.

There has been a plethora of reports into the matter completed by various organisations, both statutory and voluntary, a number of which are listed in Further reading on p146. A good example is Barnardo's *Puppet on a String: The urgent need to cut children free from sexual exploitation* (Barnardo's, 2011), which helped to bring about a cross-government action plan on tackling child sexual exploitation.

The definition of child sexual exploitation used by the Department for Education describes this form of child abuse as:

'Child sexual exploitation is a form of child sexual abuse. It occurs where an individual or group takes advantage of an imbalance of power to coerce, manipulate or deceive a child or young person under the age of 18 into sexual activity (a) in exchange for something the victim needs or wants, and / or (b) for the financial advantage or increased status of the perpetrator or facilitator. The victim may have been sexually exploited even if the sexual activity appears consensual. Child sexual exploitation does not always involve physical contact; it can also occur through the use of technology.'
(DfE, 2017)

Types of sexual exploitation

The four main types of child sexual exploitation are:

■ Inappropriate relationships: usually involving a sole perpetrator who has inappropriate power or control over a child (physical, emotional, financial) and uses this to sexually exploit them. One indicator may be a significant age gap. The child believes they are in a loving relationship.

■ The 'boyfriend' model of exploitation: in the boyfriend model, the perpetrator befriends and grooms a child into a 'relationship', and then coerces or forces them to have sex with friends or associates. The child believes they are in a loving relationship.

■ Peer exploitation model: a child is invited (often by same-sex friends), or forced by peers or associates, to engage in sexual activity with several, or all, of the children present at the time. There is no pretence of a special or intimate relationship with any of the perpetrators.

- Organised/networked sexual exploitation: children (often connected) are passed through networks, possibly over geographical distances between towns and cities, where they may be forced/coerced into sexual activity with multiple men. Often this occurs at 'sex parties' organised by perpetrators, at which victims are given drugs and alcohol before they are sexually abused. The children who are involved may be used as agents to recruit others into the network. Some of this activity is serious organised crime and can involve the organised 'buying and selling' of children by perpetrators (DoH, 2014).

The type of child sexual exploitation that multi-agency professionals will encounter most frequently is the second type, the 'boyfriend' model. This makes it especially hard to get the child to disclose information as they don't believe or understand that they are a victim.

Risk factors and indicators of abuse

There are number of risk factors and indicators of CSE, and any multi-agency professionals who work with or come into contact with children should be aware of the following 'red flags':

- Living in a chaotic or dysfunctional household (including parental substance use, domestic violence, parental mental health issues and parental criminality).

- A history of abuse (including familial child sexual abuse, risk of forced marriage, risk of 'honour' based violence, physical and emotional abuse and neglect).

- Risk of forced marriage and/or 'honour' based violence.

- Recent bereavement or loss.

- Gang association, either through relatives, peers or intimate relationships (in cases of gang associated child sexual exploitation only).

- Attending school with young people who are sexually exploited.

- The presence of learning disabilities in the child.

- Children who are unsure about their sexual orientation or who are unable to disclose their sexual orientation to their families.

- Children who are friends with young people who are sexually exploited.

- Homeless children.

- Children who are lacking friends from the same age group.

- Those living in a gang neighbourhood.

- Those living in residential care.

- Children living in hostels, bed and breakfast accommodation or a foyer.

- Children with low self-esteem or self-confidence.

- Young carers.

The following signs and behaviours are generally seen in children who are already being sexually exploited:

- Missing from home or care.

- Physical injuries.

- Drug or alcohol misuse.

- Involvement in offending.

- Sexually transmitted infections, pregnancy and terminations.

- Absence from school.

- Change in physical appearance.

- Evidence of sexual bullying and/or vulnerability through the internet and/or social networking sites.

- Estrangement from their family.

- Receipt of gifts from unknown sources.

- Recruiting others into exploitative situations.

- Poor mental health.

- Self-harm.

It is perhaps a good idea to display these lists in a prominent position in workplaces to allow staff to refresh their memories and to remain mindful of these warning signs.

It is important to note that children who go missing either from home or in particular from care, are at an extremely high risk of being sexually exploited. This group are considerably overly represented in all research and statistics that look at children and young people who have been subjected to CSE, and multi-agency professionals must therefore be alert to any indicators of CSE when dealing with these missing children.

If a multi-agency professional has suspicions and some of the indicators highlighted above are present in a child or young person they have dealings with, they need to refer on their concerns. An increasing number of local authorities have in place referral pathways specifically for CSE, normally to a Multi-Agency Safeguarding Hub if one is in place (MASH – see Chapter 9), or to children's social care. Some areas have in place a Missing, Exploited and Trafficked hub that looks at and analyses the referrals. A number of areas have also developed a specific CSE referral form and hold a panel on a regular basis to consider children that have been referred. Local areas are increasingly developing specialist teams made up of social workers, police officers and, on occasion, other specialists, including from the voluntary sector.

Case study: Estelle Thain (principal social worker)

Girl A is a young person who has suffered horrific sexual exploitation at the hands of a group of males.

Having identified that Girl A was a victim of exploitation at some level, she was accommodated into a local authority care placement far away from the area of concern. Once in the safety of a care placement she began to disclose, and when I think back to the first occasion when she was able to do this, it remains very clearly in my mind. We sat together on the sofa in the living room at the placement, she withdrew into the corner of the sofa and pulled her knees up to her chest, she stretched her sweatshirt over her knees and pulled her sleeves over her hands and we sat quiet and still for a few moments, and this was unusual; she was always very fidgety and chatty, giggling and laughing when she was nervous, but on that day she was different. I asked her what she wanted to tell me and she began to talk, describing the very frightening things she had experienced only a few months earlier. This was the start of a very long and emotional journey for her and those closest to her.

She was always my focus, the priority of everything I did regarding the criminal investigation of those who had exploited her, and as more victims were identified the same principle applied – we worked to ensure they could cope with the process, remembering at all times they had suffered terrible abuse and, although convicting those who had abused them was extremely important, it was not the priority.

The child sexual exploitation team was established and I, along with four colleagues, worked to support the criminal process. As a newly formed social work team, our priority was to protect the girls from further harm and support them to achieve the justice they deserved through the court system. Over the coming months we committed a lot of time and energy to achieving this. Finishing work at 5pm was not an option. The hurt and confusion the girls felt did not stop in the ➔

afternoon because we finished our working day, and it was important that if they needed us we were available, making visits and phone calls and supporting them through new and sometimes distressing experiences: meeting new people, visiting new places – all a necessary part of the criminal process for us, but an often difficult part of the process for them.

Identifying key professionals and maintaining that consistency was vital. It was as important for the girls to build a relationship with the police as it was with their social worker, and so having the same police officer do the interviews and the victim liaison work helped to foster a feeling of trust and reliability. Not having to retell their story over and over to new people was important, so a team of social workers and police who shared information and worked closely together was very important to the success of this process.

In the months between the police interviews and the trial there were numerous occasions when the girls would feel anxious about the trial. I found with Girl A, because of her learning disability, that timing was a big issue for her, and so we created a wall chart that she could use to count the days until the trial. I also wrote things down that I had told her so that she could look at it when I was not there. Things that seem small to us made a big difference to her.

As the trial drew closer, we focused our efforts on supporting the girls to give their evidence in court. It was immensely stressful for all of them, and there were times when the enormity of what they had to do was overwhelming for them.

At that time we were all learning, and the dedicated CSE team was critical. It gave us time to develop relationships that would prove to be crucial, not only with the victims, but with each other and with our police colleagues. Those close working relationships provided us all with much needed emotional support. Too often there is a lack of communication between agencies, but throughout this investigation social workers and police worked closely together at every level, sharing information and listening to each other.

Developing close relationships with the victims and their families was the most important part of the process, to be prepared to go above and beyond, to pull out all the stops and to ensure they know they can trust you implicitly, and that they are your priority and your focus at all times.

The past 18 months have perhaps been the most challenging of my career, but they have also been the most rewarding. I feel so very proud of the girls and immensely privileged to have been part of their journey, to have shared their experiences and supported them through the highs and lows of the process. →

Although the outcome of the criminal process is extremely important, the work we do as social workers doesn't end there. Our commitment to these girls needs to continue, but with a different focus. We now need to help the girls pick up the pieces of their lives so that they can grow into adults and have healthy relationships and a chance of a safe and positive future, and the relationships we have built with the girls thus far will give us the best possible chance of doing this.

Key learning

■ CSE is child abuse.

■ The four main types of abuse are: inappropriate relationships; the boyfriend model; peer exploitation; organised networks.

■ There a number of risk factors that professionals need to be aware of, with missing from home or care being a key one, and this includes absence from education.

■ Referral pathways specific to CSE need to be utilised if CSE is suspected.

■ Only one professional should work with the child to help build a trusting relationship – they should not keep changing, and they need to work hard to build up a mutually trusting relationship.

Independent Inquiry into Child Sexual Abuse (IICSA)

In recent years there have been increasing reports of child sexual abuse in a number of institutions, including in the BBC, the NHS, in children's homes and in schools. Allegations of sexual offending involving children have been made against people with prominent positions in public life, including those in the media, in parliament, and in the church, and children sent abroad as part of a migration programme have also been victims. At the same time there have been growing reports of failures within the police to investigate allegations of child sexual abuse, and failures within the Crown Prosecution Service to prosecute the alleged abusers. Together, these reports demand a comprehensive and joined-up response. The Independent Inquiry into Child Sexual Abuse was established as a statutory inquiry on 12 March 2015 to consider the growing evidence of institutional failures to protect children from child sexual abuse, and to make recommendations to ensure the best possible protection for children in future.

This inquiry has already published reports for its legal investigations, research work and the Truth Project, as well as an Interim Report, which included recommendations to parliament. There has also been reports published into the Church of England, Rochdale, Custodial situations etc.

Further information is available at: www.iicsa.org.uk.

Female genital mutilation

Female genital mutilation (FGM) is child abuse. There is no health reason for any person, including a medical practitioner, to carry out the procedures associated with the removal of part or whole of the external female genitalia.

Working Together to Safeguard Children (Department for Education, 2010) outlines what these procedures mean.

FGM is a collective term for procedures that include the removal of all or part of the external female genitalia for cultural or other non-therapeutic reasons. The practice is medically unnecessary, extremely painful, and has serious health consequences, both at the time when the mutilation is carried out and in later life. The procedure is typically performed on girls aged between four and 13, but in some cases FGM is performed on new born infants or on young women before marriage or pregnancy. A number of girls die as a direct result of the procedure from blood loss or infection, either following the procedure or subsequently in childbirth.

The NHS describes four main types of FGM:

- Type 1: clitoridectomy – removing part or all of the clitoris.

- Type 2: excision – removing part or all of the clitoris and the inner labia (lips that surround the vagina), with or without removal of the labia majora (larger outer lips).

- Type 3: infibulation – narrowing of the vaginal opening by creating a seal, formed by cutting and repositioning the labia.

- Other harmful procedures to the female genitals, which include pricking, piercing, cutting, scraping and burning the area.

It has been a criminal offence in the UK since the Prohibition of Female Circumcision Act (1985) was passed. The Female Genital Mutilation Act (2003) replaced the 1985 act. It is an offence to:

- perform FGM (including taking a child abroad for FGM)
- help a girl perform FGM on herself in or outside the UK
- help anyone perform FGM in the UK
- help anyone perform FGM outside the UK on a UK national or resident
- fail to protect a girl for whom you are responsible from FGM.

Anyone who performs FGM can face up to 14 years in prison. Anyone found guilty of failing to protect a girl from FGM can face up to seven years in prison.

There is also requirement for regulated health and social care professionals and teachers in England and Wales to report 'known' cases of FGM in under 18s to the police. (For more information, see Home Office (2016) Mandatory reporting of female genital mutilation – procedural information.)[4]

FGM is much more common than many of us would think. It is reportedly practiced in 30 African countries and in parts of the Middle and Far East, but is increasingly found in Western Europe. The World Health Organization (2018) have estimated that more than 200 million girls and women alive today have undergone female genital mutilation in the countries where the practice is concentrated. Furthermore, there are an estimated three million girls at risk of undergoing female genital mutilation every year. The majority of girls are cut before they turn 15 years old. There are an estimated 137,000 women and girls affected by FGM in England and Wales (Macfarlane & Dorkenoo, 2015). Since July 2015, 205 Female Genital Mutilation Protection Orders have been made to safeguard girls from female genital mutilation (MoJ, 2018).

If any multi-agency practitioner suspects that a child may be, or has been, subject to FGM, they should report their concerns without delay to their local children's social care department, as the child or young person is at risk of significant harm under section 47 of the Children Act (1989). The school holidays are when girls are most at risk and school staff should be alert to any signs that this could be about to occur.

The Department of Health has published guidance for multi-agency practitioners, which can be found at: www.nhs.uk/conditions/female-genital-mutilation-fgm/ (accessed September 2019).

Another good source of information is available from the National FGM Centre, which can be found at: http://nationalfgmcentre.org.uk/fgm/fgm-direct-work-toolkit/ (accessed September 2019).

---

4   Available at: www.gov.uk/government/publications/mandatory-reporting-of-female-genital-mutilation-procedural-information

Key learning

- FGM is the removal of part or all of the external female genitalia for cultural or other non-therapeutic reasons.
- FGM is a criminal offence.
- School holidays are when children are at highest risk.

In March 2019, a 37-year-old mother was jailed after becoming the first person in the UK to be convicted of female genital mutilation (FGM). The Ugandan woman mutilated her three-year-old daughter at their family home in east London in 2017. She was jailed for 11 years. Sentencing at the Old Bailey, Mrs Justice Whipple said the act was 'a barbaric and sickening crime'.

'FGM has long been against the law and let's be clear FGM is a form of child abuse,' she added.

Forced marriage and honour-based violence

The term 'forced marriage' should not be confused with the term 'arranged marriage', which is a highly respected custom in many cultures. 'Forced marriage', however, is not acceptable, and everyone should have the right to choose whom they marry. Forcing a child to marry, sometimes as young as 12 years old, is not acceptable and multi-agency professionals should prevent this from happening.

Working Together to Safeguard Children (DfE, 2010) defines forced marriage as:

'*... marriage conducted without the full consent of both parties and where duress is a factor. There is a clear distinction between forced marriage and an arranged marriage. In arranged marriages, the families may take a leading role in arranging the marriage, but the choice whether or not to accept remains with the prospective spouses. In a forced marriage, one or both spouses do not consent to the marriage. The young person could be facing physical, psychological, sexual, financial or emotional abuse to pressure them into accepting the marriage.*'

The majority of forced marriage cases reported to date in the UK involve South Asian families, although there have been cases involving families from across Europe, East Asia, the Middle East and Africa. Some forced marriages take place in the UK with no overseas element, while others involve a partner coming from overseas or a British national being sent abroad. In 2017 the government introduced lifelong anonymity for victims of forced marriage to encourage more victims of this hidden crime to come forward.

The offenders are normally a parent, carer or other member of the family such as an aunt, uncle or older sibling. Other offences of abduction, threatening behaviour and physical assaults often take place, and sexual intercourse with anyone under 16 years is also an offence.

At the beginning of 2005, the Home Office and the Foreign and Commonwealth Office set up a joint unit called the Forced Marriage Unit, which in 2018 gave advice or support related to a possible 1,196 cases of forced marriage. These figures include contact that has been made to the FMU through the public helpline or by email in relation to a new case.

If any multi-agency professional has concerns that a child or young person is likely to be made to have a forced marriage, the professional should make a referral through their local procedures as the child could be at risk of significant harm. They should also contact the Forced Marriage Unit, which runs a helpline[5] that is not only to support victims, but also to help professionals dealing with a case.

There is a specific criminal offence in England and Wales of 'forcing someone to marry' in the Anti-Social Behaviour, Crime and Policing Act (2014). This also covers situations in which the marriage is likely to or takes place overseas if the victim is normally resident in the UK or a British national. Marrying someone who lacks the mental capacity to consent to the marriage (whether they're pressured to or not) or breaching a Forced Marriage Protection Order is also a criminal offence. The civil remedy of obtaining a Forced Marriage Protection Order through the family courts will continue to exist alongside the new criminal offence, so victims can choose how they wish to be assisted.

Anyone threatened with forced marriage, or forced to marry against their will, can apply for a Forced Marriage Protection Order. Third parties, such as relatives, friends, voluntary workers and police officers, can also apply for a protection order from the court. Fifteen county courts deal with applications and make orders to prevent forced marriages. Local authorities can now seek a protection order for vulnerable adults and children without leave of the court.

Multi-agency professionals need to be aware that it is estimated that hundreds of children are forced into marriage each year. Those working in education need to be especially alert as a young person may disclose that they are worried about being taken out of education and sent abroad, or directly disclose that they are worried they will be forced to marry.

---

5   The helpline number is 0207 008 0151. Out of hours: 020 7008 1500 (ask for the Global Response Centre)

There is a really informative video campaign by HM Government called 'Right to Choose' as well as additional and focused statutory guidance called *The Right to Choose: Multi-agency statutory guidance for dealing with forced marriage* (HM Government, 2010), which is aimed at senior executives and managers. Multi-agency practitioners can also access *Multiagency Practice Guidelines: Handling cases of forced marriage* (HM Government, 2014), which provides detailed advice and support to frontline practitioners.

Further information available at www.gov.uk/guidance/forced-marriage (accessed September 2019).

Key learning

- Forced marriage is a marriage conducted without the full consent of both parties and where duress is a factor.
- Forced marriage is now a criminal offence and professionals can take out a Forced Marriage Protection Order.
- School holidays are the most likely time that this could occur.
- The Forced Marriage Unit is a vital place to seek support from: fmu@fco.gov.uk.

Fabricated or induced illness

Fabricated or induced illness (FII) – once known as Munchausen's syndrome by proxy – is a form of child abuse in which someone who is caring for a child fakes or deliberately causes symptoms of illness in the child. The definition was changed by health professionals in 2002 to 'fabricated or induced illness', to consciously move the focus away from the offender to the child, as the victim.

While the perpetrators of FII are sometimes outsiders to a family, such as a nurse as in the well-known Beverley Allitt case, the guidance we are going to look at here will not look at harm by an outsider but by a parent or carer.

There are two key documents that professionals will need to consider further if they suspect they have a case of FII. These are:

- *Fabricated or Induced Illness by Carers (FII): A practical guide for paediatricians* (Royal College of Paediatrics and Child Health, 2009). (The RCPCH have been trying to update this guidance but as of 2019 this has not yet happened.)

- *Safeguarding Children in Whom Illness is Fabricated or Induced* (DCSF, 2008). This is supplementary guidance to *Working Together to Safeguard Children* (Department for Education, 2006).

- NHS pages on FII are available at: www.nhs.uk/conditions/fabricated-or-induced-illness/symptoms/ (accessed September 2019).

There are three main ways that FII can occur:

- Fabrication of signs and symptoms. This may include fabrication of past medical history.

- Falsification of hospital charts, records and specimens of bodily fluids. May also include falsification of letters and documents.

- Induction of illness by a variety of means, for example poisoning or causing physical injury like smothering.

Signs for professionals to look out for that may indicate a child is being subjected to FII include the following:

- The parent or carer reports signs and symptoms that are not explained by any known medical condition.

- Physical examination and diagnostic tests do not explain the reported signs and symptoms.

- The affected child has an inexplicably poor response to medication or other treatment.

- The only person claiming to see noticeable symptoms is the parent or carer.

- If a particular health problem is resolved, the parent or carer suddenly begins reporting a new set of symptoms.

- The child's daily activities are being limited far beyond what you would usually expect as a result of having a certain condition, for example they never go to school or have to wear leg braces even though they can walk properly.

- The parent or carer seeks multiple opinions from a range of different healthcare professionals.

- The parent or carer often has good medical knowledge or a medical background often learnt from the internet.

- The parent or carer often tries to maintain a close and friendly relationship with medical staff but can quickly become abusive or argumentative if their own views on what is wrong with the child are challenged.

- The parent or carer encourages medical staff to perform often painful tests and procedures on the child (tests that most parents would only agree to if they were persuaded that it was absolutely necessary).

- The parent or carer has a history of frequently changing GPs or visiting different hospitals for treatment, particularly if their views about the child's treatment are challenged by medical staff.

It is important that all multi-agency staff are familiar with the above, especially those who work in hospitals or other medical settings, and it may be useful to have the above list displayed somewhere that all staff can see it.

Reported symptoms

Parents or carers involved in fabricating or inducing illnesses usually describe symptoms that only happen at certain times, such as seizures (fits) and vomiting. The most commonly reported symptoms in cases of FII are listed below, in order of most to least common:

- Seizures (fits).

- Apparently life-threatening events, for example a mother may claim that her baby suddenly stopped breathing for a few minutes.

- Being unusually drowsy.

- Vomiting blood or passing blood in their stools.

- Feeding difficulties.

- Bowel disturbances, such as constipation and diarrhoea.

- Asthma.

- Vomiting.

FII can involve children of all ages, but the most severe cases usually involve children under five. In approximately 90% of reported cases of FII the child's mother is responsible for the abuse. However cases have been reported in which the father, foster parent, grandparent, guardian or a healthcare or childcare professional was responsible. It is not fully understood why FII occurs. In cases where the mother is responsible, it could be that she enjoys the attention or playing the role of a 'caring mother' (NHS Choices, 2014).

A large number of mothers who have been involved in cases of FII have had a previous history of unresolved psychological and behavioural problems, such as a history of self-harming or drug or alcohol misuse, or have experienced the death of another child. In particular, a high proportion of mothers involved in FII have been found to have a type of mental health problem called borderline personality disorder, which is characterised by emotional instability and disturbed thinking. There have been several reported cases where illness was fabricated or induced for financial reasons, such as to claim disability benefits.

Safeguarding in FII

FII is a child protection issue and cannot be treated by a single agency alone. Professionals who suspect FII is taking place should liaise with social services and the police, and must follow local child protection procedures. If you suspect that someone you know may be fabricating or inducing illness in their child, it is recommended that you do not speak to them about your suspicions as they may become more dangerous after this conversation.

If the senior paediatrician also suspects FII, they will put together a detailed record of all the available information that is related to the child's medical history. This is known as a chronology. They will also contact the local authority's child services to inform them that concerns have been raised about the child's safety and that an investigation is under way.

The senior paediatrician can call a strategy meeting and they will become the responsible paediatrician. At this meeting, other professionals that are involved with the child's welfare, such as their school or social services, may be contacted in case they have information that is relevant to the chronology – it is good practice to develop an integrated chronology. The police also need to be at this meeting as a crime may have been, or is, actually occurring.

Covert video surveillance may be used to collect evidence that can help to confirm a suspicion of FII. Only the police have the legal authority to carry out covert video surveillance and it will only be used if there is no other way of obtaining information to explain the child's symptoms. This authority is rarely used in practice, but if the police decide that there is sufficient evidence to bring criminal charges, they will begin to investigate the case.

Although there is no specific offence of FII, the offences that will be investigated are for example neglect, cruelty, GBH or assault.

Key learning

- FII used to be called Munchausen's syndrome by proxy.

- There are three main types: fabrication of symptoms, falsification of charts, medical records etc; induction of illness.

- The offender is usually the mother, and motivation includes attention or sympathy, but can also be financial.

- A multi-agency approach is required, led by a paediatrician.

- Chronologies are very useful.

Child death

The close liaison and collaboration of multi-agency professionals in child deaths has always been in place, in particular between the police, primarily in their role as coroner's officers, and health professionals. However, this became a statutory liaison, as detailed in Chapter 7 of *Working Together to Safeguard Children* (2006) (Chapter 5 of the 2018 version). Baroness Kennedy QC chaired a working group and as a result of this, in 2004 there were a series of recommendations on good practice to be used in cases of child death, for example taking samples from the child. In 2016 following a request from the Royal College of Pathology and RCPH Baroness Kennedy reconvened a Working Group to update the guidance and published in November 2016 'Sudden unexpected death in infancy and childhood', which is a multi-agency protocol for the handling of sudden infant death. This guidance is available at: www.rcpath.org/discover-pathology/news/new-guidelines-for-the-investigation-of-sudden-unexpected-death-in-infancy-launched.html (accessed November 2019).

The *Working Together* (2018) guidance deals with all deaths of children under 18 year.

There are two inter-related, multi-agency processes detailed in the statutory guidance:

- A Child Death Review Process by a group of key professionals, who come together for the purpose of enquiring into and evaluating each death of a child. This process will include a joint agency response where it is an unexpected death of the child.

- An overview of all child deaths in the area, undertaken by a panel (child death overview panel).

The Child Death Review Partners (CCG and Local Authority) for each area have to ensure that they have in place procedures for dealing with both the Joint Agency Response and the child death overview process, and full details of their policies will be available on their multi-agency safeguarding partners' websites.

The below flow chart from *Working Together* (2018), which is also in Child Death Review (statutory and operational guidance (England) 2018), outlines the statutory process to be followed in full by all agencies.

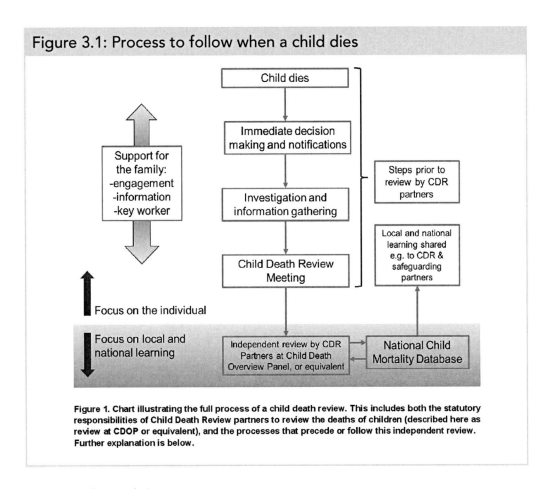

Figure 1. Chart illustrating the full process of a child death review. This includes both the statutory responsibilities of Child Death Review partners to review the deaths of children (described here as review at CDOP or equivalent), and the processes that precede or follow this independent review. Further explanation is below.

(© Crown Copyright)

When dealing with the death of a child or infant, all agencies should follow five common principles, as detailed in the Baroness Kennedy guidelines (2016). (This is also in *Working Together*, 2018, p100 para 20, and the importance of adhering to the Baroness Kennedy 2016 guidelines is highlighted in para 21 *Working Together* 2018):

- Establish, as far as is possible, the cause or causes of the infant's death.

- Identify any potential contributory or modifiable factors.

- Provide ongoing support to the family.

- Ensure that all statutory obligations are met.

- Learn lessons in order to reduce the risks of future infant deaths.

The current National Police Guidance (2014) – especially when having contact with family members – states that professionals should consider:

- a balanced approach between sensitivity and the investigative mind-set (sometimes known as being a compassionate cynic).

- A multi-agency response.

- Sharing of information.

- Appropriate response to the circumstances.

- Preservation of evidence.

When a child has died unexpectedly and is taken into hospital, a number of steps and procedures need to take place. First, once all attempts of resuscitation have failed, and if a cause of death is unknown, the lead paediatrician and other key professional, namely the police, have to work together as a joint agency response team (formally known as rapid response). Some of these steps are:

- Respond quickly to the unexpected death of a child, through a Joint Agency Response.

- Make immediate enquiries into, and evaluating the reasons for and circumstances of, the death, in agreement with the coroner (this will include examining the child's body and taking samples, known as Kennedy samples).

- Undertake the types of enquiries/investigations that relate to the current responsibilities of their respective organisations when a child dies unexpectedly. This includes liaising with those who have ongoing responsibilities for other family members (this also includes checking those organisations' information systems to see if anything is known about the child or family to make sure that any surviving siblings are not at risk).

- Collect information in a standard, nationally agreed manner. Speak to the parents and carers, which is often called history taking.

- Provide support to the bereaved family and, where appropriate, refer on to specialist bereavement services.

Child death review partners should ensure that a designated doctor for child deaths is appointed to any multi-agency panel (or structure in place to review deaths). The designated doctor for child deaths should be a senior paediatrician who can take a lead role in the review process.

The flow chart below is more detailed than the one in *Working Together* (2018) and is taken from page 23 of the Child death review guidance 2018. It clearly shows the steps that professionals need to take where a Joint Agency Response is required.

Figure 3.2: Joint Agency Response

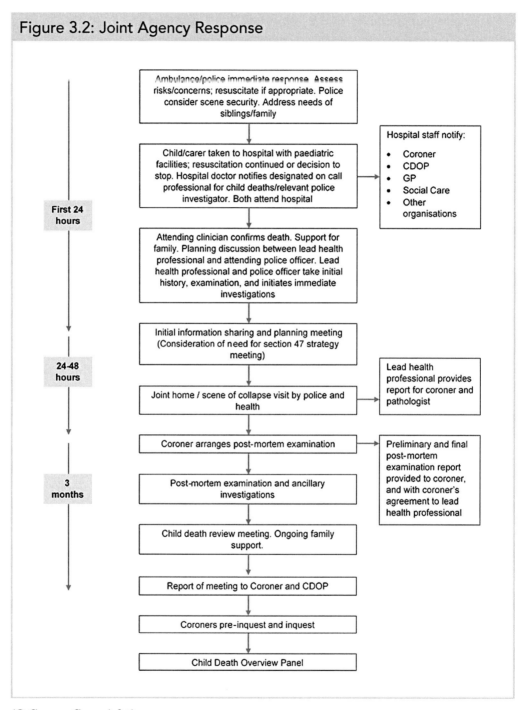

(© Crown Copyright)

What is the prevalence of child deaths?

There has been a huge reduction in unexpected infant deaths, in children under one year old, over the last 20 years, largely brought about by education campaigns for new parents such as the 'Back to Sleep' campaign, which dates from 1991. Despite this reduction, every year in England and Wales several hundred children will die before they reach the age of one. The majority of these deaths occur as a result of natural causes such as disease or physical defects. A relatively small number of deaths are, however, caused deliberately by violence or neglect. For the years 2016/17, The NSPCC state in *How Safe Are Our Children* (NSPCC, 2018) that there were 98 child homicides across the UK, 91 of which were in England – this is the highest it has ever been in England. Police-recorded homicide statistics should accurately reflect the number of child homicides reported each year. However, they will only record cases where there is sufficient evidence to suspect that a homicide has taken place. Studies have indicated that the number of child deaths where abuse or neglect is suspected as a factor is higher than shown in the police-recorded homicide figures (Sidebotham *et al*, 2016).

Child homicides are most commonly perpetrated by someone known the child. For example, proportionally few homicides of those aged under 16 were committed by strangers, the victim was known to have been killed by a stranger in only three offences in the year ending March 2016 (4%) (Office for National Statistics, 2018).

Sudden infant death syndrome

Often known by the term 'cot death', the general definition of sudden infant death syndrome (SIDS) widely used by professionals throughout the world, including sub-categories of the death, is:

'The sudden unexpected death of an infant <1 year of age, with onset of the fatal episode apparently occurring during sleep, that remains unexplained after a thorough investigation, including performance of a complete autopsy and review of the circumstances of death and the clinical history.'

There are some risk factors to be aware of in relation to SIDS:

- Intrinsic to child: congenital anomalies; low birth weight; prematurity; poor postnatal growth; certain genetic polymorphisms; male gender.
- Parental: young maternal age; maternal smoking during pregnancy; alcohol/ drugs; high parity; family history of SIDS.

- Environmental: smoking in the house; prone sleeping position; head covering during sleep; inappropriate sleeping environment; overheating; crowded housing; unsupported mother; low income.

- It is worth noting the high risk caused by maternal smoking in pregnancy and after birth smoking in the household.

Abusive head trauma (shaken baby syndrome)

When dealing with child deaths, multi-agency professionals will at times come across this type of injury, including those occasions where the child survives. Paediatric ophthalmological assessment should quickly reveal the presence of retinal haemorrhages or other head injuries indicative of abusive head trauma (sometimes known as shaken baby syndrome, however most if not all professionals do not use this term now).

The triad of injuries most commonly found and known to be consistent with shaking are:

- subdural haemorrhages (bleeding around the surface of the brain)
- brain encephalopathy (brain swelling)
- retinal bleeding.

These injuries are caused when the brain moves inside the skull, causing damage and shearing the bridging veins. Infants are particularly susceptible because of their relatively large heads, heavy brains and weak neck muscles. These injuries can also be caused by a sudden violent throw, which causes the head to jolt backwards and forward and undergo rotational forces. However, bear in mind that this is not the opinion of all paediatric specialists.

As a guide, some of the specialised investigation techniques that should be employed include:

- a full skeletal survey from head to finger and toe tips, properly interpreted by a paediatric radiologist
- ultraviolet photography
- thorough ophthalmologic examination, including specialised retinal photography, examination of eyes as soon as possible (while the child is still in the emergency department) as the picture will deteriorate and the timing of when things are observed, as well as excluded, is very relevant.

- MRI and CT scans – ensuring that the machine is set up for brain matter and a child-sized brain

- full post-mortem ophthalmologic examination carried out in a specialised laboratory

- full post-mortem examination of the brain carried out in a specialised laboratory.

For more information, see www.cps.gov.uk/legal-guidance/non-accidental-head-injury-cases-nahi-formerly-referred-shaken-baby-syndrome-sbs (accessed September 2019). This should be considered in all such cases.

Risk factors indicating a suspicious child death

The key information below is taken from *Risk Factors for Intra-familial Unlawful and Suspicious Child Deaths* (Mayes *et al*, 2010), and suggested further reading can be found in *Effective Investigation of Child Homicide and Suspicious Deaths* (Marshall, 2012). A very similar list of factors that suggest that a death may be suspicious is included at Appendix 2 in Baroness Kennedy, 2016.

There are a number of risk factors to look out for when a child has died in suspicious circumstances (in order of priority of suspicion):

- A parent or carer has a history of violence towards children.

- They provide an inconsistent account of events.

- The presence of mental health issues in a parent or carer.

- There have been previous atypical hospital visits.

- A parent or carer has a history of alcohol abuse.

- The child is over one year old.

- They are on a child protection plan.

- They are known to social services.

- A parent or carer has a history of drug abuse.

- There is a history of domestic violence.

- A parent or carer has a criminal record.

- Another sibling has previously died.

It is worth noting that the above list is not exclusive to unlawful deaths, and would be useful in any case where there was a suspicion of child abuse.

Case study: Joanne Early

In 2008 I gave birth to twins; a boy and a girl. I was a new mum and it was the happiest time of my life. Little did I know that three months later my son would be dead (the cause was shaken baby syndrome) and my daughter taken into foster care as a result. At the time of their birth I enjoyed a full-time career as an ambulance services manager and I'd been in a relationship with my husband for nearly 10 years. I'd never been in trouble with the police or any other authority and it was inconceivable to think I could ever be in this situation. The whole thing came as a huge shock and the minute my son died it felt like time had stopped. I do remember clearly, however, that when I was spoken to by both medical professionals and the police my account of what I knew never changed.

My husband was charged with murder and GBH and it took me a long time to believe that not only had my son been killed, but that the perpetrator was actually a man I loved and trusted. I was also arrested. I researched on the internet, looking for other causes of shaken baby syndrome, and spoke to various pressure groups and lawyers. The time between Charlie's death and the end of both care and criminal proceedings was an incredibly stressful and traumatic experience, however I was able to identify both positive and negatives and record them in a written diary I kept throughout this time.

Positives

Building agency relationships – communication and transparency

Having been arrested and investigated, my sense of trust in the authorities had completely diminished. However all the professionals involved were investigating what happened to my children, which made them incredibly important people to me. I needed to know they were getting it right. At first these were exceptionally difficult relationships, balancing trust and distrust. My long-term belief system was challenged when I was arrested as I was raised to respect and trust authority, and my arrest made me question this. I asked questions in order to understand the process of each agency involvement. I had a fear of the unknown, making it imperative to know what lay ahead. →

Initial police/social services contact

At the beginning, both the police and social services made initial contact. They clearly explained their roles and the reasons for their involvement. Although I was traumatised at the time and could barely digest the information, it helped me to record these conversations and refer back to them when I was able. This effective communication process worked for me. I also found staff sensitive and empathetic as they acknowledged the terrible situation. I heard the words 'I'm so sorry for your loss', which meant a lot, and I became receptive as a result.

Negatives

Initial contact with hospital staff

When my son was admitted to hospital, I found the doctors' attitudes harsh and critical. My experience was a negative one which took place before the national rapid response guidelines were introduced. I experienced a lack of sensitivity as I was repeatedly questioned and told, 'your son is the sickest patient on the ward – if he dies you will both be arrested and questioned as part of a murder investigation'. I became defensive as a result and felt the need to defend myself instead of being open and communicative. This didn't work for me at all.

Parents' expectations of the medical evidence

When the police started their investigation, they instructed medical experts to produce reports for the prosecution. Those reports were nearly impossible to understand. However, I was determined to understand them – after all, they were about my children. I wanted all the reports to tell me the exact answers about what happened to Charlie and why. But some reports were inconclusive and others contradicted each other, which proved very frustrating to me as Charlie's mother.

My advice to multi-agency practitioners is to not judge parents and do whatever you can to find out why the child died, and to not use complicated medical terminology.

Key learning

- Multi-agency liaison is essential.

- Child Death Review involves good information sharing as well as support for the family.

- Unexpected child death requires a joint agency response of professionals.

- The child death overview process exists to prevent future deaths.

- A balanced approach between sensitivity and the investigative mind-set is needed, or to be a compassionate cynic, where no cause of death is readily available.

- Standard medical tests need to take place, including taking samples.

- History taking is important.

- In SIDS under 12 months, smoking a significant risk factor.

- Abusive head trauma is indicated by a triad of injuries. In order to prosecute there will need to be an additional other factor(s) to this triad of injuries.

- Toxic trio – domestic abuse, substance misuse and parental mental health feature highly as factors to raise suspicion.

Serious Case Reviews – Child Safeguarding Practice Reviews

After the death of Jasmine Beckford in the 1980s, regular reviews of child deaths began. These serious case reviews (SCRs) were called at this time 'Part 8 reviews'. After Lord Laming's review of the death of Victoria Climbié and the Children's Act (2004), carrying out SCRs became statutory and governed by LSCBs. The Child and Social Work Act (2017) abolished LSCBs and, through Chapter 4 of *Working Together to Safeguard Children* (DfE, 2018), it created Child Safeguarding Practice Reviews. The local responsibility for these sits with the multi-agency safeguarding partners as described in Chapter 1 of this book, while the national responsibility sits with the Child Safeguarding Practice Review Panel.

When do Child Safeguarding Practice Reviews take place?

Child Safeguarding Practice Reviews take place where abuse or neglect of a child is known or suspected and a child has died or been seriously harmed. This may include cases where a child has caused serious harm to someone else.

The term 'Seriously harmed' is defined by *Working Together* (2018) as follows:

'Serious harm includes (but is not limited to) serious and/or long-term impairment of a child's mental health or intellectual, emotional, social or behavioural development. It should also cover impairment of physical health. This is not an exhaustive list. When making decisions, judgment should be exercised in cases where impairment is likely to be long-term, even if this is not immediately certain. Even if a child recovers, including from a one-off incident, serious harm may still have occurred.'

Local authorities must notify the Child Safeguarding Practice Review Panel and the multi-agency safeguarding partners in their area (and in other areas if appropriate) within five working days if they know or suspect that a child has been seriously harmed or died as a result of abuse or neglect, and notify the Secretary of State and Ofsted where a looked after child has died, whether or not abuse or neglect is known or suspected.

The Multi-agency safeguarding partners must initiate a rapid review of the case to identify any immediate action to ensure a child's safety, consider the potential for identifying learning and help inform a decision about whether to undertake a child safeguarding practice review. If a rapid review is carried out well, the learning may already be evident and could be used on the basis of the rapid review alone.

A copy of the rapid review must be sent to the Child Safeguarding Practice Review Panel along with their decision about whether to carry out a local child safeguarding practice review, and whether they think a national review may be more appropriate.

There are two types of reviews, that could then be commissioned:

National reviews: These take place where the Child Safeguarding Practice Review Panel considers that a case raises issues which are complex or of national importance. The Panel may also commission reviews on any incident(s) or themes they think relevant. They also oversee the review of local cases, and have to set up a pool of potential reviewers who can undertake national reviews, a list of whom must be publicly available.

Local reviews: These take place where safeguarding partners consider that a case raises issues of importance in relation to their area. At a local level, the safeguarding partners must make arrangements to:

- identify and consider serious child safeguarding cases which raise issues of importance in relation to their area

- commission and oversee child safeguarding practice reviews of those cases where they consider it to be appropriate.

Meeting the criteria does not mean that safeguarding partners must automatically carry out a local child safeguarding practice review. Decisions on whether to undertake reviews should be made transparently and the rationale communicated appropriately, including to families.

It is essential to ensure that practitioners, families and surviving children are fully involved in reviews and invited to contribute their perspectives without fear of being blamed for actions they took in good faith. All child safeguarding practice reviews should:

- reflect the child's perspective and the family context

- be proportionate to the circumstances of the case

- focus on potential learning

- establish and explain the reasons why the events occurred as they did.

The final report should include:

- a summary of recommended improvements to safeguard and promote the welfare of children

- an analysis of any systemic or underlying reasons why actions were taken or not taken.

Child safeguarding practice reviews normally take at least six months to complete and, depending on the type of review, have to be published. An action plan with learning for the partnership will also be completed. A number of safeguarding partnership boards now carry out what is known as 'systems reviews', and a key part of these is to hold practitioners' workshops. Multi-agency professionals that have been involved in the case will be invited to attend and the learning is further helped as reviewers develop an understanding of what happened in the case and why.

Learning lessons[6]

In order to learn a lesson from Child Safeguarding Practice Reviews, and formerly SCRs, there has been a number of research papers and a series of analysis reviews of these papers. One such series is the biennial reviews completed by the University of East Anglia. They have then combined together with Warwick University to complete the last two triennial reviews.

The first time the UEA carried out their research and analysis, their researchers commented:

'The findings about the children and their circumstances make powerful and painful reading. Prevention of child death or injury through abuse or neglect is uppermost in the minds of practitioners and managers working with children and families.'

Some of the key lessons from the biennial research and Ofsted research are highlighted below, and it must be emphasised that it is the same lessons that come out time and time again:

■ In many cases, parents were hostile to helping agencies and workers were often frightened to visit family homes. These circumstances could have a paralysing effect on practitioners, hampering their ability to reflect, make judgments and act clearly (Brandon *et al*, 2008).

■ There was hesitancy in challenging the opinion of other professionals which appeared to stem from a lack of confidence, knowledge, experience or status (Brandon *et al*, 2008).

■ Supervision helps practitioners to think, to explain and to understand. It also helps them to cope with the complex emotional demands of work with children and their families (Brandon *et al*, 2008).

■ Practitioners and managers need to be curious, to be sceptical, to think critically and systematically but to act compassionately (Brandon *et al*, 2010).

■ High levels of current or past domestic violence and/or parental mental ill health and/or parental substance misuse, often in combination, were apparent throughout, and this is a major feature throughout all of the years that SCRs have been analysed (Brandon *et al*, 2009).

■ The police tended to be the agency most involved with these families, which often involves domestic or community conflict or violence. Also, with cases of substance misuse involving the family (Brandon *et al*, 2008).

---

6   This section was first published in *Effective Investigation of Child Homicide and Suspicious Deaths* (2012) by David Marshall and is repeated here with his permission.

- There was sometimes a lack of awareness on the part of health staff and some branches of the police force of the link between domestic violence and the risk of harm to the child (Brandon *et al*, 2008).

- Half of the parents/carers had criminal convictions. Many families were overwhelmed, with poor or negative family support. Nearly three-quarters of the children lived with past or present domestic violence and/or past or present parental mental ill health, and/or past or present parental substance misuse. These three parental characteristics often co-existed (Brandon *et al*, 2009).

- Three-quarters of the 40 families did not co-operate with services. Patterns of hostility and lack of compliance included: deliberate deception, disguised compliance and 'telling workers what they want to hear', selective engagement, and sporadic, passive or desultory compliance. Reluctant parental co-operation and multiple moves meant that many children went off the radar of professionals (Brandon *et al*, 2009).

- While the youngest children are the most vulnerable to death from abuse or neglect, the next most vulnerable group were adolescents (Brandon *et al*, 2009).

- As last time, these young people might have been amenable to help if they had been offered the right approach. Some young people were seen as a nuisance and not easy to work with (Brandon *et al*, 2009).

- There is less public concern, however, on behalf of the vulnerable adolescents who feature repeatedly in serious case reviews and homicide statistics (Brandon *et al*, 2009).

- This suggests a level of 'agency neglect' of this vulnerable group of young people, many of whom are on the cusp of adulthood (Brandon *et al*, 2009).

- The tendency towards 'silo practice' that we found, where professionals preferred to work within the comfort zone of their own specialism, underlines the importance of joint child protection training. This should continue to be offered not just for those working with children but also to the adult workforce and any groups of workers coming into contact with children and families (Brandon *et al*, 2009).

- Professionals' working together can be tentative with the perceived responsibilities and priorities of separate agencies overshadowing the safeguarding responsibility (Brandon *et al*, 2009).

- This is possibly the single most significant practice failing throughout the majority of the serious case reviews – the failure of all professionals to see the situation from the child's perspective and experience; to see and speak to the children; to listen to what they said, to observe how they were and to take serious account of their views in supporting their needs (Ofsted, 2008).

The 2016 triennial review of SCRs, by Dr Peter Sidebotham *et al*, on behalf of the Department for Education, titled *Pathways to Harm, Pathways to Protection*, found the following are of significance in the serious case reviews looked at.

Figure 3.3: Cumulative risk of harm

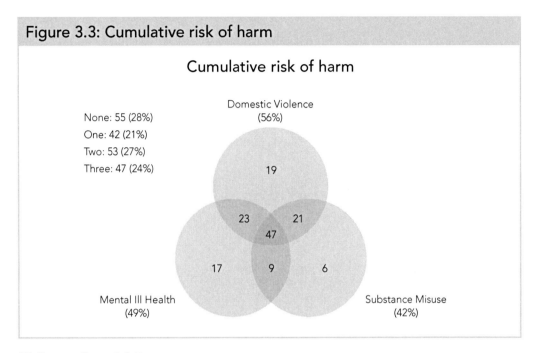

(© Crown Copyright)

As can be seen, the toxic trio of domestic abuse, substance misuse and parental mental health features significantly.

As stated by Professor Marion Brandon in the first UEA review:

'Serious Case Reviews present a lasting testimony and memorial to children who die in horrific circumstances. This must be remembered in order to learn from these reviews.'

Key learning

■ Child Safeguarding Practice Reviews take place when a child has died and abuse or neglect is known or suspected.

■ They can take place when they are seriously harmed.

■ Toxic trio – domestic abuse, substance misuse and parental mental health feature highly as risk factors in SCRs.

Further reading

Child Sexual Exploitation

Barnardo's (2011) *Puppet on a String: The urgent need to cut children free from Sexual Exploitation*.

DCSF (2009) *Safeguarding Children and Young People from Sexual Exploitation: Supplementary guide to working together*.

Department for Health (2014) *Health Working Group Report on Child Sexual Exploitation*.

Children's Commissioner (2013) *If Only Someone Had Listened. The Office of the Children's Commissioner's Inquiry into Child Sexual Exploitation in gangs and groups. Final report*.

Independent Inquiry into Child Sexual Abuse (IICSA), available at: www.iicsa.org.uk

Female genital mutilation

The Department for Health published guidance in 2016 for multi-agency practitioners, which is available at: www.nhs.uk/conditions/female-genital-mutilation-fgm/ (accessed September 2019).

Information is available from the National FGM Centre at: http://nationalfgmcentre.org.uk/fgm/fgm-direct-work-toolkit/ (accessed September 2019).

Forced marriage

For more information on forced marriage, see: www.gov.uk/guidance/forced-marriage (accessed September 2019).

Fabricated or induced illness

Royal College of Paediatrics and child health (2009) *Fabricated or Induced Illness by Carers (FII): A practical guide for paediatricians.*

Department for Children Schools and Families (2008) *Safeguarding children in whom illness is fabricated or induced.*

NHS pages on FII are available at: www.nhs.uk/conditions/fabricated-or-induced-illness/symptoms/ (accessed September 2019).

Child Death Review

Department of Health (2018) Child Death Review. DH London. Available at: https://assets.publishing.service.gov.uk/government/uploads/system/uploads/attachment_data/file/777955/Child_death_review_statutory_and_operational_guidance_England.pdf (accessed September 2019).

Kennedy, Baroness H (2004) *Sudden Unexpected Death in Infancy: A multi-agency protocol for care and investigation.*

Kennedy Baroness H (2016) *Sudden Unexpected Death in Infancy: A multi-agency protocol for care and investigation* (2nd Edition), completed on behalf of the Royal College of Pathology and Royal College for child and paediatric Health [online]. Available at: www.rcpath.org/discover-pathology/news/new-guidelines-for-the-investigation-of-sudden-unexpected-death-in-infancy-launched.html (accessed November 2019).

Marshall D (2012) *Effective Investigation of Child Homicide and Suspicious Child Deaths.* Oxford, Oxford University Press.

Sidebotham P & Fleming P (2007) *Unexpected Death in Childhood: A handbook for practitioners.*

Mayes J, Brown A & Marshall D (2010) Risk factors for intra-familial unlawful and suspicious child deaths. *Journal of Homicide and Major Incident Investigation* **6** (1) 77–96.

Child Safeguarding Practice Reviews

Sidebotham P, Brandon M, Bailey S, Belderson P, Dodsworth J, Garstang J, Harrison E, Retzer A & Sorensen P (2016) *Pathways to harm, pathways to protection: a triennial analysis of serious case reviews 2011 to 2014: final report.* [London]: Department for Education.

Brandon M, Sidebotham P, Belderson P, Clever H, Dickens J, Garstang J, Harris J, Sorensen P, and Wate R (2019) *Complexity and Challenge: Triennial analysis of serious case reviews 2014 to 2017: final report.* [London]: Department for Education.

References

Barnado's (2011) *Puppet on a String: The urgent need to cut children free from sexual exploitation* [online]. Ilford: Barnado's. Available at: www.barnardos.org.uk/ctf_puppetonastring_report_final.pdf (accessed September 2019).

Brandon M, Belderson P, Warren C, Howe D, Gardner R, Dodsworth J & Black J (2008) *Analysing Child Deaths and Serious Injury Through Abuse and Neglect: What can we learn? A biennial analysis of serious case reviews 2003–2005* [online]. Department for Children, Schools and Families. Available at: http://dera.ioe.ac.uk/7190/1/dcsf-rr023.pdf (accessed September 2019).

Brandon M, Bailey S, Belderson P, Gardner R, Sidebotham P, Dodsworth J, Warren C & Black J (2009) *Analysing serious case reviews and their impact'. A biennial analysis of serious case reviews 2005-2007* [online]. Nottingham: Department for Children, Schools and Families. Available at: http://dera.ioe.ac.uk/11151/1/DCSF-RR129%28R%29.pdf (accessed September 2019).

Brandon M, Bailey S & Belderson P (2010) *Building on the Learning from Serious Case Reviews: A two-year analysis, 2007-2009.* London: Department for Education.

College of Policing (2014) *Homicide* [online]. Available at: www.app.college.police.uk/app-content/major-investigation-and-public-protection/homicide/ (accessed September 2019).

DCSF (2008) *Safeguarding Children in Whom Illness is Fabricated or Induced* [online]. London: Department for Children, Schools and Families. Available at: www.gov.uk/government/publications/safeguarding-children-in-whom-illness-is-fabricated-or-induced (accessed September 2019).

DCSF (2009) *Safeguarding Children and Young People from Sexual Exploitation: Supplementary guide to working together.* London: Department for Children, Schools and Families.

Department for Education (2006) *Working Together to Safeguard Children.* London: HM Government.

Department for Education (2010) *Working Together to Safeguard Children.* London: HM Government.

Department for Education (2017) *'Child sexual exploitation Definition and a guide for practitioners, local leaders and decision makers working to protect children from child sexual exploitation'.* London HM Government.

Department for Education (2018) *Working Together to Safeguard Children.* London: HM Government.

Department of Health (2011) *Female Genital Mutilation: Guidelines to protect women and children* [online]. Available at: www.gov.uk/government/publications/female-genital-mutilation-multi-agency-practice-guidelines (accessed January 2015).

Duncan JR & Bayard RW (2018) *SIDS – Sudden infant and early childhood death: The past, the present and the future.* Adelaide. University of Adelaide Press.

Hardcastle K & Bellis M (2018) *Routine enquiry for history of adverse childhood experiences (ACEs) in the adult patient population in a general practice setting: A pathfinder study.* Public Health, Wales.

HM Government (2009) *Multiagency Practice Guidelines: Handling cases of forced marriage* [online]. Available at: www.gov.uk/government/uploads/system/uploads/attachment_data/file/35530/forced-marriage-guidelines09.pdf (accessed September 2019).

HM Government (2010) *The Right to Choose: Multi-agency statutory guidance for dealing with forced marriage* [online]. Available at: www.gov.uk/government/uploads/system/uploads/attachment_data/file/35532/fmu-right-to-choose.pdf (accessed January 2015).

HM Government (2016) *Multi-agency statutory guidance on female genital mutilation* [online]. Available at: https://www.gov.uk/government/publications/multi-agency-statutory-guidance-on-female-genital-mutilation

Jutte S, Bentley B, Miller M & Jetha N (2014) *How Safe Are Our Children?* London: NSPCC.

Kennedy Baroness H (2004) *Sudden Unexpected Death in Infancy: A multi-agency protocol for care and investigation* [online]. Available at: www.rcpath.org/NR/rdonlyres/30213EB6-451B-4830-A7FD-4EEFF0420260/0/SUDIreportforweb.pdf (accessed February 2015).

Kennedy Baroness H (2016) *Sudden Unexpected Death in Infancy: A multi-agency protocol for care and investigation* (2nd Edition) [online]. Available at: https://www.rcpath.org/uploads/assets/uploaded/af879a1b-1974-4692-9e002c20f09dc14c.pdf

Krous HF (2004) Sudden infant death syndrome and unclassified sudden infant deaths: a definitional and diagnostic approach. *Paediatrics* **114** (1) 234–8.

Macfarlane A & Dorkenoo E (2015) *Prevalence of female genital mutilation in England and Wales: national and local estimates* [online]. Available at: www.nspcc.org.uk/preventing-abuse/child-abuse-and-neglect/female-genital-mutilation-fgm/ (accessed September 2019).

Marshall D (2012) *Effective Investigation of Child Homicide and Suspicious Child Deaths.* Oxford: Oxford University Press.

Mayes J, Brown A & Marshall D (2010) Risk factors for intra-familial unlawful and suspicious child deaths. *Journal of Homicide and Major Incident Investigation* **6** (1) 77–96.

Ministry of Justice (2018) Family court statistics quarterly, England and Wales: annual 2017 including October to December 2017.

NHS Choices (2014) *Fabricated or Induced Illness* [online]. Available at: www.nhs.uk/Conditions/Fabricated-or-induced-illness (accessed September 2019).

NSPCC (2018) *How Safe are Our Children?*

ONS (2019) *Homicide in England and Wales: Year ending March 2018.*

Ofsted (2008) *Learning lessons, taking action: Ofsted's evaluations of serious case reviews 1 April 2007 to 31 March 2008.* London: Ofsted.

Royal College of Paediatrics and Child Health (2009) Fabricated or Induced Illness by Carers (FII): A practical guide for paediatricians. London: RCPCH.

Sidebotham P, Bailey S, Belderson P & Brandon M (2011) Fatal child maltreatment in England 2005–2009. *Child Abuse & Neglect* **35** (4) 299–306.

Sidebotham P, Brandon M, Bailey S, Belderson P, Dodsworth J, Garstang J, Harrison E, Retzer A & Sorensen P (2016) *Pathways to Harm, Pathways to Protection: A triennial analysis of serious case reviews 2011 to 2014: final report.* [London]: Department for Education.

World Health Organization (2018) *Female Genital Mutilation* [online]. Available at: www.who.int/mediacentre/factsheets/fs241/en/ (accessed September 2019).

Chapter 4: Domestic violence and abuse

By Russell Wate

Chapter overview

- A definition of domestic abuse.
- Domestic abuse, stalking and harassment risk assessment.
- Independent domestic violence advisors.
- Multi-agency public protection conference.
- Civil orders.
- Domestic homicide reviews.

Introduction

Domestic abuse (DA) is a complex safeguarding issue and all multi-agency professionals have a role to play in keeping victims, their families, children and other affected people safe. Professionals will come across victims of DA on a regular basis, whether they are displaying physical signs of any injuries or not. One of the difficulties professionals may encounter is getting the victim to appreciate the situation they are in and to persuade them to access help to make them safe. The police, however, can take positive action even if the victim doesn't consent.

A key point to remember is that if there is a child present within a household they also are affected by domestic abuse, and a way to protect the adult victim may be through safeguarding the child. Multi-agency professionals need to be alert to those cases in which a woman is the victim of men who are sometimes referred to as the 'invisible' men in a household.

The actual scale of the DA problem within the UK is impossible to measure exactly. It is acknowledged by professionals, though, that there has been little change in the prevalence of DA, as supported by the latest figures from the Crime Survey for England and Wales. In the year ending March 2018, an estimated two million adults aged 16 to 59 years experienced domestic abuse in the last year (1.3 million women, 695,000 men).

In the year ending March 2018 the police recorded 599,549 domestic abuse-related crimes. This was an increase of 23% from the previous year, perhaps due in part to an increased willingness by victims to come forward. This in part reflects police forces improving their identification and recording of domestic abuse incidents. These figures represent five million females and 2.9 million male victims. An interesting point to note is that this number is only 50% of the DA incidents that were reported to the police, so recorded crime is not the best guide of the level of DA occurring in England and Wales.

The figures quoted in this chapter come from the ONS report *Domestic abuse in England and Wales: year ending March 2018* (2018), which further stated that there was a total of 400 domestic homicides recorded by the police in England and Wales between April 2014 and March 2017. This represents 25% of all homicides during this time period where the victim was aged 16 years and over. The majority of victims of domestic homicides were female (73%, or 293), with 27% of victims being male (107); four in five female victims of domestic homicide were killed by a partner or ex-partner (82% or 239), of which the majority of the suspects were male (238).

Anecdotally it is said that, on average, by the time a victim informs the police they will have been subjected to domestic abuse on 35 previous occasions. There are a number of barriers to reporting, some of which are highlighted in this chapter. These include the feeling by victims of the overwhelming desire to keep the family unit together, and the belief that it might not happen again. There are particular challenges and barriers within the BME/immigrant community to the reporting to statutory agencies, and professionals need to work hard to build up trust to overcome them.

Multi-agency professionals may wonder why victims don't report more often or sooner than they do, or why they don't leave the situation they are currently in. There are often barriers to the reporting of DA and there are many reasons why victims stay. Asking an individual why they stay may be seen as blaming them, but it is important to consider their reasons, such as children, extended family, the fact that it's all they know and their natural reluctance to leave the familiar – home, neighbours, pets, financial dependency etc. If they do leave, this may in some cases increase the risk, as the known surroundings and friends and family may no longer be there to support them. The 2018 SafeLives impact report made the following comment which professionals need to take into account: '*…we need to stop asking why doesn't she leave and start asking why doesn't he stop.*'

Referrals made to specialist domestic abuse services, including independent domestic violence advisors (IDVAs) and multi-agency risk assessment conferences (MARACs), were most commonly made by the police in the year ending March 2018. While other agencies such as social care and health care services are already involved in the response to domestic abuse, such involvement is not widespread and could be improved.

The Home Office published another research report in 2019 titled *Economic and Social Costs of Domestic Abuse*. This report aimed to estimate the costs of domestic abuse in England and Wales for the year ending 31 March 2017 to highlight the impact of these crimes. It estimates the cost of domestic abuse for victims over this period to be approximately £66 billion.

Since 2010, the government and all agencies have adopted a strategy titled *Call to End Violence Against Women and Girls* (HM Government, 2011). With the strategy is an action plan that every area has adopted, and progress is being made to make the necessary changes. Tackling domestic abuse is a major feature within the action plan (some areas interpret 'girls' to cover all children)[7].

There are a number of significant voluntary sector organisations that provide essential services to victims of domestic abuse, including a national 24-hour helpline. This National Domestic Violence Helpline is run in partnership between Women's Aid and Refuge. The free phone number for this service is 0808 2000 247 and more information can be found at www.nationaldomesticviolencehelpline.org.uk/

The below websites for some nationally significant domestic abuse organisations are listed in no particular order of priority or significance. Their websites have an incredible amount of extremely useful information for not only victims and their families, but also for multi-agency professionals:

- www.refuge.org.uk/
- www.safelives.org.uk/
- www.standingtogether.org.uk/
- www.womensaid.org.uk/

[7] The current action plan 2016-2020 is available at: https://assets.publishing.service.gov.uk/government/uploads/system/uploads/attachment_data/file/522166/VAWG_Strategy_FINAL_PUBLICATION_MASTER_vRB.PDF

Defining DA

Over the years there have been a number of different definitions of what was originally known as domestic violence, but is now more commonly known as domestic abuse. The current cross-government definition is:

'Any incident or pattern of incidents of controlling, coercive, threatening behaviour, violence or abuse between those aged 16 or over who are or have been intimate partners or family members regardless of gender or sexuality. The abuse can encompass but is not limited to:

- *psychological*
- *physical*
- *sexual*
- *financial*
- *emotional.'*

This definition was introduced in April 2013 and extended the term to include 16- and 17-year olds, and to include coercive behaviour. A point that is not always fully understood by multi-agency practitioners is that it not only includes intimate partners, but also familial domestic abuse involving other adult family members.

With the exception of coercive and controlling behaviour, which was introduced as a criminal offence on 29 December 2015, other acts of domestic abuse fall under generic offence categories in police recorded crime and criminal justice data, such as assault with injury.

'Controlling behaviour' is defined as a range of acts designed to make a person subordinate and/or dependent by isolating them from sources of support, exploiting their resources and capacities for personal gain, depriving them of the means needed for independence, resistance and escape, and regulating their everyday behaviour.

'Coercive behaviour' is defined as an act or a pattern of acts of assault, threats, humiliation and intimidation or other abuse that is used to harm, punish or frighten their victim.

Evan Stark (2007) describes this form of DA: 'Not only is coercive control the most common context in which [women] are abused, it is also the most dangerous'.

He also states that it is the removal of liberty for the victim: *'Intimidation (including threats, surveillance, stalking, degradation and shaming), Isolation (including from family, friends and the world outside the home); and Control (including control of family resources and 'micromanagement' of everyday life').'*

One of the challenges to tackling this type of DA is the failure to recognise coercive control and harassment cases by professionals who work with victims of DA. These include, to name just a few, police officers, probation officers, drug and alcohol workers, and health professionals. An evaluated training package based around coercive control, called *DA Matters*, is being introduced in many areas and has been developed by Safelives.

The DA definition also includes so-called 'honour' based violence (HBV), female genital mutilation (FGM) and forced marriage (FM), and victims are not confined to one gender or ethnic group. Chapter 3 looked in detail at what is meant by FM and FGM, and although in that context it was discussed as complex child abuse, it is important to remember that FGM and FM occur in adults as well, and this must be regarded by multi-agency professionals as domestic abuse and dealt with accordingly.

Honour-based violence is a form of domestic abuse that is carried out in the name of so-called 'honour'. This 'honour' is breached by male and female relatives who do not abide by the rules of the family and/or the community they come from. They are then punished for bringing shame on the family or community. Breaches of honour may include a woman having a boyfriend, rejecting a forced marriage, interfaith relationships, inappropriate dress or wearing make-up, for example. Males can also be victims, sometimes as a consequence of a relationship which is deemed to be inappropriate, or if they have assisted a victim. This is a form of DA which is not committed only by men, but female relatives can support, incite or assist. It is a particularly hidden form of DA, as often victims are too scared, shocked or tied by family or community loyalties to speak out.

If victims are from the lesbian, gay, bisexual and transsexual community (LGBT) there will be extra barriers to reporting, and there is a real need for sensitivity when dealing with victims and completing the DASH forms as highlighted in the next section. Further information in relation to LGBT and domestic violence is available at: http://www.brokenrainbow.org.uk/

The psychological and emotional impact on a victim of DA by stalking and harassment must not be underestimated. This can be carried out not only through conventional means, but also through social networks and other forms of modern technology. Victims highlight the controlling, frightening and debilitating impact this has on them. The police recorded 106,905 domestic abuse-related stalking and harassment offences in the year ending March 2018, accounting for just under one-fifth (18%) of all domestic abuse-related offences. Over half of these offences were harassment (54%, or 57,840 cases) and 40% were malicious communications. A joint inspection by HMIC and HMCPSI (2017), in a report titled *The Living in fear – the police and CPS response to harassment and stalking*, stated that harassment and stalking are crimes of persistence. It is the unrelenting and repeated behaviour by the perpetrator experienced in its totality, which seems inescapable and inevitable, that has such a detrimental effect on the victim. The actions in themselves may seem unremarkable, and this may partly explain why some victims suffer repeat behaviour over a prolonged period before reporting it to police, or do not report it at all. Harassment and stalking can often also be crimes of control. This is particularly the case when the victimisation is associated with a current or previous controlling and coercive relationship

In March 2018 the government launched a consultation to seek views on legislation, as well as other steps that can be taken to tackle the harms caused by domestic abuse, and to support victims and survivors to rebuild their lives. They stated that domestic abuse comes in many forms, shattering the lives of victims and their families, and in recognition of this the government has put forward proposals for new laws which would transform our approach to this terrible crime. The consultation has now concluded.

Forthcoming legislation

The government has produced a draft domestic abuse bill, and any prospective legislation and other measures will progress through the legislative process. The Domestic Abuse Bill will:

- define domestic abuse in law to underpin other measures in the bill

- establish a Domestic Abuse Commissioner, to stand up for victims and survivors, raise public awareness, monitor the response of local authorities, the justice system and other statutory agencies and hold them to account in tackling domestic abuse

- provide for a new Domestic Abuse Protection Notice and Domestic Abuse Protection Order

- prohibit perpetrators of abuse from cross-examining their victims in person in the family courts →

- create a statutory presumption that victims of domestic abuse are eligible for special measures in the criminal courts (for example, to enable them to give evidence via a video link)

- enable domestic abuse offenders to be subject to polygraph testing as a condition of their licence following their release from custody

- place the guidance supporting the Domestic Violence Disclosure Scheme ('Clare's law') on a statutory footing

- ensure that where a local authority, for reasons connected with domestic abuse, grants a new secure tenancy to a social tenant who had or has a secure lifetime or assured tenancy (other than an assured short hold tenancy) this must be a secure lifetime tenancy.

More information is available at: www.gov.uk/government/publications/domestic-abuse-bill-2019-factsheets (accessed September 2019).

Identifying domestic abuse, stalking and harassment

All professionals need to be aware of the risks posed to victims of DA and how to identify those risks. In order to do this, most areas and organisations are now using 'domestic abuse, stalking and harassment' (DASH) risk identification, assessment and management model, which was developed from a research and evidence base. The risk assessment form was then adopted after extensive consultation. An example of this assessment form can be found at: www.safelives.org.uk/sites/default/files/resources/Dash%20for%20IDVAs%20FINAL_0.pdf (accessed September 2019).

The National Police Chiefs Council (NPCC) has adopted DASH. They feel it is a good model to assess risk, which will help protect victims if all multi-agency practitioners fill it in on every possible occasion. Although police forces fill in DASH, and other multi-agency professionals use CAADA DASH, in some areas, other agencies use the NPCC DASH rather than the CAADA DASH.

Figure 4.1 shows the areas of risk that the form seeks to identify. As it identifies these areas, it helps to build up a picture of the level of risk.

Figure 4.1: Areas of risk

(Reproduced here with permission of SafeLives. For more information see www.safelives.org.uk)

After the DASH form is completed it will provide a score as a number which indicates a person's level of risk – if a victim scores 14 points or more they are classified as high risk. If they are high risk the victim's case should be discussed at a Multi-Agency Risk Assessment Conference (MARAC) (see p161). Some police forces had been calling a MARAC meeting only after 17 points but this has now changed in the majority of areas to fit in with the 14 points recommended by CAADA. Some MARAC processes also accept professional judgement rather than achieving the 14 points.

However, even though a victim may not be regarded as high risk, and may only score 'medium' or 'standard' risk, they are still at risk of further victimisation and positive action is still required of all agencies. Also bear in mind that the Children Act (1989) highlights the 'risk of significant harm', and section 120 of the Adoption and Children Act (2002) extended the definition of 'significant harm' to children to include the harm caused by witnessing or overhearing the abuse of another, especially in the context of domestic abuse.

It is important to note that in 2018 the College of Policing developed a new domestic abuse risk assessment (DARA) tool. This tool has been piloted in a few police areas, and a report has been compiled. DCC Louisa Rolfe the NSPCC lead for DA stated to author of this chapter, that:

'DASH has been one of the most contentious issues with many academics questioning its validity and the research upon which it is based. Numerous inspections identified that officers did not use it effectively and victims complained that officers did not explain why the questions were asked. The creators of DASH were reluctant to change, claiming that officers were insufficiently trained and that more training (supplied by them) would resolve the matter.

I therefore commissioned The College of Policing Evidence Based Policing Team to identify an improved approach to DA risk assessment. The College worked with Cardiff University Women's Safety Unit (Professor Amanda Robinson) and a number of other universities to initially conduct an evidence evaluation (i.e. what is out there already in terms of relevant research) and then to develop an improved approach. Conscious that the DASH model is used by many partner agencies and charities, the research considered DASH and also focused upon a tool for responding officers that would be compatible with tools relied upon by partners.

The research found that a shorter tool, with less 'yes / no' questions and a greater emphasis upon open questions to identify what lies behind abuse / coercion and control was (a) better understood and used more effectively by first responders and (b) better identified risk, particularly high risk coercive and controlling behaviour. Throughout the process the College have run a steering group with stakeholders from all the key charities and the founders of DASH.'

As a result of this, the DARA approach is being adopted by the police and hopefully, in due course, by other partners.

Barnardo's Domestic Violence Risk Assessment model for children

A number of areas use the Domestic Violence Risk Identification (DVRIM) model for children, which was developed and established by Barnardo's. The model has a system of threshold risk factors, vulnerabilities and protective factors, which allows analysis and assessment of risk, and enables professionals to make decisions about appropriate interventions. The DVRIM can be used by professionals to assist in identifying domestic abuse and assessing its impact on children within the household.

Key learning

- DASH is a risk assessment and management tool used to identify high risk victims of domestic abuse

- It is a checklist that covers different areas of risk. This helps ensure all areas of risk to the victim are taken into account.

- All victims of domestic abuse require positive action even though they may not be classified as high risk.

- Barnardo's DV risk assessment model is also used if there are children in the household

Independent Domestic Violence Advisors (IDVAs)

A few years ago, the Home Office introduced an initiative for every area to have a number of independent domestic violence advisors (IDVAs), with the aim of reducing incidents of DA and thereby the number of domestic related homicides. Depending on the numbers of IDVAs available in areas, they tend to focus on the high-risk victims by supporting them, putting in place safeguarding actions for both them and their children if they have them. IDVAs in some areas aren't directly accessible by the public – i.e. they only work with high-risk cases identified by the police or via MARAC.

A further part of their role involves supporting victims as they go through the court process and civil courts, if required. IDVAs are a voluntary service not statutory, and they require consent to work with DA victims to provide them with information and options, to try to empower them to make choices. They work with victims to identify bespoke risks and then devise together an independent safety plan. In identifying the risks, IDVAs will work with victims to signpost them to other services that will strengthen them, with support with civil orders, criminal court proceedings, safe accommodation, immigration, and with referrals to mental services, drug and alcohol services, counselling, CBT, and accredited DA support groups.

Some areas have a specialist domestic violence court (SDVC), and these are showing real benefits to victims. The IDVAs can inform the courts of the victim's wishes regarding bail conditions and restraining orders. Victims have said how safe and protected they feel while the IDVAs are supporting them. IDVAs are mostly funded by the local authority but there might be additional ones funded by the police. As well as IDVAs there are other support agencies for victims of DA such as refuges, outreach workers, victim support etc.

Key learning

IDVAs:

■ Provide advice in relation to domestic abuse.

■ Assist with safety planning.

■ Provide support through court proceedings, both criminal and civil.

■ Help to signpost other specialist services e.g. housing, refuge locations.

■ Assist as a voice in the Multi Agency Risk Assessment Conference (MARAC) process.

Multi-Agency Risk Assessment Conferences (MARACs)

MARAC is, in essence, a process designed to keep high-risk victims of DA safe. When they submit their DA referral, multi-agency professionals will have it assessed to see if the victim is high risk. If they are, a referral form is submitted to the MARAC co-ordinator and this victim will then be included in the next MARAC meeting. The main part of this is a multi-agency meeting to exchange information about these cases. No one agency has the complete picture of what has happened in each case. The key representatives at the meeting should be police, IDVAs, health, housing, LA and other specialists from the voluntary sectors such as Women's Aid or other similar organisations.

Once the information has been shared, the representatives discuss and decide what needs to be done to try and keep the victim and any children they may have safe. It will also produce an action plan. Although the meeting is focused on the victim, they can also discuss the alleged perpetrator. On average 16 cases are discussed at each meeting. Information shared at the MARAC is confidential, for use by the agencies involved in carrying out the actions. There are approximately 290 MARACs across the UK. MARAC data is submitted to SafeLives by individual MARACs on a quarterly basis.

The victim should be asked if they consent to the referral to MARAC, but even a refusal doesn't stop their case being discussed. The victim does not normally attend but the IDVA can be there on their behalf. The alleged offender of the abuse should not be informed of the MARAC Referral.

In the last year, the total number of cases discussed was 96,537, which is a 5% increase on the previous year. These figures are encouraging, and show that areas are increasing the identification and referrals of high-risk domestic abuse cases to MARAC nationally.

The success of the MARAC process is increasing pressure on local areas to service the number of high-risk victims. This then affects the availability of resources to fully consider the risk to medium and standard risk victims. Some areas with multi-agency safeguarding hubs are carrying out what could perhaps be referred to as a 'MARAC-lite' process on a daily basis. This involves a group of multi-agency professionals considering all of the DA cases that have occurred within the last 24 hours and deciding jointly what actions need to be taken in order to keep victims and their children (if they have any) safe.

Key learning

- It is vital to know the process for dealing with high-risk victims.

- High-risk is determined by the completion of the ACPO DASH for police and CAADA DASH for all other agencies.

- Victims do not need to consent to their information being shared at a MARAC.

- Where children are identified as being at risk of harm, professionals have a duty to make a safeguarding referral to children's services with or without the consent of the adult.

Legal considerations and police powers

Section 76 of the Serious Crime Act (2015) created a new offence of controlling or coercive behaviour in an intimate or family relationship. Before the introduction of this offence, case law indicated the difficulty in proving a pattern of behaviour amounting to harassment within an intimate relationship. The offence, which does not have retrospective effect, came into force on 29th December 2015. There is no other specific criminal offence of domestic abuse, although as discussed there is a new Domestic Violence Bill currently going through parliament which will create a specific offence of DA if it comes into force. However, there are criminal offences for which perpetrators could be prosecuted, ranging from murder and rape to physical assaults. Other offences such as threatening behaviour and stalking and harassment should also be considered.

The police and the Crown Prosecution Service (CPS) do not always need the victim to consent as they can use other forms of evidence such as other witnesses or images captured on body-worn cameras.

Civil actions to protect victims of domestic abuse have been in place for many years. The Domestic Violence Crime and Victims Act (2004) amended previous legislation to two important civil remedies: non-molestation orders and occupation orders. The Protection from Harassment Act (1997) also introduced important civil and criminal remedies, including restraining orders.

A non-molestation order can prohibit either particular behaviour or general molestation. The 2004 Act made a breach of a molestation order a criminal offence with effect from 1 July 2007. This has led to a marked reduction in the use of these as a civil order. The Protection of Freedoms Act (2012) created two offences – stalking, and stalking involving fear of violence or serious alarm and distress. The technology of social media is very often used to commit these offences.

Domestic Violence Protection Orders (DVPOs) and Domestic Violence Protection Notices (DVPNs) were introduced across all police forces in England and Wales in 2014. A DVPN is the initial notice issued by the police to provide emergency protection to an individual believed to be the victim of domestic violence. This notice, which must be authorised by a police superintendent, contains prohibitions that effectively prevent the suspected perpetrator from returning to the victim's home or otherwise contacting the victim. Almost all DVPNs applied for are granted by the superintendent. A DVPN may be issued to a person aged 18 years and over if the police superintendent has reasonable grounds for believing that:

- the individual has been violent towards an associated person

- the individual has threatened violence towards an associated person

- the DVPN is necessary to protect that person from violence or a threat of violence by the intended recipient of the DVPN.

DVPOs are a civil order that provide protection to victims by enabling the police and magistrates' courts to put in place protective measures in the immediate aftermath of a domestic violence incident. DVPOs are often used where there is insufficient evidence to charge a perpetrator and provide protection to a victim via bail conditions.

A DVPO can prevent the perpetrator from returning to a residence and from having contact with the victim for up to 28 days. An application for a DVPO by the police to a magistrates' court should be completed within 48 hours of the DVPN being served on the perpetrator. Magistrates grant the vast majority of DVPOs applied for.

The proposed new domestic abuse bill states that the government wants to introduce a new Domestic Abuse Protection Notice (DAPN) and Domestic Abuse Protection Order (DAPO). These will combine the strongest elements of the various existing orders and provide a flexible pathway for victims and practitioners.

Most victims of DA don't see criminal justice as a route to a positive outcome. Only the police and CPS seemingly describe it as that. Most victims just want the abuse to stop, and they may not want an arrest or court process. Transform Justice published a report in 2018 by Penelope Gibbs titled *Love, Fear and Control: Does the criminal justice system reduce domestic abuse?* The quote below is taken from the report's conclusion:

'Criminal sanctions rarely reduce abuse, and the DVPO is not cost-effective. The most serious offenders need to be charged, prosecuted and very possibly detained, to protect current and future victims. But the vast majority of offences dealt with in the magistrates' court could be dealt with out of court, with deferred prosecution, out of court disposals and/or restorative justice. Above all we need to continue to explore how to motivate perpetrators to understand the damage they wreak and to learn to behave differently.'

Domestic Violence Disclosure Scheme (Clare's Law)

In 2012 the Home Office carried out a pilot that allowed the police to disclose information to individual members of the public about a partner's previous violent offending with the purpose of empowering people to make an informed decision about the future of their relationships. This scheme is called the Domestic Violence Disclosure Scheme, which is better known as Clare's Law[8]. The scheme has been national policy since March 2014.

The DVDS has two routes:

■ 'Right to ask' – this enables someone to ask the police about a partner's previous history of domestic violence or violent acts.

■ 'Right to know' – the police can proactively disclose information in prescribed circumstances.

Every request under the DVDS is thoroughly checked by a panel made up of police, probation services and other agencies to ensure information is only passed on where it is deemed lawful, proportionate and necessary. Individual processes in place across forces for considering and approving applications may vary. Trained police officers and advisers are then on hand to support victims through the difficult and sometimes dangerous transitional period.

Both of the above schemes are carried out by the police. The scheme is going to be available online. This will help ease the ability for those concerned people to make a request. This is seen as a positive step by all professionals involved in DA.

---

8   Named after Clare Wood, who was murdered by her ex-boyfriend in 2009.

Case study

DT and PD have been in a relationship for 16 years and they have a son together who is 16 years old.

Throughout their relationship, PD controlled DT by asking her where she was going, asking her to ring him when she got to the supermarket and ring again when she was leaving. He would make her wear his choice of clothes and would not allow her to wear make-up. He was a manipulative and controlling character throughout their relationship.

On 20th November 2012, DT celebrated her 40th birthday. It was on this day that DT found the courage to tell PD that their relationship was over and that she was now in a newly formed relationship with a work colleague. During the early hours of 21st November 2012, PD called DT to say he was at the railway tracks and was threatening suicide. He then arrived home a few minutes later and was threatening to slash his wrists with a Stanley knife, so DT took him to the hospital and he was released to see his own GP.

At 9am on 21st November 2013, PD was at home with DT. Their son had gone to school. PD left the house and went into the garden saying he was fixing the gears on his bike. DT saw him go to the garage and then walk to the shed carrying the grinder; she heard the grinder start and at this point she went into the downstairs toilet. When she came out of the toilet moments later PD was standing there and confronted her, asking if she still loved him. She said, 'only as the father to our son'. He then stabbed her in the throat with a screwdriver and continued his frenzied attack stabbing her all over her body including her back, abdomen and breasts.

She was left fighting for her life, but she managed to get to the phone and dial 999. She fled to a neighbouring address while still talking to the police operator. Police attended and found DT with a number of stab wounds. She was rushed to hospital and later transferred to a specialist unit due to the deterioration in her condition.

Police officers from the specialist domestic abuse investigation unit (DAIU) attended the hospital to see DT. PD had made good his escape and phoned the victim on her mobile, which was answered by a friend in the presence of the police. PD confirmed he could see the police in the area and even at this point was trying to control the situation, suggesting where he will meet the police and on his terms. The police operator quickly took control and issued him with strict instructions. Armed officers quickly detained him. He was later interviewed and he answered all questions with 'no comment'. →

The case was taken to the CPS who authorised a charge of attempted murder. DT remained in hospital for three days and was treated for a collapsed lung. By all accounts she was lucky to be alive. She was then interviewed by specially trained officers from the DAIU on video where she gave a comprehensive account of the history between her and PD, and the day of the attack.

She was appointed an IDVA and she was regularly contacted by the officer in the case and kept apprised of the investigation and impending court case.

The son was interviewed by police to provide background to the relationship and he was placed in the unenviable position of having to give evidence at court when the case eventually came to be heard. This was only because the defendant would not accept the evidence and wanted the opportunity to control the family. PD pleaded guilty to GBH with intent but pleaded not guilty to attempted murder.

During his time on remand, PD regularly wrote letters to his son and sent them via the police to the case officers. The officers had to review all this material on a regular basis and deal with it accordingly. It was evident that PD wanted to control things even from prison.

DT gave evidence under special measures from behind a screen in the witness box. She came across as a credible, courageous and honest witness who had to share many intimate details of her relationship with the court room. Her son also gave evidence via video link.

The trial concluded after a number of witnesses had given evidence and the playing of the crucial 999 recording made by DT shortly after the attack. PD was found guilty of attempted murder after only 40 minutes of deliberation and later sentenced to 18 years' imprisonment. He was also given a lifetime restraining order not to contact DT.

Since the conclusion of the trial, contact has been maintained by the officers and the IDVA with the victim and her son. There continues to be issues surrounding the defendant and his on-going need to have control over his son. Police are currently addressing those issues.

The victim is now receiving counselling. She remains with her new partner and is now in a supportive and loving relationship. Her son lives with them and he too has received counselling although he is still trying to come to terms with what happened. He doesn't want contact from his father at this time.

Education

A number of areas have adopted Operation Encompass, which is a police and education early information sharing partnership which enables schools to offer immediate support for children and young people experiencing domestic abuse. Information is shared by the police, after they obtain consent, with a school's trained Key Adult (DSL) prior to the start of the next school day after officers have attended a domestic abuse incident. This enables appropriate support to be given, dependent upon the needs and wishes of the child.

There are other preventative education and awareness campaigns, available both in schools and in the wider community. These are an essential part of preventing domestic abuse. Schools run various programmes, one of which is a Home Office campaign 'This is abuse', which aims to get young people to realise what constitutes DA. However, it is not mandatory and not all schools provide DA awareness.

Perpetrator programmes

Another useful programme is 'The Freedom Programme', which was created and run by Pat Craven and which evolved from her work with perpetrators of domestic violence. The programme was primarily designed for women as victims of domestic violence, but can also include a programme for men, whether abusive and wishing to change their attitudes and behaviour, or victims of domestic abuse themselves. All group work, however, is single sex/sexuality and will not take place in a mixed group. The Freedom Programme's aim is to help victims to make sense of and understand what has happened to them. It also describes in detail how children are affected by being exposed to this kind of abuse and, importantly, how their lives are improved when the abuse is removed. More information is available at: www. freedomprogramme.co.uk/

An accredited programme for perpetrators of domestic abuse is called 'Building Better Relationships' (BBR). The intervention is aimed at those male offenders convicted of serious domestic violence, in particular those with an entrenched pattern of violence and aggression. It aims to reduce re-offending and promote the safety of current and future partners and children. It helps men achieve a better understanding of why they use violence and aggression in their intimate relationships, the attitudes and beliefs that underpin their behaviour and what factors reinforce and maintain their use of that behaviour. More information on this programme is available for multi-agency practitioners from their local area probation service. The programme is not readily available in every area. There are, however, in most areas, voluntary perpetrator programmes which are separate from the BBR and are more publicly accessible.

A highly regarded programme is 'DRIVE>', which is about responding to high-risk perpetrators of domestic abuse – increasing safety for victims and children. This is now in its third year, and, as stated, is highly regarded. Further information is available at www.driveproject.org.uk

There is also a charity that specialises in tackling perpetrator behaviour to prevent DA called Respect. More information and resources are available at https://respect. uk.net/

Key learning

- Stalking and stalking involving fear of violence are now offences.
- Civil actions include non-molestation, occupancy and residency.
- The domestic violence disclosure scheme (Clare's law) will allow people to find out about a new partner's past.
- Domestic violence protection orders can be in place for 28 days.

Education programmes such as 'This is Abuse' and 'Freedom Programme' are in place in some areas.

Domestic Homicide Reviews (DHRs)

DHRs have been carried out in some areas for a number of years. However, it only became a statutory duty to conduct a formal multi-agency review about the death of a person in the context of domestic abuse in 2009. This is a parallel process to a coroner's inquest or any criminal investigation. In accordance with the provisions of the Domestic Violence, Crime and Victims Act (2004), Section 9, DHRs came into force on 13th April, 2011. The act states that a DHR should be a review:

'Of the circumstances in which the death of a person aged 16 or over has, or appears to have, resulted from violence, abuse or neglect by:

(a) a person to whom he was related or with whom he was or had been in an intimate personal relationship, or

(b) a member of the same household as himself, held with a view to identifying the lessons to be learnt from the death'

A Community Safety Partnership (CSP) will be the body that organises and manages the DHR process.

A good DHR should always have the victim at the centre of the review, which includes getting views from their family, neighbours and the community within which they lived. Families can get advocacy to support them in the review process and a good source for this advocacy is a charity called Advocacy After Fatal Domestic Abuse. They have a website which can be accessed at: https://aafda.org.uk/

There are occasions when a Domestic Homicide Review will be conducted jointly with a Child Serious Case review. A good example of this working effectively was in the case of the murder of Child J (17 years old) who was killed by her partner. The Review was commissioned jointly by the Oxfordshire Safeguarding Children Board (OSCB) and the South and Vale Community Safety Partnership, (S&VCSP). The review into the circumstances of the death of Child J highlighted a number of issues for the local partnership, but also nationally. The first is the effectiveness of work with adolescents. The second, more specifically relevant to this chapter, is the level of understanding and response to adolescents who are experiencing domestic abuse in peer relationships. The review can be found at www.oscb.org.uk

Lessons learned

The Home Office runs a quality assurance panel that examines all DHRs. They then feed back to the Community Safety Partnerships their thoughts on the reviews they have seen. They have now published two learning lessons reports, first in 2013 and then again in December 2016.

In November 2013, after the panel had viewed 54 completed reports, they published a newsletter titled *Domestic Homicide Reviews: Common themes identified as lessons to be learned* (Home Office, 2013).

The key points from this newsletter were:

- **Awareness raising and communication**. A number of reports identified the need for improved training and awareness on domestic violence and abuse for GPs and healthcare professionals.
- **Risk assessment**. The importance of a consistent approach to risk identification, assessment and management for all professionals was identified in a number of reports.
- **Information sharing and multi-agency working**. In some cases, information sharing was identified as inadequate where individual agencies had some

knowledge of the victim and/or the perpetrator, but this was not shared, even where it was lawful to do so to give a full picture of the situation and ultimately a full understanding of the potential risks.

- **Complex needs**. In a number of cases the victim and/or the perpetrator had complex needs, which could include domestic violence and abuse, sexual abuse, alcohol, substance misuse and mental health illness.

- **Perpetrators and bail**. There needs to be improvements in compliance with existing processes and procedures specifically in relation to bail management, including breach of bail, as this is critical in protecting victims and managing suspects.

- **Awareness of the safeguarding needs of children**. There were cases in which children were in households where domestic violence and abuse occurred between adults, but the impact on the children was not necessarily considered.

In December 2016 the Home Office published *Key Findings From Analysis of Domestic Homicide Reviews*, which identified a series of common learning themes from all of the reviews that they examined:

- **Record Keeping**. There was lots of examples of poor quality and incomplete records, particularly in GP records.

- **Risk Assessment**. These were not always completed fully, were of poor quality and incidents were looked at in isolation.

- **Communication/information sharing between agencies**. Information was regularly slow or not shared and no communication took place.

- **Identification and understanding of DA**. Risk factors were not understood, vulnerabilities were overlooked.

- **Organisational policy**. There was a lack of policy in some places, and failures to understand or implement policies where they were in place.

- **Competence, knowledge and skills**. There was a lack of upskilling the workforce.

- **Multi-Agency work**. There were incidences of people thinking someone else was doing something when they weren't.

- **Referrals**. There were errors in referrals, or referrals were not taking place when they should have.

- **Training**. There was a lack of training in all agencies.

- **Public awareness**. In all cases, violence was known by family, neighbours or work colleagues. None of this was reported to professionals.

Similar themes are raised here to those seen in serious case reviews for children. Information sharing and multi-agency working is something that comes up time after time. There is also other really useful research carried out into domestic homicide, for example 'Standing Together Against Domestic Violence' has completed a case analysis of DHRs which is available at: www.standingtogether.org.uk/sites/default/files/docs/STADV_DHR_Report_Final.pdf (accessed September 2019).

The case study below is from a DHR that involved the murders of Claire and Charlotte Hart by their husband/father. Luke and Ryan, two survivors of their fathers' domestic abuse, are advocates in memory of their mother and sister striving to tackle coercive and controlling behaviour. They have a website at www.operationlighthouse.co.uk/. They have also co-authored a book about their experience called *Remembered Forever*, which is available through all good booksellers.

Case study: coercive control

On the morning of July 19th 2016, a man drove to the leisure centre in the town of Spalding with a shotgun and ammunition and waited. His wife, Claire Hart, who had recently separated from him, came out the swimming pool some while later with their 19-year-old daughter Charlotte. As Claire and Charlotte walked towards their car, he confronted them both. Claire evidently saw him approaching and had raised her arms. He shot them both at close range.

Claire was struck in the abdomen and died almost immediately. He re-loaded the weapon and shot Charlotte, before again re-loading and instantly killing himself. While being given first aid, Charlotte told a witness that it was her dad who had shot her. She suffered catastrophic injuries and died despite the efforts to save her. Claire's two grown-up sons knew instantly when they heard media reports that it was their mother and sister who had been shot.

They have now given heartrending accounts about how their father bullied them as children and the rest of their family was harassed and oppressed on a daily basis. This man came to control every aspect of their lives including his wife's finances and movements. To the rest of the outside world all appeared fine, and only occasional comments about problems were made to local doctors when discussing medical problems and ailments. The sons worked closely with their mother and sister to re-locate them to a house in the area and escape this abuse. At no time did anyone in the family try to seek external help, as at no time was violence used against them.

Since this tragedy, both sons have appeared on national television to tell what happened to them, and what happened to their mother and sister. In doing ➔

so they hope that more people will see that what happened in this case and any similar circumstances is a crime of 'coercive and controlling behaviour', recently created under Section 76 of the Serious Crime Act (2015).

What did we learn?

Despite the way this perpetrator completely dominated and oppressed the entire family, nobody in this situation thought at the time that they were victims of DA. Everyone in the family had a strong view that DA involved some sort of physical violence, and so despite bullying, controlling and dominating every aspect of their lives, the perpetrator was not committing DA.

This is of course incorrect, but from within the situation the victims did not think they could turn to others, like the police, for help. This means it is vital for all professionals to be able to recognise the criminal cases of coercive and controlling behaviour and respond to them as the victims themselves either may not see themselves as victims, or may not be physically able to break free.

Whenever there is a glimpse into such oppressive situations through a chance remark or a tentative disclosure, professionals must feel responsible for following up such insights to establish the true reality of the situation. This lack of awareness is not confined to those suffering coercive or controlling behaviour. Most of the general public are not familiar with this form of DA and are unable to recognise it if their family, friends or work colleagues are subjected to it. There needs to be a co-ordinated awareness-raising campaign particularly involving professional agencies, including medical GPs and in schools where such disclosures may be made.

Cases of coercive control damage families and young people to a devastating degree and the victims become an isolated, mutually supporting group. Through adopting a wide definition of coercive and controlling behaviour (which recognises that violence is not always a key part of the offending), as professionals we can start to prevent future cases such as this.

■ All professionals should make sure they know what the new offence of coercive and controlling behaviour involves. Just because there is no violence doesn't mean it is not domestic abuse.

■ Be professionally curious! GPs and others should ask those difficult questions if someone hints that they are being controlled. Look out for signs and symptoms.

■ Spread awareness about coercive behaviour. Most times even the victims themselves, especially children, fail to recognise the situation they are in.

For more information, see: www.lincolnshire.gov.uk/safer-lincolnshire-partnership/domestic-abuse/domestic-homicide-reviews/132347.article (accessed September 2019).

The triennial review of serious case reviews looked at domestic abuse in detail and how it affected children, and it contained the following statement that all multi-agency practitioners should be aware of:

'Learning from these serious case reviews, it is our view that a step-change is required in how we as professionals and as a society respond to Domestic Abuse.' (Sidebotham *et al*, 2016)

Further reading

There is a range of resources and information available on the following domestic abuse charity websites:

- www.refuge.org.uk/
- www.safelives.org.uk/
- www.standingtogether.org.uk/
- www.womensaid.org.uk/
- www.respect.uk.net/

References

Gibbs P (2018) *Love, Fear and Control: Does the criminal justice system reduce domestic abuse?* Transform Justice. London.

Home Office (2013) *Domestic Homicide Reviews: Common themes identified as lessons to be learned* [online]. London: Home Office. Available at: www.gov.uk/government/publications/domestic-homicide-review-lessons-learned (accessed September 2019).

Home Office (2016) *Domestic Homicide Reviews, Key findings from analysis of domestic homicide reviews* [online]. London: Home Office. Available at: https://assets.publishing.service.gov.uk/government/uploads/system/uploads/attachment_data/file/575232/HO-Domestic-Homicide-Review-Analysis-161206.pdf (accessed September 2019).

Home Office (2019) *The Economic and Social Costs of Domestic Abuse: Research Report 107*. London, Home Office. Available at: https://assets.publishing.service.gov.uk/government/uploads/system/uploads/attachment_data/file/772180/horr107.pdf (accessed September 2019).

HM Government (2011) *Call to End Violence Against Women and Girls* [online]. London: HM Government. Available at: https://www.gov.uk/government/uploads/system/uploads/attachment_data/file/97905/vawg-paper.pdf (accessed September 2019).

HM Government (2018) *Ending Violence Against Women and Girls: Stretegy 2016-2020* [online]. Available at: https://assets.publishing.service.gov.uk/government/uploads/system/uploads/attachment_data/file/522166/VAWG_Strategy_FINAL_PUBLICATION_MASTER_vRB.PDF (accessed September 2019).

HMIC and HMCPSI (2017) *Living in Fear: The police and CPS response to harassment and stalking*. HMIC and HMCPSI. London.

Office for National Statistics (2018) Domestic Abuse in England and Wales: Year ending March 2018. London: ONS. Available at: www.ons.gov.uk/peoplepopulationandcommunity/crimeandjustice/bulletins/domesticabuseinenglandandwales/yearendingmarch2018 (accessed September 2019).

SafeLives (2019) *Our Impact: Getting it right first time* [online]. Available at: www.safelives.org.uk/news-views/annual-impact-report-2018 (accessed September 2019).

Sidebotham P, Brandon M, Bailey S, Belderson P, Dodsworth J, Garstang J, Harrison E, Retzer A & Sorensen P (2016) *Pathways to Harm, Pathways to Protection: A triennial analysis of serious case reviews 2011 to 2014: final report*. [London]: Department for Education.

Stark E (2007) *Coercive Control: The entrapment of women in personal life*. U.S.A: Oxford University Press.

Chapter 5: Safeguarding vulnerable adults

By Nigel Boulton

Chapter overview

- Introduction.
- Adult safeguarding.
- Transitioning: Child Needs Assessments
- The aims of adult safeguarding.
- Seven stages of the adult safeguarding process.
- Seven core aims.
- Six key principles.
- Making Safeguarding Personal (MSP).
- 10 key areas of abuse and neglect.
- Coercive and controlling behaviour.
- Mental Capacity Act (2005).
- Deprivation of Liberty: Authorisation of arrangements enabling care and treatment.
- Independent advocacy.
- Local authority responsibilities.
- Carers.
- Local procedures.
- Review meetings.
- Victim and witness evidence and interviewing.
- Intimidated witnesses.
- Intermediaries.
- Vulnerable adults with children.

Introduction

For many years the safeguarding of vulnerable adults was not enshrined in law. Professionals involved in this area of public protection activity looked to and relied upon the government guidance *No Secrets: Guidance on developing and implementing multi-agency policies and procedures to protect vulnerable adults from abuse* (Department of Health, 2000). This sought to ensure statutory and other agencies worked together effectively and efficiently as safeguarding partners in order to promote the welfare and uphold the rights of vulnerable adults under the Human Rights Act (1998), and to ensure they received protection and support.

Professionals who worked in both child and adult protection long hoped for legislation that would legally ensure the safeguarding of vulnerable adults and ensure the multi-agency collaboration required to do so effectively. The Care Act (2014) (see Further reading on page 207) delivered this mandate for the first time in England and Wales, and required all statutorily defined organisations to co-operate to ensure the safeguarding of vulnerable adults.

Updated statutory guidance to accompany the Care Act (2014) was published in the autumn of 2018 and clearly builds upon the practice and evolution of adult safeguarding. The statutory guidance replaced *No Secrets*.

This chapter draws heavily on and clearly reflects the new and long-awaited legislation. It should, however, be read in conjunction with:

- the Care Act (2014) itself

- the *Care and Support Statutory Guidance* (Department of Health, 2018)

- the Association of Chief Police Officers (ACPO) guidance for the safeguarding and investigation of vulnerable adults (ACPO & NPIA)

- practice guidance from the Association of Directors of Adult Services (ADASS, 2011; ADASS & LGA, 2013)

- safeguarding resources (Local Government Association & Association of Directors of Adult Services)

- Guidance: Inter-Authority Safeguarding Arrangements (ADASS, 2016)

As with all public protection activity, each local area should have local procedures agreed and published for all to see, and every professional involved in safeguarding should be familiar with them. Again, as with all public protection and safeguarding practice, the Human Rights Act (1998) and the articles enshrined within it (see

Further reading on page 207) should always be uppermost in the mind of the professional when considering any action or decisions in relation to an adult who may be at risk or who is believed to be vulnerable.

The delivery of the statutory process to safeguard a vulnerable adult is not a replacement for the delivery and oversight of excellent care and support, nor does it remove or replace the statutory and common law duties of the police to prevent and detect crime as well as protect life and property. Safeguarding, as stated in the statutory guidance, should be 'person led and outcomes focused'.

The safeguarding and investigation of vulnerable adults is very much akin to the safeguarding of children in terms of its operational delivery, and there are many similarities in relation to the partnership work that is required. As with children, it is paramount that agencies work together efficiently and effectively. The service requirements across a range of cases are rarely deliverable by one service but by an integrated and co-ordinated approach. This runs true for both the delivery of criminal investigations into the abuse of vulnerable adults led by the police, and for the delivery of support and care in communities to allow adults at risk to lead independent lives. There is no single agency or service who delivers in totality, albeit one may take the lead. The range of those involved, the complexity of multi-agency protection plans and the mix of partners, should be designed on a case-by-case basis.

So, in essence, whether you work for a local authority, a health service, probation, police, education or a private or voluntary sector provider supplying services to one of those public bodies, you have a duty to safeguard adults just as has been the case for children for many years. The responsibilities, the need to work closely, effectively and efficiently as partners, and the particular agencies charged with being responsible are also similar in many respects.

Safeguarding children is everybody's responsibility, with the child being at the centre of all enquiries. The Care Act (2014) dictates the same concentration and attention from agencies and individual professionals for vulnerable adults who are at risk.

Just as with children, the overriding ethos of working together is paramount, effective communication is essential and confidence and trust between partners a necessity. The rights and desires of the adult also need to be respected.

Adult safeguarding

Vulnerable adults defined

A vulnerable adult is defined in section 42 of the Care Act (2014) as:

An adult who:

- has needs for care and support (whether or not the local authority is meeting any of those needs)
- is experiencing, or at risk of, abuse or neglect
- as a result of those care and support needs is unable to protect themselves from either the risk of, or the experience of, abuse or neglect.

Adult safeguarding relates to any individual who has reached the age of 18 years. If the person is still receiving services from a children's service department of a local authority then they should be involved, but the case will be owned and co-ordinated by adult services.

Transitioning: child needs assessments

The Care Act (2014) makes provision for the local authority children's service to carry out an assessment before a child turns 18.

Section 58 (1) states:

'Where it appears to a local authority that a child is likely to have needs for care and support after becoming 18 the authority must, if it is satisfied that it would be of significant benefit to the child to do so and if the consent condition is met assess:

(a) Whether the child has needs for care and support and, if so, what those needs are, and

(b) Whether the child is likely to have needs for care and support after becoming 18 and, if so, what those needs are likely to be.'

Section 58 (2) identifies this requirement as a child needs assessment. Section 58 (3) identifies when the consent condition is met, and Section 58 (4) stipulates that even if consent is not in place the local authority must still carry out the assessment if the child is experiencing, or at risk of, abuse or neglect.

Section 59 identifies that the child, a parent, carer, or any person the child wishes, should be involved in the assessment with an indication as to needs for care and support which have been identified, and advice concerning how best the needs for care and support can be provided. The local authority will make a decision as to whether the assessment should be used as a needs assessment when the child turns 18 as if it had been carried out after the person had become 18.

Child's needs assessments are intended to ensure a seamless transition for a child when they turn 18 in relation to the identification and provision of care and support.

Safeguarding means protecting a vulnerable adult's right to live in safety, free from abuse and neglect. It is about people and organisations working together to prevent and stop both the risks and experience of abuse or neglect, while at the same time making sure the adult's well-being is promoted.

Any person, professional or otherwise, can and should identify concerns in relation to an adult who may be vulnerable and at risk of abuse or neglect. These concerns should be made known to the local authority for the area where the adult is residing or present at that time. Each local authority area will have published guidance as to how this is done locally and may well publish guidance concerning levels of harm and thresholds that may be used to support decisions.

In many areas, local authorities have integrated their referral pathways into a Multi-Agency Safeguarding Hub (MASH) or similar partnership model, where all partners are able to share information and assess risk very dynamically. MASH is dealt with in greater depth in Chapter 9, but, in brief, they consist of a team of multidisciplinary professionals who can meet and bring together any relevant information for a particular case, allowing for greater communication and a consistent, coherent and quick response.

All safeguarding professionals should identify any risk of harm to a vulnerable adult and take action to remove or reduce the risk if this is deemed necessary.

The aims of adult safeguarding

The Care Act (2014) statutory guidance (Department of Health, 2018) identifies seven core aims of adult safeguarding:

1. Stop abuse or neglect.

2. Prevent harm and reduce the risk of abuse or neglect to adults with care and support needs.

3. Safeguard adults in a way that supports them in making choices and having control about how they want to live.

4. Promote an approach that concentrates on improving life for the adults concerned.

5. Raise public awareness so that communities as a whole, alongside professionals, play their part in preventing, identifying and responding to abuse and neglect.

6. Provide information and support in accessible ways to help people understand the different types of abuse, how to stay safe and what to do to raise a concern about the safety or well-being of an adult.

7. Address what has caused the abuse or neglect.

These aims reinforce the two key outcomes of adult safeguarding: to stop or prevent harm and to enable as much as possible the highest quality of life for those who may be at risk.

The Care Act (2014) statutory guidance also identifies six key principles that underpin adult safeguarding:

1. **Empowerment** – people being supported and encouraged to make their own decisions and informed consent.

2. **Prevention** – it is better to take action before harm occurs.

3. **Proportionality** – the least intrusive response appropriate to the risk presented.

4. **Protection** – support and representation for those in greatest need.

5. **Partnership** – local solutions through services working with their communities. Communities have a part to play in preventing, detecting and reporting neglect and abuse.

6. **Accountability** – accountability and transparency in delivering safeguarding.

What is abuse and neglect?

There is no definitive description of what forms abuse and neglect as it can occur in many ways. It is therefore essential that each case is considered individually, taking account of the specific circumstances and whether it fits the definition of a safeguarding concern within section 42 of the Care Act (2014), as explained in Box 5.1.

The statutory guidance for the Care Act (2014) identifies ten areas that may constitute abuse or neglect. These can be single incidents or multiple occurrences over a period of time affecting one person or more. It is important for professionals to consider patterns in relation to harm. Repeated incidents of poor care, for example, may indicate a more serious problem that could be categorised as organisational abuse.

Box 5.1: 10 Key types of abuse and neglect

Physical abuse – including assault, hitting, slapping, pushing, misuse of medication, restraint or inappropriate physical sanctions.

Domestic violence – including psychological, physical, sexual, financial, emotional abuse and so-called 'honour' based violence. The age range for this abuse type covers everyone 16 years and over. It can be a single event or a number of incidents and can include coercion or controlling behaviour as well as violence and abuse.

Sexual abuse – including rape, indecent exposure, sexual harassment, inappropriate looking or touching, sexual teasing or innuendo, sexual photography, subjection to pornography or witnessing sexual acts, and sexual assault or sexual acts to which the adult has not consented or was pressured into consenting.

Psychological abuse – including emotional abuse, threats of harm or abandonment, deprivation of contact, humiliation, blaming, controlling, intimidation, coercion, harassment, verbal abuse, cyber bullying, isolation or unreasonable and unjustified withdrawal of services or supportive networks.

Financial or material abuse – including theft, fraud, internet scamming, coercion in relation to an adult's financial affairs or arrangements, including in connection with wills, property, inheritance or financial transactions, or the misuse or misappropriation of property, possessions or benefits. ➔

Modern slavery – encompasses slavery, human trafficking, forced labour and domestic servitude. Traffickers and slave masters use whatever means they have at their disposal to coerce, deceive and force individuals into a life of abuse, servitude and inhumane treatment.

Discriminatory abuse – including forms of harassment, slurs or similar treatment because of race, gender and gender identity, age, disability, sexual orientation or religion.

Organisational abuse – including neglect and poor care practice within an institution or specific care setting such as a hospital or care home for example, or in relation to care provided in one's own home. This may range from one-off incidents to on-going ill-treatment. It can be through neglect or poor professional practice as a result of the structure, policies, processes and practices within an organisation.

Neglect and acts of omission – including ignoring medical, emotional or physical care needs, failing to provide access to appropriate health, care and support or educational services, the withholding of the necessities of life, such as medication, adequate nutrition and heating. Neglect is not always intentional and may be due to carers not coping or struggling to cope.

Self-neglect – this covers a wide range of behaviour that neglects to care for one's personal hygiene, health or surroundings and includes behaviour such as hoarding. Self-neglect, although recognised for many years, is now specifically identified in the Care Act (2014) and the statutory guidance, but it must be appreciated that it may not necessarily prompt a safeguarding enquiry.

The Serious Crime Act (2015) created an offence of coercive and controlling behaviour. This offence closed a gap concerning these issues and provides protection for victims experiencing continuous abuse and sends a clear message that it is unacceptable to violate the trust of those who are or were close or intimate within a relationship.

A statutory guidance framework is available covering the issues of controlling or coercive behaviour.

As with all abuse and crimes of this nature, abuse can be long-term within a family; serial abuse by an individual who has sought out and groomed the victim for the very reason of abusing them; as well as single and opportunistic crimes such as theft. Anyone can be a perpetrator of abuse and neglect including absolute strangers. It is, however, more likely that an abuser will be known to the individual and be in a position of trust and/or power. It can occur anywhere, including in a person's home, a hospital or a care home. Domestic abuse isn't always committed by a partner and it is important to remember that it can and is perpetrated by other family members.

Everyone in society can help to identify the signs of abuse or neglect. Being vigilant is the key, and then being aware of what to do and where to seek help and advice if one believes something is not right. Supporting adults to be safe and make safe choices is also important in combatting abuse and neglect.

The indications, signs or triggers may not be easy to see but a concern from one person, professional or otherwise, when shared with the appropriate professionals, may add to another and more easily identify that abuse and neglect are present. All professionals who have concerns should share their information with the local authority about the person's welfare if they believe they are suffering or likely to suffer abuse or neglect. The identification of harm in this way is dealt with in greater detail in Chapter 8.

Once reported as a concern, the circumstances of the case will obviously shape the response. Safeguarding the individual will always be the primary focus. Once a concern is highlighted then the causes can be understood. It is the identification and communication of the concern that is crucial. Professionals should never assume someone else is going to report the issue, nor should they be embarrassed. If in doubt, seek advice from a colleague or directly from the local authority. If a professional believes a crime may have been committed then the police should also be told.

While there many similarities between the abuse of children and that of adults, there are also clear differences which need to be understood and considered. All vulnerable adults have the same rights as any other person and their views need to be taken into account. Adults are presumed to be in a position to make decisions concerning themselves and the risks they may face unless it is deemed that they cannot due to a mental incapacity (see p187).

Identifying harm and risk to adults is somewhat more difficult than to children, on the whole, as they are less visible to society than children, who will in the normal course of events be seen regularly by teachers, doctors and other professionals or volunteers. Front line services such as police, health and carers as well as family members therefore have the best opportunity of identifying concerns or suspicions.

Making Safeguarding Personal (MSP)

As has been stated above, the Care Act (2014) statutory guidance identifies six key principles, the first of which is to empower service users to make their own decisions with informed consent through being supported and encouraged. The guidance also identifies seven core aims of adult safeguarding which clearly state adult safeguarding practice needs to be delivered in a way that supports them in making choices and having control about how they want to live.

To ensure this focus on the service user, an initiative entitled Making Safeguarding Personal (MSP), which has been running since 2010 and was created by the adult safeguarding sector supported by the Association of Directors of Adult Social Care (ADASS), came more into focus in supporting the overall aims of the Care Act (2014).

MSP aims to develop an outcome focus to adult safeguarding work, and a range of responses to support people to improve or resolve their circumstances. It also aims to ensure that practice embraces the core statutory principles of both the Human Rights framework and the Mental Capacity Act (2005). There are tools available to support the initiative, to measure effectiveness and to improve safeguarding practice.

Making Safeguarding Personal now sits firmly within the Care and Support Statutory Guidance, as revised in 2018, that supports the Care Act (2014).

It means safeguarding adults is:

■ person-led

■ outcome-focused

■ engages the person and enhances involvement, choice and control

■ improves quality of life, well-being and safety.

(paragraph 14.15)

MSP must not simply be seen in the context of a formal safeguarding enquiry (a Care Act (2014), Section 42 enquiry), but as part of the whole spectrum of care and support activity.

A person-centred approach

Professionals must be mindful and respect the views, wishes, feelings and beliefs of an adult at all times, especially when deciding on any action. Any intervention in family or personal relationships needs to be carefully considered, and any action which may jeopardise or remove all contact with family members may be experienced in a negative way by the adult and risk breaching their fundamental human right to family life if not justified or proportionate.

Decision making within adult safeguarding has to balance the requirement to protect an individual from harm with respect for their individual and personal rights to freedom, family life etc. The risk of harm to vulnerable adults is therefore a very complex issue, in part because the law clearly identifies an adult's right to make choices and decisions about their own lives. This includes decisions about their own safety and perceptions of vulnerability.

The ability of an individual to make such decisions is of course, on occasions, an issue in itself. This is expanded on below, but it is the responsibility of all frontline professionals who may come into contact with a vulnerable adult to ensure immediate safeguarding actions are taken and to identify cases where support or assessment may be appropriate.

As with all decisions, best practice and guidance suggests good quality and accurate records should be kept and each decision considered in terms of necessity and proportionality.

Mental Capacity Act (2005)

The Mental Capacity Act (2005) (MCA) as amended by the Mental capacity (Amendment) Act (2019) enshrines in law the best practice and common law principles in relation to people who may lack the necessary capacity to make decisions for themselves. The act is underpinned and supported by a code of practice that provides advice and guidance on how professionals should interpret and apply the law.

The Mental capacity (Amendment) Act (2019) amended two specific areas of law in relation to the Deprivation of Liberty of individuals who require care and treatment as well as the authorisation of steps necessary for life-sustaining treatment or another vital act. The act also amended the Codes of Practice to the Mental Capacity Act (2015).

There are five straightforward key principles within the act which should be adhered to at all times when considering actions concerning the mental capacity of vulnerable adults. It is important to be aware that an assessment of mental capacity is always based on a decision-by-decision basis and is not generic – just because a person is assessed as unable to make one particular decision does not mean they are unable to make any other decisions, and a separate assessment will be needed each time.

The statutory principles aim to:

- protect people who lack capacity
- help them take part, as much as possible, in decisions that affect them.

They aim to assist and support people who may lack capacity to make particular decisions, not to restrict or control their lives.

Mental Capacity Act (2005): five statutory principles

1. **Presumption of capacity**. A person must be assumed to have capacity unless it is established that they lack capacity.
2. **Individuals should be supported to make their own decisions**. A person is not to be treated as unable to make a decision unless all practicable steps to help him to do so have been taken without success.
3. **Unwise decisions**. A person is not to be treated as unable to make a decision merely because he makes an unwise decision.
4. **Best interests**. An act done, or decision made, under this Act for or on behalf of a person who lacks capacity must be done, or made, in his best interests.
5. **Less restrictive option**. Before the act is done, or the decision is made, regard must be had to whether the purpose for which it is needed can be as effectively achieved in a way that is less restrictive of the person's rights and freedom of action.

There are two stages identified within the MCA for suitably qualified professionals to consider when determining if an individual has the necessary capacity. This assessment of capacity is carried out by the most relevant person. It is possible that a carer can assess if the person has the capacity to decide on what they might have for supper. For more important decisions, a social work or health professional who has the training and experience should undertake the assessment. The underlying considerations are, however, useful to all professionals who are in a position where they need to consider immediate action or in considering harm and risk to an adult.

Stage 1

Does the person have an impairment of the mind or brain, or is there some sort of disturbance affecting the way their mind or brain works? (It doesn't matter whether the impairment or disturbance is temporary or permanent.)

If a professional does not believe this to be the case then they will not lack capacity under the act and their decisions are to be respected. A bad decision is to be supported.

The act and codes of practice identify the many types of impairment or disturbance. The decision concerning impairment, however, must never be made on issues such as age, conditions such as Down's syndrome or cerebral palsy, or appearance or personal choices of dress, body art, skin colour or cultural influence. It depends upon the ability to understand the issue and the consequences of the decision.

Stage 2

If so, does that impairment or disturbance mean that the person is unable to make the decision in question at the time it needs to be made?

If it is a temporary impairment, one must consider if it is appropriate in the circumstances to wait until the capacity to make decisions returns.

The act suggests a person needs to be able to understand and remember the information about the decision and use it as part of the decision-making process. It is also relevant whether or not a person is able to communicate the decision in any manner. It must be remembered that this can include verbal, written, signed or any other type of communication and may be through an intermediary or translator.

If a person is deemed not to have the capacity to make a particular decision, it is necessary to call a best interest meeting at which relevant people should consider the issue and a decision will be made which must be in the best interests of the person. This could well be a decision that might be considered unwise but which is believed to be what the person would have wanted when balancing their views when they had the capacity to make them.

The MCA introduced a new criminal offence under Section 44 to ill-treat or wilfully neglect any person who lacks the required mental capacity. Police are now required to investigate such allegations. The offence is usually committed by those who are caring for, or who have legal responsibility over, a person who lacks the mental capacity required to make decisions about specific issues.

These types of offence require careful consideration even before recording them as crimes and the police are likely to seek legal advice from the Crown Prosecution Service. Any subsequent investigation will require expert evidence to prove a lack of mental capacity. The police will use the balance of probability test in relation to whether an alleged incident is the result of a criminal act under this section. If they believe it is likely, they are duty bound to record it as a crime and investigate it.

Deprivation of Liberty: Authorisation of arrangements enabling care and treatment

The Mental Capacity (Amendment) Act (2019), Schedule AA1, replaced the Deprivation of Liberty Safeguards (commonly known as the DoLs by safeguarding professionals), which formed part of the Mental Capacity Act (2005).

The schedule applies to arrangements for enabling the care or treatment of a person, the 'cared for person', that give rise to a deprivation of the cared-for person's liberty, and that are not excluded by Part 7 of the schedule.

They apply to a cared for person who:

- is aged 16 or over
- lacks capacity to consent to the arrangements
- has a mental disorder.

The deprivation of a person's liberty in these circumstances has to be approved by an 'Approved Mental Capacity Professional' defined within part 4 of the schedule.

The authorisation can only be made where the following conditions are met:

- The cared-for person lacks capacity to consent to the arrangements.
- The cared-for person has a mental disorder.
- The arrangements are necessary to prevent harm to the cared-for person and are proportionate in relation to the likelihood and seriousness of harm to the cared-for person.

The schedule makes it clear that the cared for person, any appropriate person and any independent mental capacity advocate, must be provided with a copy of the authorisation to deprive them of their liberty and be informed of the nature of the arrangements being put in place.

The schedule states an Independent Mental Capacity Advocate who supports and represents the cared-for person must be appointed if a cared-for person has capacity and asks for such, or if they lack capacity unless it is felt the appointment would not be in the person's best interests.

An Independent Mental Capacity Advocate may not be appointed if an appropriate person is deemed suitable, consents to representing the cared-for person and is not involved in care or treatment of them.

Independent advocacy

The Care Act (2014) makes specific provision for independent advocates. Chapter 7 of the statutory guidance (Department of Health, 2018) provides a comprehensive knowledge base in this area. It states that local authorities must involve people in decisions concerning them and their care and support, regardless how complex a person's needs are. A local authority must make a judgement about whether a person has substantial difficulty in being involved with the decisions and discussions. If the local authority believes a person will have difficulty being involved in a process and there is no appropriate person such as a carer, family member or friend to support and represent them, then they must arrange for an independent advocate to support and represent them.

Section 67(2) of the Care Act (2014) creates the statutory duty on local authorities to arrange for an independent advocate for a vulnerable adult when they are the subject of an assessment or care plan[9] or when a vulnerable adult is involved in safeguarding enquiries and reviews[10]. Only an urgent enquiry or review to commence can take place without an independent advocate, as allowed by section 68(6).

The Mental Capacity (Amendment) Act (2019) also makes provision for Independent Mental Capacity Advocates (IMCAs) and, as the title implies, these are independent of the local authority and the NHS. The Mental Capacity (Amendment) Act (2019) allows a suitable and appropriate person to represent and support the cared for person. If this was the case then the functions of an Independent Mental

---

9   As identified in Section 68(3).

10 Section 68(2).

Capacity Advocate can be provided by the same individual to ensure a vulnerable adult receives seamless advocacy and does not have to repeat their story to different advocates.

Independent Mental Capacity Advocates are especially relevant to adult safeguarding cases where an individual lacks capacity and is suspected of being abused or neglected or is suspected of abusing or neglecting another person. In these circumstances an IMCA can be appointed even if the person has family and friends available to support them.

The statutory guidance issued under Schedule AA of the Mental Capacity (Amendment) Act (2019) should be the reference point for practitioners when considering these issues.

Local authority responsibilities

A local authority is statutorily responsible under the Care Act (2014) to:

■ Make enquiries, or cause others to do so, if it believes a vulnerable adult is experiencing, or is at risk of, abuse or neglect. This should establish whether any action needs to be taken to prevent or stop abuse or neglect, and if so, by whom.

■ Set up a local Safeguarding Adults Board (SAB).

■ Arrange, where appropriate, for an independent advocate to represent and support an adult who is the subject of a safeguarding enquiry or Safeguarding Adult Review (SAR).

■ Co-operate with each of its relevant partners (as set out in Section 6(7) of the Care Act (2014)) in order to protect the vulnerable adult and promote their welfare. Conversely, each partner must co-operate with the local authority.

Local authorities may choose to undertake safeguarding enquiries for people where there is not a section 42 enquiry duty, if they believe it is proportionate to do so, and will enable the local authority to promote the person's well-being and support a preventative agenda.

These requirements in many ways follow the law and practice for children as defined in the Children Act (1989) and (2004), and this is very much the case when one examines the list of partner agencies required by law to co-operate with the local authority.

These agencies are:

- A district council, if they exist within the area of a local authority (usually within a county council).

- Another local authority that it would be appropriate to co-operate with.

- All NHS bodies within the local authority area (listed in Section 6(8)).

- The police covering the area, or part of it.

- Social security, employment and training (in England).

- The prison service (in England).

- Probation services.

- Any organisation involved in activities or providing a service relating to vulnerable adults.

Section 6(6)(a) identifies that it is a statutory duty for a local authority and its relevant partners to co-operate in promoting the well-being of adults with needs for care and support, and Section 6(6)(d) identifies that they need to co-operate to *'protect adults with needs for care and support who are experiencing, or at risk of, abuse or neglect'*.

So, as in Section 11(2)(a) of the Children Act (2004), the two core co-operation activities of promoting welfare and safeguarding are identified.

Safeguarding therefore requires collaboration between partners in order to create a framework of inter-agency arrangements to enable timely and effective prevention and responses to abuse and neglect. To do this, there needs to be a widespread understanding among all professionals of the roles and responsibilities of others. It is vital that all professionals know their own responsibilities as well as what others can deliver and how they will do so.

Partners, both statutory and other, on many occasions have an essential part to play in safeguarding and ensuring that vulnerable adults live as independent lives as possible and must share the overall responsibility. These partnerships need to create strong, positive learning environments which seek to break down cultures and which don't seek to blame practitioners or find scapegoats when things go awry.

One important way in which a partnership ensures it is able to achieve its aims of safeguarding vulnerable adults and has a partnership mechanism to oversee and enhance delivery is through a Safeguarding Adults Board (see p196).

Local authority enquiry

If a local authority reasonably suspects that an adult is vulnerable and experiencing or is at risk of experiencing abuse and neglect, they must make enquiries or ensure that others do so, such as care providers or a partner or group of partners within a multi-agency plan, overseen by the local authority. The whole point of the enquiry is to decide if something needs to be done to help or protect the adult or adults. As stated earlier, this must take into account the wishes of those adults involved. This action may well involve a criminal investigation by the police if a crime is suspected.

Many local authority areas have published adult safeguarding procedures, and within many of these the safeguarding process is identified in seven clear stages. However, it is always advisable to be aware of the requirements within your own local procedures. They may differ!

Box 5.2: Seven stage safeguarding process

Stage 1 – Raise an alert and make a decision as to whether to refer to the local authority. Any immediate action to protect the adult or others should be taken.

Stage 2 – Make the referral and decide if a safeguarding plan is appropriate. Gather information from all agencies involved and seek the adult's wishes to inform a risk assessment. The risk assessment will determine and underpin any interim protection plan.

Stage 3 – Evaluate the risk and decide if an investigation is needed and who will conduct it. If a safeguarding adult intervention is not required, then appropriate action is agreed and the case is closed. This part of the process is carried out either through a strategy discussion or a strategy meeting.

Stage 4 – The investigation. This may be carried out by a myriad of organisations according to the circumstances, including employers who may be responsible for care delivery. (See p197 for further detail on criminal investigations by the police.) The evidence and information is then shared across all involved partners.

Stage 5 – A case conference is held and, based on the evidence and information gathered, risk is re-assessed and a protection plan is agreed. Attendees will also identify the review process with timescales for the case. The adult may attend or be represented, possibly by an independent advocate if appropriate.

Stage 6 – Hold a review meeting to look at the protection plan and re-assess the risk. Again, the adult may attend or be represented.

Stage 7 – Close the case and disseminate learning. Decide whether a serious case review is required.

Carers

A carer, who may be a family member or friend, might become involved in a situation where a safeguarding response is needed to prevent neglect or abuse. They may, for example, be a witness or identify concerns, they may suffer some harm from the person they are trying to care for or from those who are in contact with the adult, or they may well be the person who intentionally or otherwise harms or neglects the person they are caring for. A carer may be a vulnerable adult or may have physical or mental needs of their own, which have to be taken into account, or which may even make them unable to care adequately for the adult. Each case will demand a different response depending on the circumstances.

It is important that a carer is listened to if they raise concerns, and a suitable safeguarding response delivered. In different circumstances it may also be appropriate to assess the carer and the adult to establish if there is information or support available, such as training that would prevent the harm from continuing. Similarly, if a carer experiences harm themselves, whether intentional or not, an assessment may identify remedial measures that might mitigate the harm and support the carer to continue.

It is possible that the abuse could be part of a life-long pattern and part of the relationship. Care is needed to ascertain if a vulnerable adult would choose for it to continue given their expressed wishes in the past, even if they lack the capacity to decide at this stage of their lives. This must be balanced with the professionals and wider family trying to improve matters. It is fraught with difficulty.

Professionals can find more detailed advice in relation to these difficult issues in their local safeguarding procedures. The Association of Directors for Adult Safeguarding (ADASS) published useful guidance in 2011, *Carers and Safeguarding Adults: Working together to improve outcomes*.

Local procedures

If society is to respond appropriately to abuse and neglect of vulnerable adults, then anyone who comes into contact with such an individual must know what to do if they suspect it and know where to go for advice and guidance. Every organisation and all local authority areas in the country will have procedures published that, if followed, will ensure an appropriate response to reduce, remove or accept the risks to the person in question. These procedures should be constantly reviewed and updated by the local Safeguarding Adults Board, ensuring learning and best practice is available to all who require it.

Safeguarding Adult Boards (SABs)

Safeguarding Adult Boards were made statutory by Section 43(1) of the Care Act (2014) and in essence replicated, in structure and governance, the long-established Local Safeguarding Children's Boards (LSCBs). The government commissioned a review of safeguarding arrangements, which recommended the abolition of LSCBs and as a result The Children and Social Work Act (2017) abolished the functions of LSCBs in favour of new multi-agency safeguarding arrangements. The review did not consider Safeguarding Adults Boards (for more on LSCBs and multi-agency safeguarding arrangements, see Chapter 1).

Many areas already had safeguarding adult boards before the act made them statutory, and in some areas adult and children's safeguarding arrangements are very closely related; many share business managers and independent chairs. Safeguarding Adults Boards should have representation from all the organisations involved in the safeguarding of adults within a local authority area. The boards have many responsibilities listed within the act. These include:

- Identifying the roles, responsibilities and accountability with regard to the action each agency should take to ensure the protection of adults.

- Understanding through data analysis the prevalence of abuse and neglect locally, and developing strategies to reduce and prevent it.

- Carrying out Safeguarding Adult Reviews (SARs).

- Promoting multi-agency and specialist training.

Safeguarding Adult Boards should also ensure that they create effective links to other related partnerships that will oversee essential work within an area in relation to risk and harm to individuals, families and communities. These include Community Safety Partnerships, Local Children Safeguarding Boards, Health and Wellbeing Boards, Clinical Commissioning Group Boards and Health Overview and Scrutiny Committees (OSCs).

Safeguarding Adult Reviews

Safeguarding Adult Boards under Section 44 of the Care Act (2014) must arrange a Safeguarding Adult Review (SAR) when an adult in its area dies as a result of abuse or neglect, whether known or suspected, and there is concern that partner agencies could have worked more effectively to protect the adult. A SAR should also be carried out if an adult has not died but the SAB knows or suspects that the adult has experienced serious abuse or neglect.

SARs should be designed and agreed by the members of the SAB to promote effective learning and to improve procedures to prevent future deaths or serious harm occurring again. The review should aim to understand how organisations can work better together to prevent and reduce abuse and neglect of adults, but also to identify areas of good practice. Terms of reference for a SAR should reflect the six key principles of safeguarding (see p182) and be independently led. The core approach of any SAR should be one which is proportionate to the circumstances of the case and one that engenders learning and improvement across the partnership responsible for safeguarding adults.

Learning Disabilities Mortality Reviews (LeDeR)

The persistence of health inequalities between different population groups has been well documented, including the inequalities faced by people with learning disabilities. Today, people with learning disabilities die, on average, 15-20 years sooner than people in the general population, with some of those deaths identified as being potentially avoidable with access to good quality healthcare.

The aim of the LeDeR Programme (delivered by the University of Bristol and commissioned by the Healthcare Quality Improvement Partnership on behalf of NHS England) is to drive improvement in the quality of health and social care service delivery for people with learning disabilities and to help reduce premature mortality and health inequalities in this population, through mortality case reviews. These reviews are intended to support health and social care professionals and policy makers to clarify the contribution of various causes of death to the overall burden of excess premature mortality for people with learning disabilities; identify variation and best practice; and identify key recommendations for improvement.

Every area in the country should have in place their own LeDeR review process, beginning the process of learning from these deaths both locally and nationally to improve both the quality of life and the mortality rate for people living with learning disabilities.

More information is available at:
www.bristol.ac.uk/sps/leder/ (accessed September 2019).

Criminal investigation of vulnerable adult cases

Once a referral or a concern has been identified to the local authority adult services, a decision will be made at stage three of the seven-stage process (see Box 5.2 on p194) as to who is the organisation or person who should investigate the circumstances surrounding the case.

As has been stated, the local authority has a duty to safeguard an individual who is believed to be vulnerable but they are not always the most appropriate agency to carry out the investigation. When criminal offences are identified or suspected, the police should be involved as early as possible.

The police are the only agency who can decide if a crime is suspected or has been committed and whether and when they need to be involved to pursue a criminal investigation, and they are therefore vital in a local authority's decision making. As with the investigation of any crime, securing evidence, and in particular forensic evidence, at the earliest stage is paramount so that it is not lost or contaminated.

All vulnerable adult criminal investigations will be led by the police but they will involve social workers, health professionals and any relevant partner or agency in order to co-ordinate the best response. Safeguarding the victim, which will be co-ordinated by the local authority, needs to be considered in tandem with the criminal investigation and only through a true multi-agency integrated approach is it possible to achieve this. Harm is not always visible to one agency, but when added to the knowledge of others it comes into focus and can be acted upon. This concept is discussed further in Chapter 8. A constant assessment of the risks to the vulnerable adult victim should be made by the local authority to ensure their best interests and well-being are met.

The Association of Chief Police Officers (ACPO) has published the guidance document *Safeguarding and Investigating the Abuse of Vulnerable Adults* (ACPO, 2012).

Along with abuse and neglect as defined within the Care Act (2014) (see p183), ACPO also defines 'serious abuse', which covers serious violent offences including murder, death of a vulnerable adult through negligence, and serious sexual crimes. It also includes financial crimes requiring specialist investigative expertise, and computer crime where vulnerable adults are at risk. These types of crimes and abuse will attract a greater level of police resourcing or expertise.

ACPO also identify 'serious incidents' in relation to the abuse of vulnerable adults. These include where the offences have taken place in a hospital or care setting, those committed by a carer, where there are multiple victims or those that have a high media profile. The police will always treat the death of a vulnerable adult who is already subject to an investigation, or where an incident poses a threat to life, such as arson, as a serious incident.

If an incident or set of circumstances suggests the effectiveness of a police response is likely to have a significant impact on a victim, family or community, they will identify it as a 'critical incident' and it is very likely that a senior officer will take overall command and a Community Impact Assessment will be undertaken in order to inform and shape the response. It is more than likely that the police will form a multi-agency group to consider the wider community issues involved. The term 'critical incident', as used by the police, is not solely applied to vulnerable adults' cases but for any incident that fits the definition.

On occasions, the police can support the safeguarding of the victim. One such example is the ability of the police to issue Domestic Violence Protection Notices (DVPN) and then subsequently seek a Domestic Violence Protection Order (DVPO) from a magistrate's court. The notices and orders are designed to give immediate breathing space for victims and DVPOs are specifically designed to protect victims for a maximum of 28 days, during which time further considerations and assessments concerning how best to safeguard the victim can be made. DVPN and DVPOs are governed by the Crime and Security Act (2010).

The police are also able to ensure that witnesses who need protection receive it, as well as potentially connecting the person to organisations and individuals who can provide victim support.

Non-reporting of crimes

We must accept that there are many barriers to adults reporting crimes. These can include the fear that they will not be believed, the perception that reporting will have an adverse effect on their own care or family needs, or they may, as is the case with many victims, be embarrassed or feel too ashamed to report and discuss the circumstances of a crime. There are many more reasons that can feel very real to the person who is or has experienced the abuse or neglect. Professionals can and should therefore support vulnerable adults to report crimes to prevent further harm to themselves and possibly others.

Some victims do not wish to pursue allegations of crime and this, as with all victims, must be respected. The police, however, may need to continue if others are at risk or the circumstances demand that they do. When the police choose to respect the wishes of an individual victim and not pursue an investigation (it will still be recorded as a crime), it is still likely and good practice for the safeguarding partners to share information if it is appropriate to do so in order to check that the adult is not being coerced into making the decision. It may well also be appropriate to share information to ensure that no other vulnerable individuals are at risk or suffering abuse or harm from the alleged perpetrators or others.

Whistleblowing

Similarly, members of the private, public and voluntary sectors who are delivering care and support may feel worried about identifying concerns or 'whistleblowing'. The Public Interest Disclosure Act (1998) provides a legal support framework to protect people in a workplace from suffering victimisation or harassment when they raise genuine concerns about malpractice.

The investigation processes

Vulnerable adults may be identified either as at risk of harm or as potential perpetrators through the investigation of various associated crime types. These include domestic abuse, hate crimes of all types (including against disabilities), forced marriage cases, honour-based violence and anti-social behaviour.

Each crime type has both local procedures and national guidelines for professionals to follow.

The management of offenders through the Multi Agency Public Protection Arrangements (MAPPA) and as 'potentially dangerous persons' can also identify vulnerable adults and the abuse of them. These arrangements are examined in detail in Chapter 8.

Many investigations into crimes where a vulnerable adult is the victim will be dealt with by a uniformed officer who may be part of a neighbourhood policing team or be a response officer. Cases that fall into the definitions identified earlier of serious abuse or serious incidents will normally be dealt with by a specialist officer who is likely to be part of a police force's public protection department or command. Some forces have officers who specialise in vulnerable adult cases but many utilise public protection specialists who work on a range of investigations, for instance child abuse and domestic abuse.

Where there is a report that a vulnerable adult has been the victim of abuse or neglect and a crime has or may have been committed, the police will be made aware. In fact, the police may in many circumstances be the organisation identifying the issue, and will deal with it accordingly. If this is the case, they will notify the local authority.

The police will commence an investigation in the manner they would for any crime and take immediate action to identify all evidence and witnesses. In the majority of cases this will mean they immediately attend the scene or scenes. Forensic evidence in many cases is paramount and the securing and protection of this from contamination will be uppermost in their minds.

Safeguarding thresholds

Whether the police, another organisation or an individual has referred the case, the local authority will make a decision as to whether the referral meets the local threshold for safeguarding. As mentioned, each local area should have published both the threshold at which safeguarding needs to take place, as well as policy and procedure documents. These should be considered along with national guidance in relation to any action taken. In effect, the process of referral places the case within a multi-agency context, which is essential for any action that is deemed necessary and if a crime needs to be investigated.

The local authority will consider which other partners it will consult with, if any, in making a decision, for example a health professional who may be working with the adult in question.

On some occasions the local authority may not believe the local threshold has been reached and a safeguarding response will therefore not be delivered. The police, however, may well still continue with their investigation if they believe a crime has been committed.

Strategy meetings

Once the decision has been made that a safeguarding response is appropriate, a strategy discussion or meeting will be held to assess the risk to the adult, agree a multi-agency response and consider any criminal investigation. The most immediate actions needed will be to protect the adult and these actions will be agreed together with the immediate investigative activity that is required. Safeguarding activity and investigation of crimes committed against or by those being safeguarded are clearly woven together. It is this agreement for the delivery of a multi-agency plan that enables the partners to achieve a wide range of activities in concert with each other while ensuring the priorities of each is achieved.

Agreements of this nature can be reached very swiftly by phone or video conference if there is an urgent need or if the nature and type of the allegation demands it. If not, it is likely a meeting with all relevant partners will be held within a defined time period. The local authority is responsible for co-ordinating this meeting and the formulation of the Safeguarding Assessment Strategy that is produced. Any partner can request a discussion or meeting. The victim's views and wishes should be presented during this process but they or their family do not attend.

On occasions, professionals have to be pushy and insist on being heard. Every local safeguarding partnership should have an escalation policy agreed across all the professions for occasions when one partner disagrees with the decision of another. This includes decisions by the local authority. Escalation policies are just what they suggest – they enable an issue to be escalated to a more senior level across the partnership to ensure clarity of discussion and decisions, and to make a judgement where there is disagreement between partners. These conversations, which should always be accurately recorded, may or may not change the decision, but they are an essential part of the management of very complex processes between organisations which think and deliver on a day-to-day basis in very different ways.

There is a plethora of evidence to show that, where the required integrated partnership approach is either weak or non-existent, then communication between the professions will not be robust or effective, issues will be hidden or misunderstood, and opportunities will be missed. The strength of inter-professional practice needed to deliver strong and meaningful safeguarding activity together with any type of investigation, criminal or otherwise, cannot be over stressed. It is the bedrock of all safeguarding, and the safeguarding of vulnerable adults is no different.

If the police have identified a criminal offence and they believe there is an urgent need to safeguard the adult or take urgent investigative action to secure evidence of some type, they will do so. However, it is accepted that a discussion or meeting will be called as soon as possible and when the immediate so-called fast track actions have been completed. It is also very likely on occasions that the police will have to act outside office hours when it may be difficult to gain immediate access to other professional colleagues. Whether the response to safeguard or investigate a crime is planned or is an immediate and urgent response, the case will very swiftly enter the multi-agency context for assessment, discussion and agreement on a strategy or plan.

The strategy meeting allows the multi-agency team to address many issues and make decisions about many actions. This will include how best to deal with risk, who will investigate an allegation (it will always be the police if a criminal offence is suspected), agree the sharing of information, which organisation will lead any safeguarding activity and identify the roles, responsibilities and actions of individual organisations. In some cases, a media and communication strategy may be discussed and agreed. The Safeguarding Assessment Strategy is articulated and agreed. If a victim subsequently withdraws an allegation of abuse, the multi-agency strategy discussion will still take place and investigate if any intimidation or coercion is present.

Whatever investigation is to be undertaken, the high-level activities are very similar. They will involve gathering evidence by various means (documentary, witnesses, forensic or medical) while at the same time continually assessing and dealing with the risk and support needs of the adult. The outcome of this activity should be to reach a conclusion as to whether abuse or neglect has taken place and ensure current and future risks to the adult and others involved is understood and minimised. The local authority will minute the strategy meeting and ensure these are circulated. All professionals involved in such meetings should ensure they are accurate.

If a criminal investigation does take place, there may be occasions where other investigations by employers or inspecting bodies will have to take place at the same time. It may be necessary to deal swiftly with employment matters, for example.

The risks to other persons who may be vulnerable should be discussed at the strategy meeting. There may be a need to consider suspension or removal of a member of staff from a care setting and this will be the responsibility of any employer. It is usual for any disciplinary investigation to be conducted once a criminal investigation has been completed, but this may not always be possible.

Ongoing police investigations

Some investigations concerning abuse and neglect to adults can and will take many months, or even years. They are extremely complex and obtaining evidence from both witnesses and other sources can be extremely time consuming (and rightly so). The police will always try to expedite their enquiries in a reasonable timeframe, but it must be understood this is not always possible. The police should ensure robust supervision by their own management occurs across all such investigations, especially those which are of a protracted nature. Timescales and progress can and should be discussed and challenged at ongoing strategy meetings with partner organisations as the case progresses.

All professionals must be aware that any action they take should not adversely affect the criminal investigation. If in doubt, a conversation with the investigating officer should be sought, or, in terms of a serious incident, the Senior Investigating Officer (SIO).

Strategy update meetings can and should be requested by any partner involved in the case. The police will request a meeting if there are any significant changes in the case or if information comes to light which may change an assessment of risk to the victim or others who may be vulnerable, and this request should be acted on quickly. Other issues concerning access to the victim or witnesses or the withdrawal of co-operation by the victim will again call for a new discussion of the case in partnership. Should the adult die during the investigation, this too should be discussed.

Case conferences

Once an investigation (of whatever nature) has been concluded to a point where all organisations have collated their information and have assessed the ongoing protection of any victim, the local authority or an independent person contracted by them will chair a case conference of all interested partners. The adult and a representative have a right to attend and express their views.

The case conference will discuss the wide range of issues concerning the case, the ongoing welfare and protection of the adult and any issues identified as the result of the investigation. Case conferences, however, may well be held long before the conclusion of a criminal investigation and even before suspects have been arrested. All professionals need to be sensitive to the fact that a suspect in a criminal investigation may on occasions not know they are deemed to be such. It is therefore very important for the police to identify such issues to the local authority chair of the meeting and for all to respect the confidentiality of any relevant conversations.

The conference will agree a plan with timescales for the ongoing delivery of any criminal investigation and/or the continued protection and support of the adult or adults. A review meeting will be agreed, usually within six months.

Review meetings

There may be one or many review meetings before a case is finally closed. The meetings will, again, be chaired by the local authority and the decision to close a case rests with them. On each occasion each partner must ensure they attend and provide the latest update of information and intelligence to the meeting. Things change and any updating of a risk assessment or protection plan requires the best possible information from across the partnership.

Victim and witness evidence and interviewing

When interviewing victims and witnesses in a vulnerable adult abuse investigation, police officers and their social work colleagues will interview in line with the *Achieving Best Evidence in Criminal Proceedings guidance* (Ministry of Justice, 2011) commonly known as ABE (Achieving Best Evidence).

The police and other criminal justice agencies are obliged by law through *The Code of Practice for Victims of Crime* (Ministry of Justice, 2015) to provide an enhanced service for vulnerable and intimidated victims and witnesses. Police officers will identify individuals as vulnerable or intimidated based on definitions within the Youth Justice and Criminal Evidence Act (1999) (YJCE Act). They must then ensure they deliver their specific responsibilities under the act which includes identifying the wishes of a witness in relation to any special measures that are defined within the same act, informing any suspect of their intention to use special measures at the point of arrest, bail or charge, and ensuring victims receive updates and any support for individual needs.

Special measures include screens around a witness box to shield the victim or witness from the accused, or the use of video link to give evidence without attending court.

YJCE definitions

Section 16 of the YJCE Act defines vulnerable adult witnesses as those who have a:

- mental disorder as defined in Mental Health Act (1983)
- significant impairment of intelligence and social functioning
- physical disability or physical disorder.

Individuals within these criteria can only receive special measures if the quality of their evidence is going to be diminished without them because of their disability or disorder.

Section 17 of YJCE Act (1999) identifies individuals whose evidence will be diminished by fear or distress.

A court will take into account a range of issues in relation to the witness and the case in question.

A pivotal case in terms of the use of special measures for vulnerable adults in a criminal case is that of Regina v Watts, 2010. The case was the first of its kind where evidence from victims with profound levels of disability had been brought before a court in England and Wales.

This case was subsequently examined by the court of appeal in relation to specific arguments of law which included issues concerning evidence gathered by use of intermediaries and the use of special measures. It provides commentary on the use of both electronic communications to support the evidence of vulnerable adult witnesses and a vulnerable adult witness who could only communicate through the movement of their eyes. The court of appeal upheld the conviction but reduced the sentence.

Intermediaries

Intermediaries were introduced into criminal cases and investigations in 2004, in effect to ensure the voice of a victim or witness is properly heard if they have a difficulty in communicating or articulating the evidence themselves.

If it is deemed appropriate, an intermediary may be used to help the adult understand questions they are being asked and to ensure their answers are fully and correctly articulated. Intermediaries can be used in evidence-gathering and evidence-giving stages of a criminal enquiry. The police can advise any professional in relation to these specific matters for witnesses and victims who may fit the criteria.

Vulnerable adults with children

Finally, it is important to mention that vulnerable adults who become victims and subject of an investigation may of course be responsible for the care of children. There is also a wealth of evidence from serious case reviews that children can be placed at significant risk and have died when the mental or physical health of an adult has deteriorated.

Any investigation concerning a vulnerable adult where they have custody or care over a child or children and the vulnerability of the adult is such that it may affect the safety of the child or children, should sensibly involve children's services and police child protection specialists. If such a child is found to be suffering or likely to suffer significant harm from the adult, then child protection powers and procedures in the normal way may well need to be used. These are discussed in Chapter 1 and professionals should consult local procedures, the national guidelines, in particular *Working Together to Safeguard Children* (DFE, 2015; 2018) and above all seek advice from across the partnership.

Children can also be carers for vulnerable adults, a position which can expose them to risk for their own safety and also a risk of becoming a perpetrator of abuse upon the vulnerable adult themselves. The sharing of knowledge, experience and specialist advice in these circumstances cannot be understated. Young careers as an issue is expanded upon in Chapter 2.

Vulnerable adults might also be at risk from an adult with responsibility for a child. It is vital to consider if the child is also at risk.

Further reading

Care Act (2014) Available at: www.legislation.gov.uk/ukpga/2014/23/contents (accessed September 2019).

Crime and Security Act (2010) Available at: www.legislation.gov.uk/ukpga/2010/17/crossheading/domestic-violence (accessed September 2019).

Human Rights Act (1998) Available at: www.legislation.gov.uk/ukpga/1998/42/contents (accessed September 2019).

Local Government Association (2018) Making Safeguarding Personal Outcomes Framework: *Final report* [online]. Available at: www.local.gov.uk/our-support/our-improvement-offer/care-and-health-improvement/making-safeguarding-personal (accessed September 2019).

Mental Capacity Act (2005) Available at: www.legislation.gov.uk/ukpga/2005/9/contents (accessed February 2015).

Mental Capacity Act (2005) *Code of Practice*. Available at: https://www.gov.uk/government/publications/mental-capacity-act-code-of-practice (accessed September 2019).

Mental Capacity (Amendment) Act (2019) Available at: www.legislation.gov.uk/ukpga/2019/18/enacted (accessed September 2019).

Mental Health Act (1983) Available at: www.legislation.gov.uk/ukpga/1983/20/contents (accessed September 2019).

Mental Health Act (2007) Available at: www.legislation.gov.uk/ukpga/2007/12/contents (accessed September 2019).

Public Interest Disclosure Act (1998) Available at: www.legislation.gov.uk/ukpga/1998/23/contents (accessed September 2019).

Youth Justice and Criminal Evidence Act (1999) Available at: www.legislation.gov.uk/ukpga/1999/23/contents (accessed September 2019).

Making Decisions: A guide for a advice workers (2009) Available at: www.gov.uk/government/uploads/system/uploads/attachment_data/file/348637/OPG604_Advice-workers-MCA-decisions.pdf (accessed September 2019).

References

Association of Chief Police Officers & National Policing Improvement Agency (2012) *Guidance on Safeguarding and Investigating the Abuse of Vulnerable Adults* [online]. Available at: http://library.college.police.uk/docs/acpo/vulnerable-adults-2012.pdf (accessed September 2019).

Association of Directors of Adult Social Services (2011) *Carers and Safeguarding Adults: Working together to improve outcomes* [online]. Available at: http://static.carers.org/files/carers-and-safeguarding-document-june-2011-5730.pdf (accessed September 2019).

Association of Directors of Adult Social Services & Local Government Association (2013) *Safeguarding Adults: Advice and guidance to Directors of Adult Social Services* [online]. Available at: www.adass.org.uk/adassmedia/stories/Policy%20Networks/Safeguarding_Adults/Key_Documents/LGA%20ADASS_SafeguardingAdviceAndGuidanceToDASS_Mar13.pdf (accessed September 2019).

Braye S, Orr D & Preston-Shoot M (2011) *Self-neglect and Adult Safeguarding: Findings from research*. London: SCIE.

DfE (2013) *Working Together to Safeguard Children* [online]. London: Department for Education. Available at: www.gov.uk/government/publications/working-together-to-safeguard-children (accessed September 2019).

DfE (2015) *Working Together to Safeguard Children: A guide to inter-agency working to safeguard and promote the welfare of children* [online]. London: Department for Education. Available at: www.gov.uk/government/publications/working-together-to-safeguard-children--2 (accessed September 2019).

Department of Health (2000) *No Secrets: Guidance on developing and implementing multi-agency policies and procedures to protect vulnerable adults from abuse*. London: TSO. Available at: www.gov.uk/government/publications/no-secrets-guidance-on-protecting-vulnerable-adults-in-care (accessed September 2019).

Department of Health (2018) *Care and Support Statutory Guidance* [online]. Available at: www.gov.uk/government/publications/care-act-statutory-guidance/care-and-support-statutory-guidance#safeguarding-1 (accessed September 2019).

Home Office (2015) *Statutory guidance framework controlling or coercive behaviour in an intimate or family relationship* [online]. Available at: www.gov.uk/government/publications/statutory-guidance-framework-controlling-or-coercive-behaviour-in-an-intimate-or-family-relationship (accessed September 2019).

Ministry of Justice (2005) *The Code of Practice for Victims of Crime*. London: The Office for Criminal Justice Reform. Available at: www.cps.gov.uk/publications/docs/victims_code_2013.pdf (accessed September 2019).

Ministry of Justice (2011) *Achieving Best Evidence in Criminal Proceedings: Guidance on interviewing victims and witnesses, and guidance on using special measures*. London: TSO. Available at: www.cps.gov.uk/publications/docs/best_evidence_in_criminal_proceedings.pdf (accessed September 2019).

Regina v Watts [2010] EWCA Crim 1824.

Chapter 6: Sexual violence

By Aelfwynn Sampson (new and refreshed content) and Helen Murphy (original content) (edited by Russell Wate)

Chapter overview

- Introduction.
- Prevalence.
- Human trafficking and its link to sexual violence and CSE.
- Sexual offence law.
- Violence against Women and Girls Strategy.
- Victim support including the role of an ISVA.
- Sexual Assault Referral Centre (SARC).
- Acute and non-recent sexual offences.
- Drug and/or alcohol facilitated sexual assaults.
- CPS policy on rape.

Introduction

Rape Crisis (2019) defines sexual violence as:

'Sexual violence is any unwanted sexual act or activity. There are many different kinds, including: rape, sexual abuse (including in childhood), sexual assault, sexual harassment, forced marriage, so-called honour-based violence, female genital mutilation (FGM), trafficking, sexual exploitation (including child sexual exploitation), and others.'

As this definition makes clear, sexual violence can take many forms. And yet it is a sad fact that many victims don't always come forward, and if they do, in some cases it can be several years after the abuse occurred, which can make investigations more challenging and complex and place victims in greater need of long-term support and counselling. This chapter highlights the prevalence and forms of abuse, and the support available to victims and/or survivors, in addition to exploring the laws and tools we can use to bring perpetrators to account for their actions.

Prevalence

In 2018, the Office for National Statistics published *Sexual offending: victimisation and the path through the criminal justice system*:

'The report highlights that investigating sexual offences is challenging. Many offences don't proceed further than the police investigation due to evidential difficulties. In addition, investigations are becoming more complex due to an increase in evidence from phones, tablets, computers and social media.

'We hope that providing insights into this serious issue will assist all those working to achieve better outcomes for victims.' (Alexa Bradley (2018) Centre for Crime and Justice, Office for National Statistics)

This report highlighted that increases in the number of sexual offences handled by the police in recent years largely reflected the improvements in police recording and the fact that more victims are now willing to report. The crime survey for England and Wales (CSEW) has estimated an increase in prevalence over the same period.

The CSEW estimated that appropriately 700,000 people aged 16 to 59 years were victims of sexual assault in the last year. The majority of these cases will not enter the criminal justice system. Less than one in five victims of rape or assault by penetration reported their experience to the police. The age range within this data, i.e. 16 to 59, thus excludes people over 60 and so clearly does not capture a large proportion of the population who, according to other studies, are no less likely to be victims of domestic or sexual abuse.

In January 2013, The Ministry of Justice produced *An Overview of Sexual Offending in England and Wales*, based on data for the Crime Survey for England and Wales. It found that:

- Females were more likely than males to report sexual offences.
- Around 90% of victims of the most serious sexual offences in the previous year knew the perpetrator, compared with less than half for other sexual offences.

- Each year on average, over 400,000 females and 72,000 males said that they were a victim of a sexual offence (including attempts and ranging from the most serious offences of rape and sexual assault, to other sexual offences such as indecent exposure and unwanted touching). Eighty-five thousand women and 12,000 men are raped each year, although many don't report this to police.

- Around one in 20 females (aged 16 to 59) reported being a victim of a serious sexual offence since the age of 16. Only 15% reported the offence to the police. Reasons for not reporting included that it was 'embarrassing', they 'didn't think the police could do much to help', that the incident was 'too trivial or not worth reporting', or that they saw it as a 'private/family matter and not police business'.

In 2011/12, the police recorded a total of 53,700 sexual offences across England and Wales. The most serious sexual offences of 'rape' (16,000 offences) and 'sexual assault' (22,100 offences) accounted for 71% of sexual offences recorded by the police. This indicates that many who experience less serious offences are less likely to report them to the police. Many victims also struggle to come to terms with assaults, often blaming themselves for not fighting back or for some other aspect of what occurred. In fact, the human response to threat can mean a victim will respond by freezing or 'flopping' and appearing to comply with the perpetrator's demands.

Sometimes sexual violence is a strong feature in domestic abuse and any physical assault can mask the fact that serious sexual violence has also taken place. Professionals need to be aware of this so they don't miss underlying signs. It is essential for all agencies and multi-agency professionals to ensure that victims are treated with respect and dignity if they take the brave step to report sexual violence. A key challenge remains encouraging victims to come forward to access vital multi-agency support and report the abuse to police, which enables the criminal justice system to hold perpetrators to account and prevent future victimisation.

As covered in detail in Chapter 3, child sexual exploitation (CSE) is sexual abuse against a child. The four main types of contact child sexual exploitation are:

1. Inappropriate relationships: usually involving a sole perpetrator who has inappropriate power or control over a child (physical, emotional, financial) and uses this to sexually exploit them. One indicator may be a significant age gap. The child believes they are in a loving relationship.

2. 'Boyfriend' model of exploitation: in the boyfriend model, the perpetrator befriends and grooms a child into a 'relationship', and then coerces or forces them to have sex with friends or associates. The child believes they are in a loving relationship.

3. Peer exploitation model: a child is invited (often by same-sex friends), or forced by peers or associates, to engage in sexual activity with several, or all, of the children present at the time. There is no pretence of a special or intimate relationship with any of the perpetrators.

4. Organised/networked sexual exploitation and trafficking: children (often connected) are passed through networks, possibly over geographical distances between towns and cities, where they may be forced/coerced into sexual activity with multiple men. Often this occurs at 'sex parties' (including 'pop up parties' in hotels) organised by perpetrators for the purposes of giving victims drugs and alcohol before sexually abusing them. The children who are involved may be used as agents to recruit others into the network. Some of this activity is serious organised crime and can involve the organised 'buying and selling' of children by perpetrators.

It must be remembered in all of these types of exploitation, that no matter what the victim tells professionals, and what the victim believes, they must always be treated as a child victim. The nationally agreed National Police Chief's council definition of CSE includes a reminder of this: 'The victim may have been sexually exploited even if the sexual activity appears consensual'.

Online CSE (OSCE) is also included in the NPCC definition, which outlines that 'Child sexual exploitation does not always involve physical contact; it can also occur through the use of technology'. OCSE is a genre of internet offending which includes, but is not defined by, traditional notions of online grooming. In this context, OCSE includes the much broader threat from online communication between an adult and a child for the purposes of sexual exploitation and may include: indecent images of children (IIOC), social networking, file sharing, live video streaming and cyber bullying.

Modern slavery, human trafficking and its link to sexual violence and CSE

Modern slavery and human trafficking are strongly linked to the sexual and other criminal exploitation of both children and adults.

The Palermo Protocol was ratified in the UK in 2006 and provides an accepted definition of trafficking used in international instruments:

"Trafficking in persons" shall mean the recruitment, transportation, transfer, harbouring or receipt of persons, by means of the threat or use of force or other forms of coercion, of abduction, of fraud, of deception, of the abuse of power or of a position of vulnerability or of the giving or receiving of payments or benefits to

achieve the consent of a person having control over another person, for the purpose of exploitation. Exploitation shall include, at a minimum, the exploitation of the prostitution of others or other forms of sexual exploitation, forced labour or services, slavery or practices similar to slavery, servitude or the removal of organs' (UN, 2000)

Trafficking breaks down into three elements:

1. The act (what is done): 'Recruitment, transportation, transfer, harbouring, or receipt of persons'.
2. The means (how it is done): 'Threat or use of force or other forms of coercion, of abduction, of fraud, of deception, of the abuse of power or of a position of vulnerability or of the giving or receiving of payments or benefits to achieve the consent of a person having control over another person'.
3. The purpose (why it is done): 'For the purpose of exploitation... Exploitation shall include, at a minimum, the exploitation of the prostitution of others or other forms of sexual exploitation, forced labour or services, slavery or practices similar to slavery, servitude or the removal of organs'. (Note that there is no requirement for the purpose to have been achieved, so a person who is rescued before exploitation occurs is still a victim of trafficking.)

Children (both male and female) and adults can be trafficked into and within the UK for prostitution and child sexual or criminal exploitation, and the possibility of trafficking should always be considered when dealing with cases involving sexual exploitation.

The United Nations Office on Drug and Crime (UNODC, 2012) has created a comprehensive strategy to combat the trafficking and smuggling of migrants. Victims are likely to suffer, among other emotions, loss of dignity, loss of control, disorientation, fear, shame and a lack of self-esteem. Friends and family members may be under threat in their country of origin. In every case where human trafficking is suspected the National Referral Mechanism (NRM) form is to be completed and forwarded to the UKHTC who will review the case and make a decision as to whether an individual is a victim of trafficking or not. The EU and UNODC have launched the Global Action to Prevent and Address Trafficking in Persons and the Smuggling of Migrants (GLO.ACT), which is a four-year initiative. Further information is available at: www.unodc.org/unodc/human-trafficking/index. html?ref=menuside (accessed September 2019).

A multi-agency and safeguarding approach should be taken when dealing with trafficked individuals, and agencies involved may include social care (adults or child), the UKHTC, the UK Border Agency (UKBA) and any organisations or charities that support exploited or trafficked people such as Barnardo's.

Sexual offences

Sexual offences include a variety of crimes, including rape, exposure, sexual comments or any other form of unwanted sexual behaviour. Sexual offences are listed under the Sexual Offences Act (2003) for England and Wales, the Sexual Offences (Scotland) Act (2009), and the Sexual Offences (Northern Ireland) order (2008). There will be times, however, when a victim will report an offence that pre-dates these laws, in which case the older Sexual Offences Act (1956) is relevant.

This section will focus on the Sexual Offences Act (2003).

Section 78 of the act defines 'sexual' as follows: *'Penetration, touching or any other activity is 'sexual' if a reasonable person would consider it to be of a sexual nature'*.

In sexual assault investigations, there are often no physical injuries on a victim and no independent witnesses, and whether a person consented to sexual activity is often a key factor in sexual assault cases. Section 74 also provides the legal definition of 'consent', which can be summarised as: *'A person consents if they agree by choice, and have the freedom and capacity to make that choice'*.

The CPS has set down a standard for rape specialist prosecutors. The specialist prosecutors in each of the 42 CPS areas are expected to be trained and experienced in prosecuting rape and other sexual offence cases. Prosecutors will consider two stages:

- Whether a person has the capacity to consent or to make a choice about whether to take part in a sexual activity or not, based on factors such as their age and level of understanding. The question of capacity to consent is particularly relevant when a complainant is intoxicated by alcohol or affected by drugs.

- If they did have capacity, whether he or she was in a position to make that choice freely and was not coerced or threatened in any way. For a CPS prosecutor, the crucial question is whether the complainant agrees to the activity by choice.

The Sexual Offences Act (2003) requires the defendant to show that his belief in consent was reasonable. In deciding whether the belief of the defendant was reasonable, a jury must have regard to all the circumstances, including any steps he has taken to ascertain whether the victim consented. In certain circumstances, there is a presumption that the victim did not consent to sexual activity and the defendant did not reasonably believe that the victim consented, unless he can show otherwise. Examples of circumstances where the presumption applies are where the victim was unconscious, drugged, abducted or subject to threats or fear of serious harm.

Types of sexual violence

Police forces generally separate sexual offences as either *acute* or *non-recent*.

A case is generally categorised as acute when it is reported to the police within seven days of taking place, while non-recent offences are those reported after seven days, including those that are reported many months, years and even decades after the incident. Cases are largely divided into acute and non-recent as different investigation approaches are needed, mainly due to the likely availability of different types of evidence.

For acute crimes, a SOIT (Sexual Offences Investigation Trained) officer is usually deployed to speak to the victim first, provide the immediate support and commence the early stages on the investigation. In some police forces these officers are referred to as a SOLO (sexual offence liaison officer) or SOLO plus. Their main duties include supporting the victim through the initial process and taking an initial account of events. They will also attend the Sexual Assault Referral Centre (SARC) with the victim to ensure a forensic medical exam is conducted by a specially trained doctor.

Early Evidence Kits (EEKs) should be used in all acute investigations. The samples should be taken as soon as possible after the victim contacts the police. The type of sample collected will depend on the circumstances but may include urine samples in vaginal rape cases or if there is need to understand a level of intoxication in the victim, or mouth swabs if oral rape occurred). The aim is to capture all possible forensic evidence as quickly as possible. Many victims understandably want to wash and change their clothes as soon as possible after the assault; however, it is advised that this is avoided until such evidence has been gathered and recorded.

In the case of non-recent investigations, much of the forensic evidence such as DNA on the victim and at the location of the crime, may no longer be available and therefore the use of EEKs and forensic examinations are not necessary or helpful. However, advice is always sought from a forensic specialist if there is any potential for forensic evidence to be gathered if the case is borderline in terms of time elapsed between assault and report.

In non-recent cases, victims have often kept secret for a number of years the sexual abuse that they suffered, often since childhood. During their life they may not only have had physical but also psychological scarring as a result of the abuse. Multi-agency professionals must be alert to the extra help, needs and support the victim and their families may require.

Figures published in early 2019 by the ONS confirm that sexual offences reported to the police are still on the increase, continuing a trend that has lasted over four years.

> ## Case study: CPS
>
> Helen (name has been changed), a deeply vulnerable victim, was subjected to a long history of domestic abuse, including multiple rapes by her partner. She had previously retracted her statements detailing the abuse because of threats and intimidation by her partner. Her trust in the police and CPS was eventually secured and she provided a full statement, leading to the defendant's prosecution. In light of Helen's account, other non-recent complaints from previous partners of the defendant were identified and three victims came forward to provide evidence. All of the victims were highly vulnerable with histories of mental health issues and substance addictions. They had been targeted by the defendant because of their vulnerabilities. Complex disclosure issues were dealt with fully and bespoke special measures provided for all three victims to help them provide evidence. The defendant was sentenced to 20 years.

Drug and/or alcohol facilitated sexual assaults (DFSA)

Drug and/or alcohol facilitated sexual assault and rape is when drugs or alcohol are intentionally used to compromise an individual's ability to consent to sexual activity. In addition, drugs and alcohol are often used by perpetrators in order to minimise any resistance and impair any memory of the victim of the assault. It is difficult to estimate the prevalence of such assaults, not only because victims don't always come forward but also because victims may be unaware they have been targeted and may put the effects of the drug instead down to other factors, such as illness. Drugs, including alcohol, might have been administered to someone without their knowledge or consent, or they might have willingly consumed alcohol or drugs. Regardless of the circumstances, 100% of the responsibility for any act of sexual violence lies with its perpetrator.

In the USA, the Steubenville rape case highlighted the cultural challenges alive today that victims face. The Steubenville case centred on the sexual assault of a teenager who was incapacitated by alcohol by several members of a football team. The assault occurred in 2012 and the case, which attracted international attention, highlighted common myths and the culture of victim blaming, whereby the victim was blamed for the assault because she had been drinking, and some media sources sympathised with the loss of future for the offenders. This particular case remains a poignant example of rape myths and stereotypes which are still believed by a significant proportion of the general public today and how these myths and stereotypes often play out in both printed and social media.

If a victim decides to report an assault to the police, depending on how much time has lapsed, it is key that a responding officer utilises EEKs and captures urine samples from the victim to help understand what type and level of drink or drugs are present. The victim may require specific considerations, depending on the level of alcohol or drug used and how recently it had been administered. They will probably be in a state of confusion and may have no or only partial recollection of events. The victim may reflect upon what has happened and question whether they may have given the impression of consent. The victim is treated as a victim of rape irrespective of how confused they may be. Professionals who may assist the victim in coming to terms with the assault in the future should also be mindful to the confusion faced by the victim.

Domestic abuse and sexual violence

Chapter 4 discussed aspects of domestic abuse including so-called honour-based violence. There are strong links between sexual violence and domestic abuse, with perpetrators abusing victims sexually as well as physically and emotionally. Sexual abuse can also be seen in honour-based violence cases, with sexual assaults used to punish any person who may have caused perceived 'dishonour'.

LGBT sexual abuse

People who identify as lesbian, gay, bisexual or transgender who are victims of non-recent or acute sexual assault can face additional barriers to reporting. They may feel that they will be discriminated against by the police or feel that the other services such as counselling may not be LGBT friendly. Information from specialist agencies Broken Rainbow identify that sexual assaults can be used as a hate crime by perpetrators because of a victim's sexuality, such as a male perpetrator sexually assaulting a lesbian because of her sexuality. Like straight relationships, LGBT relationships also experience domestic and sexual abuse.

Violence Against Women and Girls Strategy

The government and all agencies adopted the *Call to End Violence Against Women and Girls* in 2010 (HM Government, 2011). In March 2016, the Minister for Crime, Safeguarding and Vulnerability, along with the government, published the new *Ending Violence Against Women and Girls* strategy (VAWG). The refreshed national strategy 2016-2020 ,includes all aspects of domestic and sexual abuse and was refreshed again in March 2019. This strategy is both relevant to this and Chapter 4: Domestic violence and abuse.

The crimes addressed through this strategy are the crimes that disproportionately affect women and girls, which are domestic abuse, sexual violence, stalking, and 'honour-based' violence, including forced marriage and female genital mutilation (FGM). The advent of the #MeToo movement has helped to raise the profile of sexual harassment and VAWG, and increased support for those who have come forward to speak publicly about their experiences.

It is also recognised that the rise in the number of people using online dating services has created new opportunities for perpetrators to target and abuse women, but equally they offer more opportunities to raise awareness of VAWG issues at an earlier stage.

Victim support and the role of an independent sexual violence advisor

Victims of sexual violence may need specific support to help them through any court process and to recover both physiologically and emotionally from abuse.

Independent sexual violence advisors

The independent sexual violence advisor[11] (ISVA) role was commissioned by Baroness Stern through the Home Office Violent Crime Unit in 2005.

The number of ISVAs varies across the country, but it is common for an ISVA to be either child victim focused or adult victim focused. They work with victims of acute and non-recent historic sexual assaults to ensure they get the best help and advice they need, including:

- what counselling and support services are available and how to access them?

- explaining the criminal justice system – 'from report to court'

- supporting them throughout their case including attending court.

A child ISVA may support a victim of child sexual exploitation if there are no dedicated child sexual exploitation workers in the area.

---

11 Sometimes referred to as advocates rather than advisors.

Key learning

ISVAs:

■ Provide advice in relation to sexual violence.

■ Provide support through court proceedings, both criminal and civil.

■ Help to signpost other specialist services e.g. counselling.

Counselling

Victims of sexual violence may need specialist counselling by those specifically trained in this area. Counsellors can listen empathetically to those in need and suggest ways to resolve or cope with issues relevant to the victim.

Sexual Assault Referral Centre

A Sexual Assault Referral Centre (SARC) offers specialist medical and forensic services and support for victims of serious sexual offences in both the short and long term, whether or not they have reported the offence to the police. SARCs are generally funded by police and health services and often employ health professionals and those who work in charity organisations, such as Rape Crisis. What is available in a SARC varies from area to area and in some cases they are referred to as 'havens'. They have several functions, including:

■ forensic medical examinations

■ sexual health screening including HIV testing and medication

■ counselling

■ confidential reporting – victims can choose to have their samples stored while they are considering what to do next, so evidence is captured if they report to the police at a later stage.

CPS policy on rape

The CPS policy on rape explains how it deals with cases where an allegation of rape has been made.

It gives advice and provides guidance as to the definition of rape, how rape cases are prosecuted and the role of the CPS, how they assess if there is enough evidence to prosecute, what victims can expect from the CPS and the special measures and support available to victims as they attend court.

It is available on the CPS's website and it is recommended that any professional who may support a rape victim, or any police officers who may investigate rape, read and understand it. For more information, see: www.cps.gov.uk/publication/cps-policy-prosecuting-cases-rape (accessed September 2019).

Case study: Mary

Mary was in a relationship with Peter for 10 months before she fell pregnant. Although the couple were initially pleased with the pregnancy, the relationship quickly deteriorated as Peter became more jealous and controlling. Peter also began to abuse Mary verbally and emotionally. One night when Mary was five months pregnant, Peter began pressurising Mary for sex although she said no. Mary was scared and felt she had no option other than to have oral, vaginal and anal sex with Peter. She cried throughout the ordeal and Peter left the address shortly afterwards.

Mary rang her close friend who visited her at her address and persuaded her to contact the police straight away. A SOIT officer attended who took Mary's initial account, captured a urine sample using an EEK and transported her to the SARC. After a specialist forensic examination, Mary was able to give an Achieving Best Evidence (ABE) interview to the investigating officers

Peter was arrested and after investigation he was charged by the CPS with rape. Research showed he had been violent with previous partners, including committing a serious physical assault against a previous girlfriend. Mary had not known about his violent past.

An ISVA worked with Mary to support her through the court process. When Peter's family threatened and intimidated her into dropping the charges, the ISVA reported this to the police on her behalf and also offered safety advice. Mary was scared to attend court. The ISVA escorted Mary to a court room before the event so she knew what to expect and the police officers offered her special measures for court to support her to give her evidence. After trial, Peter was found guilty of rape and sentenced to eight years in prison and required to complete a sex offender register form.

Key learning

- Sexual violence incorporates a number of crimes covered under the Sexual Offences Act (2003) for England and Wales.

- Many victims never report to the police and those who do may wait several years before they come forward.

- In serious sexual offence cases like rape, the victim and perpetrator are often known to each other.

- Often victims have no physical injuries and there are no witnesses. Many cases rely on establishing whether the victim consented or not. Consent is defined as follows: 'A person consents if they agree by choice, and have the freedom and capacity to make that choice'.

- There is a range of support available to victims including specialist counselling and access to a SARC.

- ISVAs often work with child or adult victims of recent and historic sexual assaults to ensure they get the best help and advice they need.

Further reading

A Call to End Violence Against Women and Girls: Action plan 2014 [online]. London: HM Government. Available at: www.gov.uk/government/uploads/system/uploads/attachment_data/file/287758/VAWG_Action_Plan.pdf (accessed September 2019).

A Call to End Violence Against Women and Girls [online]. London: HM Government. Available at: www.gov.uk/government/uploads/system/uploads/attachment_data/file/97905/vawg-paper.pdf (accessed September 2019).

Ending Violence against Women and Girls 2016 – 2020 Strategy Refresh [online]. Available at: https://assets.publishing.service.gov.uk/government/uploads/system/uploads/attachment_data/file/783596/VAWG_Strategy_Refresh_Web_Accessible.pdf (accessed September 2019).

Broken Rainbow is a helpline providing information and support to LGBT victims of domestic abuse. Their website can be found at: www.brokenrainbow.org.uk/

CPS Policy for Prosecuting Cases of Rape (2018) [online]. Crown Prosecution Service. www.cps.gov.uk/publication/cps-policy-prosecuting-cases-rape (accessed September 2019).

Ending Violence Against Women and Girls (2013) Available at: www.gov.uk/government/policies/ending-violence-against-women-and-girls-in-the-uk (accessed September 2019).

Galop is a lesbian, gay, bisexual and transgender community safety charity. Their website can be found at: www.galop.org.uk/

References

Bows H & Westmarland N (2017) Rape of Older people in the United Kingdom: Challenging the 'real-rape' stereotype. *British Journal of Criminology* **57** (1).

HM Government (2011) *A Call to End Violence Against Women and Girls* [online]. London:

HM Government. Available at: www.gov.uk/government/uploads/system/uploads/attachment_data/file/97905/vawg-paper.pdf (accessed September 2019).

Ministry of Justice (2013) *An Overview of Sexual Offending in England and Wales* [online]. London: Ministry of Justice, Home Office & ONS. Available at: www.gov.uk/government/statistics/an-overview-of-sexual-offending-in-england-and-wales (accessed September 2019).

ONS (2018) Sexual offending: victimisation and the path through the criminal justice system. ONS. Available at: www.ons.gov.uk/peoplepopulationandcommunity/crimeandjustice/articles/sexualoffendingvictimisationandthepaththroughthecriminaljusticesystem/2018-12-13 (accessed April 2019)

Rape Crisis (2015) *Rape and Sexual Violence* [online]. London: Rape Crisis. Available at: https://rapecrisis.org.uk/get-informed/about-sexual-violence/what-is-sexual-violence/ (accessed September 2019).

UNDOC (2012) *Comprehensive Strategy to Combat Trafficking in Persons and Smuggling of Migrants* [online]. United Nations Office on Drugs and Crime. Available at: www.unodc.org/documents/human-trafficking/UNODC_Strategy_on_Human_Trafficking_and_Migrant_Smuggling.pdf (accessed September 2019).

UN (2000) *Protocol to Prevent, Suppress and Punish Trafficking in Persons Especially Women and Children, supplementing the United Nations Convention against Transnational Organized Crime.*

Chapter 7: Internet safeguarding (online safety)

By Jody Watts (refreshed content) & John Hodge (original content), edited by Nigel Boulton

Chapter overview

- Introduction.

- Grooming and sexual solicitation.

- Indecent images of children.

- Youth produced sexual images.

- Live streaming.

- Cyber bullying – mental health and self-harm.

- Online extremism and radicalisation.

- Viruses and malware.

- Professional boundaries online.

- Useful resources.

Introduction

The internet is becoming ever more integrated into our daily lives, with the number of mobile devices growing on a daily basis. Home devices such as TVs, music speakers, toys, CCTV cameras, lights, heating or kitchen appliances, being remotely controlled through smartphone apps, can bring great benefits to your daily life.

Children and young people who have lived with the internet and its associated technology for their whole lives may be comfortable with this new world, however they are often poorly equipped emotionally to deal with some of the social risks this connectivity presents, and the many and varied communication platforms associated with it can expose them to moral and sometimes physical danger. It is often very difficult for parents and carers to keep abreast of changes in technology and, as such, many feel powerless to properly supervise young people's online behaviour.

The UK government's guidance, *Child Safety Online: A practical guide for providers of social media and interactive services* (DCMS, 2016), classifies online risk into three categories:

- **Content Risk:** Children receiving mass-distributed content. This may expose them to age-inappropriate material such as pornography, extreme violence, or content involving hate speech and radicalisation.

- **Conduct Risk:** Children participating in an interactive situation. This includes bullying, sexting, harassing, being aggressive or stalking; or promoting harmful behaviour such as self-harm, suicide, pro-anorexia, bulimia, illegal drug use or imitating dangerous behaviour. A child's own conduct online can also make them vulnerable, for example by over-sharing their personal information or by harassing or bullying other people.

- **Contact Risk:** Children being victims of interactive situations. This includes being bullied, harassed or stalked; meeting strangers; threats to privacy, identity and reputation (for example, through embarrassing photos shared without permission, a house location being identified, someone impersonating a user, users sharing information with strangers); and violence, threats and abuse directly aimed at individual users and/or groups of users

This chapter seeks to explain and offer advice and guidance concerning many of the dangers that can be encountered by children and other vulnerable people while using the internet. It identifies the core criminal offences that aim to govern internet activity with the intention of attempting to protect the vulnerable.

Grooming and sexual solicitation

A person aged 18 or over commits an offence under Section 15 of the Sexual Offences Act (2003) if, having met or communicated with a child online, they intentionally meet them or travel with the intention of meeting that person anywhere in the 'real world' with the intention of doing anything to them of a sexual or violent nature. For an offence to be committed, the person who is being groomed has to be under the age of 16 or the offender does not reasonably believe that they are 16 or over, that is, there is not necessarily an offence if they had good reason to believe the person was over 16 when in fact they were not. The act gives further detailed explanations of the offences that are to be considered, and covers a range of sexual offences that are found within legislation currently in place in the UK.

The Serious Crime Act (2015) also introduced the offence of sexual communication with a child. This criminalises an adult who communicates with a child for the purpose of obtaining sexual gratification, where the communication is sexual or if it is intended to elicit from the child a communication which is sexual and the adult reasonably believes the child to be under 16.

The growth in online social media has changed young people's attitudes to the information they are prepared to share, not only with their friends and contacts but, sometimes unwittingly, with other people who may use it to groom them with a view to either encouraging them to engage in sexual language and posing, or to encourage them to meet in a real-world environment. Children should be encouraged to be aware of the privacy settings of social media which, although sometimes not quite as explicit as they should be, are always available and can be altered so as to allow as little information to be shared publicly as the user wishes.

Many people are not aware, for example, that all profile pictures placed on Twitter are searchable on Google and that, by default, all Facebook posts are public and Facebook profile pictures are likewise searchable on Google. Privacy rules change constantly and it is advisable to assess social media privacy settings on a regular basis.

Many old-fashioned 'stranger danger' rules are still relevant in the internet age, but with the caveat that persons who may seek to groom young people online are likely not to appear as a stranger at all, but as someone who already knows a great deal about them. Grooming is when someone builds an emotional connection with a child or young person online to gain their trust for the purposes of sexual abuse, sexual exploitation or trafficking. This can be a stranger or someone they know such as a friend, a professional or family member, a female or male, an adult or a peer.

Groomers use social media sites, instant messaging apps including teen dating apps, or online gaming platforms to connect with a young person or child. They spend time learning about a young person's interests from their online profiles and then use this knowledge to help them build up a relationship or send messages to hundreds of young people and wait to see who responds. Groomers can easily hide their identity online and pretend to be a child, then become 'friends' with children they are targeting.

Some definitions

Sexual abuse means a child or young person is being forced or persuaded to take part in sexual activity. This doesn't have to be physical contact; it can happen online. Increasingly, groomers are sexually exploiting their victims by persuading them to take part in online sexual activity.

Child sexual exploitation is a form of child sexual abuse. It occurs where an individual or group takes advantage of an imbalance of power to coerce, manipulate or deceive a child or young person under the age of 18 into sexual activity (a) in exchange for something the victim needs or wants, and/or (b) for the financial advantage or increased status of the perpetrator or facilitator. The victim may have been sexually exploited even if the sexual activity appears consensual. Child sexual exploitation does not always involve physical contact; it can also occur through the use of technology. Abuse is possible in real time using webcams to provide material for paedophile groups.

The impact on a child of online-based sexual abuse and exploitation is similar to that for all sexually abused children. However, it has an additional dimension of there being a visual record of the abuse. Online-based sexual abuse of a child constitutes significant harm through sexual and emotional abuse and Child Protection procedures should be followed accordingly.

Children, young people, parents and carers can be advised by professionals along the following lines:

- Always be aware of privacy settings and changes.

- Friend requests should not be accepted from people who aren't real-world friends, or at least well-known to them.

- Personal details such as addresses or mobile phone numbers should never be given out on social networking sites.

- Strong passwords should be used and these should never be disclosed, even to close friends. Weak passwords include those that aren't changed regularly, those that could be guessed with some background knowledge (e.g. favourite colour, football team, food etc.) or the actual word 'password', which is unfortunately still the most commonly used. However, a balance needs to be reached between setting a memorable password and setting an over complex one that has to be written down and can therefore be seen by others.

■ Where possible, Multi-factor Authentication, also known as Two Factor Authentication, should be used on accounts such as social networking sites. Multi-factor Authentication adds another layer of security, supplementing the username and password model with a pin code that only a specific user has access to. This can be via SMS message, phone call, authenticator app or email. This authentication method can be easily summed up as a combination of 'something you have and something you know'.

■ Care should be taken when uploading images, status updates and messages, even among trusted friends. Once circulated online, images can be shared widely and can be extremely difficult to block or remove.

■ No agreement should ever be made to meet a stranger in person who has previously only been an online acquaintance.

■ All users should familiarise themselves with safety functions that can be employed on social media networking sites. Many of these will have a 'block' function to stop unwanted contact with another user.

Following these simple rules can help ensure that social media remains what it is supposed to be – a socially interactive tool, rather than a place of danger. Parents and carers should be advised to have their own social media accounts so that they can get acquainted with the technology and become more confident within the environment. While their child may not be over-impressed with their parents becoming their Facebook friend or Twitter follower, it is an excellent method of understanding how young people interact on social media and ensuring they stay safe, in the same way that they would ensure that a young person stayed safe in the real world, no matter how unpopular this may be with the young person.

Anything found that is upsetting or offensive while using social networking sites should be reported. Equally, if a young person or parents suspect a child may be the victim of any form of online harassment or grooming, they need to seek help immediately. Aside from contacting the social networking site itself, serious cases that do not gain swift resolution should be reported to the police or directly to the Child Exploitation and Online Protection Centre (CEOP).

If a child is the victim of any form of harassment or abuse, ensure a record is kept of all communication to pass over to the relevant bodies. Gathering such evidence will vary dependent upon the method of communication used and it could mean securing mobile phones or personal computers. If in doubt, take advice as early as possible. If digital data is relevant then consideration should be given to the *Good Practice Guide for Digital Evidence* (ACPO, 2012), which establishes four main principles when dealing with digital evidence:

- **Principle 1:** No action taken by law enforcement agencies, persons employed within those agencies or their agents should change data which may subsequently be relied upon in court.

- **Principle 2:** In circumstances where a person finds it necessary to access original data, that person must be competent to do so and be able to give evidence explaining the relevance and the implications of their actions.

- **Principle 3:** An audit trail or other record of all processes applied to digital evidence should be created and preserved. An independent third party should be able to examine those processes and achieve the same result.

- **Principle 4:** The person in charge of the investigation has overall responsibility for ensuring that the law and these principles are adhered to.

Signs of online grooming

The majority of children who are online are not being abused and never will be. The following activities could be perfectly innocent, but it is worth being alert to potential signs:

- Becoming secretive with their phone or computer.

- Excessive use of their phone or computer.

- Showing aggression if asked about their online use.

- Change in the use of sexual language.

- Unexplained gifts or cash.

Changes in a child's behaviour may also act as indicators, and these can include:

- A change in your child's self-esteem and self-confidence.

- Withdrawal from family and friends.

- Difficulties at school.

- An increased level of anxiety.

- Sleeping and concentration difficulties.

- Becoming excessively concerned with washing and cleanliness.

Indecent images of children

Section 1 of the Protection of Children Act (1978) creates the following offences:

- To take, permit to be taken, or to make any indecent photographs or pseudo photographs of a child.

- To distribute or show indecent photographs or pseudo-photographs.

- To have in one's possession such indecent photographs or pseudo-photographs with a view to their being distributed or shown by himself or others.

- To publish or cause to be published any advertisement likely to be understood as conveying that the advertiser distributes or shows such indecent photographs or pseudo-photographs or intends to do so.

Police specialist investigators will be aware of the points to prove concerning this and all the offences identified within this chapter. Always feel confident to contact the local police and speak with a specialist investigator for advice about securing evidence and the detailed points required to prove offences.

Possession of an indecent image of a child

Section 160 of the Criminal Justice Act (1988) covers the offence of possession of an indecent image of a child. There are no requirements for a person to have any motive in relation to making or distributing the image, all that is required is that they had the image in their possession. A sad product of the internet is that people who seek indecent images of children (IIOC) can find these online with relative anonymity and do not have to physically travel to find them. The internet has also proved to be an anonymous avenue for those who seek sexual gratification from such images to endorse their own habits by gathering in forums and chat rooms where similarly minded people will assist in justifying their feelings and thoughts.

There is a significant trade in IIOC, not generally for financial gain (although this can be the case), but in exchange for other such images or for kudos among forum groups or in chat rooms. There is a particular demand for previously unseen images or particularly rare images from a given series. As time and technology has progressed the demand for still images has progressed to video footage displaying sexual acts with children, in some case extremely young and pre-pubescent, but certainly under teenage years.

Categorisation of images

While the Protection of Children Act (1978) deals with the taking, making, distribution and publishing of images, it does not take into account their categorisation. However, sentencing guidelines for indecent images of children creates useful categories dependent on image content.

These were amended and simplified with effect from 1st April 2014 by the *Sexual Offences: Definitive guidelines*, issues by the Sentencing Council (2014):

- Category A – images involving penetrative sexual activity, sexual activity with an animal or sadism.
- Category B – images involving non-penetrative sexual activity.
- Category C – other indecent images not falling within Categories A or B.

Youth produced sexual images

The Criminal Justice and Courts Act (2015) created a new statutory offence of 'disclosing private sexual photographs and films with intent to cause distress', which seeks to address the problem of 'revenge porn'. The rise of incidents of intimate images being posted online without consent has become a serious concern due to the increasingly prevalent culture of 'sexting' and the technological advances which have made it easy to reproduce and distribute photographs and videos online. This has become a particular problem among young adults and teenagers. Under Section 33 it is an offence to disclose a private sexual photograph or film if the disclosure is made without consent and with the intention of causing distress.

The definition of 'indecent' is a subjective one and relies on a Clapham Omnibus type test – would the average person see the image as indecent?

A child is defined for the purposes of the Protection of Children Act (1978) as being a person under the age of 18 and this should be provable beyond reasonable doubt. The definition of a child in relation to age has been subject to change and clarification in the last few years and is on occasions specific to particular offences.

Under the age of 18 years is a solid starting point when considering the age issue but professionals should always seek advice from specialist investigators if they are concerned about the internet-based activity of a child or young person. While some of these images are created by persons with direct access to children, many images in circulation originate from self-taken images and video footage originally sent between young people engaged in relationships and sexual experimentation, which quickly falls into the wrong hands or is obtained by trickery and then swiftly distributed through groups as described above.

Research has shown that a new image can circulate worldwide extremely quickly and even images that can be taken innocently by parents and carers (children in the bath etc.) can be used for inappropriate reasons when distributed on the internet and via social media. While there are obvious emotional and moral repercussions to images such as these being distributed, young people need to be reminded that it is an offence in the UK to take, distribute, publish or possess with a view to distribute or show an indecent image of a child, even if that is a self-taken image and/or distributed by that person. While rare in the UK and not the preferred outcome for law enforcement or prosecuting authorities, there have been occasions where young people have been prosecuted for distributing indecent images of themselves.

The College of Policing published a briefing note, *Police action in response to youth produced sexual imagery ('Sexting')*, which stated the following:

- All reported offences of youth produced sexual imagery must be recorded as a crime in line with Home Office Counting Rules (HOCR).

- At the point of report, it is vital to ascertain whether any aggravating features (e.g. an adult involved, the presence of violence) and/or known vulnerabilities are present and check the welfare of relevant parties.

- Advice should be given that enables the effective safeguarding of persons affected (e.g. where further advice/support can be found) and that also ensures they do not do anything which in effect could result in them breaking the law such as taking a copy of the image on their own device.

Background checks should be run regarding the victim(s), perpetrator(s) and location(s) (where relevant). This should include all police systems (including national (PNC/PND) and, where possible, those belonging to partners (e.g. via a Multi-Agency Safeguarding Hub (MASH) or equivalent). Where a multi-agency meeting is planned, or where there will be a discussion with the various parties directly involved, such as the children and/or their parents/carers, these checks should ideally take place before any meeting. Safeguarding concerns may require immediate action and this may prevent checks being undertaken in advance.

Where significant risks are identified or any of the involved children are found to be subject to ongoing child protection activity (e.g. in care or on a child protection plan) there is likely to be a requirement for a child protection referral and/or a strategy meeting. This should help develop measures to safeguard the child effectively and ensure relevant duties of care are followed.

Most offences involving sexual activity connected to children will raise significant safeguarding concerns. In youth produced sexual imagery cases where there are no aggravating features, it may be appropriate to take an approach that is supportive of the children involved, rather than beginning a criminal process. Decisions on the appropriate approach should be underpinned by careful assessment of the facts of the case: the presence of any aggravating features, the backgrounds of the children involved, and the views of significant stakeholders (such as parents/carers and the children's teachers).

In January 2016, the Home Office launched 'outcome 21', which states: 'Further investigation, resulting from the crime report, which could provide evidence sufficient to support formal action being taken against the suspect is not in the public interest – police decision.' This outcome code allows the police to record a crime as having happened but for no formal criminal justice action to be taken as it is not considered to be in the public interest to do so.

Outcome 21 may be considered the most appropriate resolution in youth produced sexual imagery cases where the making and sharing is considered non-abusive and there is no evidence of exploitation, grooming, profit motive, malicious intent (such as extensive or inappropriate sharing, including uploading onto a pornographic website) or it being persistent behaviour. Where these factors are present, outcome 21 would not apply.

There are a number of apps such as Snapchat and Vine which can be particularly troublesome as they encourage the sending of pictures and short videos. It is also relatively easy for recipients to screen capture an image or record a video which can then be forwarded to any number of recipients or used to blackmail young people into further acts.

Key learning

Children, young persons, parents and carers should be advised along the following lines:

- They should never take pictures (or videos) of themselves in any compromising position, especially in any stage of undress.

- Once an image or video is on the internet everyone can see it. When a picture or video of them is being taken, they should always try to imagine their loved ones, employers or respected peers viewing this image or video. They should stop and think, 'Is this something they would be OK with them seeing?' They should remember that every device that has a camera is likely to be connected to the internet in some way. →

- Friendships and intimate relationships are not always forever. Disgruntled friends, ex-boyfriends etc. are often the most active offenders in posting undesirable images or videos. Even if they completely trust the individual they are sending the images to, individuals should consider what may happen if their phone, tablet, laptop or PC were stolen or their email account was hacked. Their images could end up in the wrong hands very quickly.

- If someone takes an intimate, private, personal picture (or video) of them, they should ask them to delete it. Make sure they see that it has been deleted.

- If someone has compromising pictures or video of them, be firm in their request for it to be deleted. They should let the taker know they are serious about their privacy and security and not be intimidated. They should seek assistance from parents, school, the police or anyone with authority. In most countries, owning and distributing pictures of anyone underage is illegal.

- Parents and carers should talk to their children about the dangers of taking these types of pictures. What they see as innocent play can quickly be turned into something undesirable and often with tragic consequences. An innocent picture can find its way online all too easily.

- No images or videos of children or their friends in any state of undress, even jokingly, are acceptable.

- Young people should not allow friends to have photographs or videos taken of them in compromising positions or in any stage of undress, especially when partying. Remember, everyone at the party you are at has a camera and that camera is, generally speaking, connected to the internet.

- They should not post or upload intimate personal pictures or videos onto any website. This includes all social media and dating sites unless they want to share that picture or video with everyone on the internet – including their friends, family or employer.

- They should not be duped into taking 'pretty' pictures for a photographer who promises to make them a star.

Live streaming

Live streaming is the broadcasting of a live video recording from an internet connected device such as a phone, tablet or games console. The recorded footage is unedited and is viewed in real time by users similar to Live TV through services such as Twitch, Facebook, YouTube, Instagram, Periscope, Live.ly and

Musical.ly, which are difficult to moderate. It is possible for children and young people to view content that is inappropriate for their age even if they did not intend to watch that type of video.

Some live streaming services allow viewers to comment on a live video as it is being broadcast. Adult offenders will sometimes use tricks and dares to coerce young people into performing acts that involve nudity on camera. Younger children can be particularly susceptible to these tactics as it can be difficult for them to spot manipulative behaviour in others and stand up to pressure.

It is important to remind young people that if someone asks them to remove clothing or do anything sexual, stop and tell someone. No matter who instigated the conversation or what's been said, it is never the young person's fault. They should also be reminded that when an image is passed on, they no longer have control. It can then be posted and passed online very quickly. Encourage them to tell an adult and report to CEOP.

Cyberbullying

Cyberbullying can take many forms and, for the person affected, can lead to serious trauma, depression, self-harm and even suicide. There is no legal definition of cyberbullying within UK law but it can be defined as repeated intentional malicious threats, taunts, abuse and harassment, using phones, the internet, or any form of technology.

One person or a group of people can perpetrate cyberbullying and teenagers and younger children are usually the targets. It can take the following forms:

■ Being sent mean emails or texts.

■ Having embarrassing pictures/videos posted online.

■ Having rumours spread about them online.

Unlike traditional bullying, which requires the bully and the victim to be in the same location with the victim finding safety in their own home, cyberbullying can happen anywhere at any time by anyone who has access to the internet. Victims no longer have anywhere to hide and this can affect their emotional well-being.

The following signs and behaviours are generally seen in children experiencing cyberbullying:

1. Appears nervous when receiving a text, instant message or email.

2. Seems uneasy about going to school or pretends to be ill.

3. Unwillingness to share information about online activity.

4. Unexplained anger or depression, especially after going online.

5. Abruptly shutting off or walking away from the computer mid-use.

6. Withdrawing from friends and family in real life.

7. Unexplained stomach aches or headaches.

8. Trouble sleeping at night.

9. Unexplained weight loss or gain.

10. Suicidal thoughts or suicide attempts.

11. Closing down or creating new social networking profiles.

Guidelines issued by the Crown Prosecution Service (2018) explain how cases of cyberbullying will be assessed under current legislation.

The Defamation Act (2013), which came into force on 1st January 2014, has a bearing on the issues of cyberbullying and further information can be found at www. legislation.gov.uk/ukpga/2013/26/contents/enacted (accessed September 2019).

Box 7.1: Cyberbullying and the law

There are a number of existing UK laws that can be applied to cases of cyberbullying and online harassment.

Protection from Harassment Act (1997): This act states that a person must not pursue a course of conduct that amounts to harassment of another and which he knows or ought to know amounts to harassment. For the purposes of this offence, the person whose course of conduct is in question ought to know that it amounts to harassment if a reasonable person in possession of the same information would think it amounted to harassment.

Criminal Justice and Public Order Act (1994)
Section 154 of this act created the offence of causing intentional harassment, alarm or distress by amending Part 1 of the Public Order Act (1986) (offences relating to public order). →

'A person is guilty of an offence if, with intent to cause a person harassment, alarm or distress, he uses threatening, abusive or insulting words or behaviour, or disorderly behaviour, or displays any writing, sign or other visible representation which is threatening, abusive or insulting, thereby causing that or another person harassment, alarm or distress.'

This offence can be committed in public or private, but there are restrictions if it is committed within a dwelling and seen within the same dwelling or another. Advice should be taken from a specialist police investigator as to the relevance of all these offences.

Malicious Communications Act (1988)

Section 1 of the Malicious Communications Act (1988) makes it an offence for any person to send to another person a letter or other article which conveys a message that is indecent or grossly offensive, threatening, or which contains information that is false and known or believed to be false by the sender.

Communications Act (2003)

Section 127 of the Communications Act (2003) created an offence of improper use of a public electronic communications network. A person is guilty of this offence if he sends by means of a public electronic communication network a message or other matter that is grossly offensive or of an indecent, obscene or menacing character, or causes any such message or matter to be sent.

A person also commits an offence under this section if, for the purposes of causing annoyance, inconvenience or needless anxiety to another, he sends by means of a public electronic communications network, a message that he knows to be false, causes such a message to be sent, or persistently makes use of a public electronic communications network.

While there is therefore a legal framework to protect people against cyberbullying, it is far better to take action to minimise the effects of this behaviour before it gets to the stage where the law is involved.

The following advice may be helpful for parents and professionals to pass on to young people:

- Immediately stop replying or fighting back online and do not share any personal or private information. Replying may make things worse and you could be labelled as a 'cyberbully'.
- Block the cyberbully, and report them to the site administrator.

- Tell an adult such as a teacher or parent and keep telling someone until something is done about it.

- Find out what the respective school can do about cyberbullying.

- Do not delete any of the messages that have been sent. Show them to everyone they inform about the cyberbully as proof.

- Do not agree to meet anyone they speak to online, especially if they don't know them.

- Inform the police only if their safety and security is at risk.

If a young person becomes aware that another young person is the subject of cyberbullying then the following actions are available:

- Tell an adult.

- Report the cyberbully to the site administrator.

- Help the victim by showing they are not alone in order to show them support.

Prevention is always the best option and the following suggestions may help prevent a young person from becoming a victim of cyberbullying:

- Avoid sending or typing anything that others may find offensive.

- Never give out any personal or private information such as passwords to anyone, including your friends.

- Avoid passing on messages, especially if they contain abusive or cruel content.

- Never agree to meet anyone who is not known. The victim should always report the bullying or tell an adult if the bully insists on meeting them.

- Make sure they use privacy settings.

Actions to take when cyberbullying is reported

- **Ascertain the facts:** Obtain measured and accurate information about any alleged incident or course of behaviour from the victim. Assess whether the victim is in any immediate risk of harm. Offer reassurance and advice.

- **Gather and retain evidence:** There are many ways to record what is visible on a computer or smartphone screen and these vary from device to device. For instance, the contents of a computer screen can be captured by pressing the print screen or 'prt/scr' key, usually at the top right of a keyboard. This copies the visible area of the screen to the computer's clipboard and then this can be pasted into any image software such as Microsoft Paint. The visible screen area of an iPhone or iPad can be captured by pressing the home button and on/off button simultaneously. This will place an image of the screen into the device's images folder. For more in-depth analysis, advice should be sought from the police but, except in extremely serious cases, it is unlikely that a trained forensic examiner will be provided, so the initial action may be the only opportunity to secure evidence.

■ **Seek further advice:** After assessing the nature of the complaint, consider taking further advice from a specialist police investigator. CEOP has a reporting tool on its website at: www.ceop.police.uk/ceop-report/

Mental health and self-harm

The link between bullying and mental health issues are well established and in 2015 the Office for National Statistics found that there is a 'clear association' between the amount of time spent online and mental health problems, particularly depression, poor sleep quality and other social and emotional problems.

The London Grid for Learning published findings from a survey with 40,000 children and young people across the UK. Findings found that almost one in six children and young people had seen something that encouraged people to hurt themselves and that 'people get told to commit suicide and are sent pictures with the "correct" way to do it'. Self-harm is not only an aspect of bullying but has become a 'style' of bullying.

Young people can access harmful information on the internet or make connections with people online who encourage them to self-harm. For example, some websites imply that unhealthy behaviours, such as anorexia and self-harm, can be normal lifestyle choices. Social networking also provides the opportunity for online groups to form that promote these unhealthy behaviours.

There have been a number of high-profile cases involving cyber-bullying and suicides over the past decade and reports of suicide clusters facilitated by social media. It is very easy to find pro-suicide information, such as detailed information on methods, on the internet. Another concern is the risk of 'contagion', where young people are encouraged to take their own lives after witnessing others describing suicidal thoughts or leaving suicide notes on social media. More recently, there have been several reported incidents of young people livestreaming suicides on social media. Research on the internet and self-harm among young people found that, while young people most often use the internet to find help, there is the risk that the internet can normalise self-harm and discourage young people from talking about their problems and seeking professional help.

Digital self-harm, as it has been termed, occurs when an individual creates an anonymous online account and uses it to publicly send hurtful messages or threats to one's self. Digital self-harm is defined as the 'anonymous online posting, sending, or otherwise sharing of hurtful content about oneself'. Most commonly, it manifests as threats or targeted messages of hate – the more extreme and rare forms of cyberbullying. If professionals become aware that a child or young person appears to be accessing online content of this type, this should be raised with relevant others, including the safeguarding lead in their organisation, to ensure this information is shared appropriately and that support can be put in place.

Online extremism and radicalisation

The Racial and Religious Hatred Act (2006) makes it a criminal offence to threaten people because of their faith, or to stir up religious hatred by displaying, publishing or distributing written material that is threatening. Other laws already protect people from threats based on their race, nationality or ethnic background.

Radical and extremist groups use social media as a way of attracting and drawing in children and young people to their particular cause; this is similar to the grooming processes and exploits the same vulnerabilities. The groups concerned include those linked to extreme Islamist, or Far Right/Neo Nazi ideologies, various paramilitary groups, extremist animal rights groups and others who justify political, religious, sexist or racist violence.

A common feature of radicalisation is that the child or young person does not recognise the exploitative nature of what is happening and does not see themselves as a victim of grooming or exploitation.

Where there are concerns about a child's exposure to extremist materials, a number of agencies including the child's school may be able to provide advice and support. In accordance with the government's Prevent Duty, schools and statutory agencies are required to identify a PREVENT Lead who is the lead for safeguarding in relation to protecting individuals from radicalisation and involvement in terrorism.

Suspected online terrorist material can be reported through www.gov.uk/report-terrorism. Reports can be made anonymously, although practitioners should not do so as they must follow the procedures for professionals.

Viruses and malware

A recent government study concluded that, in 2017, 14% of UK adults surveyed reported experiencing some form of computer virus or malware. These can range from annoying adware and spyware such as those that hijack browser home pages or search engines, to more serious key logger installation (all keystrokes logged and sent to a third party resulting in compromised password and other personal data) or the whole system being compromised and used as part of a 'botnet' (the complete compromise of a computer or network which is then used to attack other computers or networks).

Most computer compromises are caused by either unpatched computer operating systems (where known vulnerabilities are not fixed, which hackers are then able to exploit to compromise the system) or the inadvertent opening of executable files or visits to websites that download executable files, which are then able to open 'backdoors' into operating systems and thereby gain control of them.

Children and young people are particularly vulnerable to attacks such as these as they are less careful when opening attachments and more likely to visit websites such as illegal music and film services. These sites often contain either executable files disguised as free media or supposed download mangers, or they are confusing as to which area to click for downloadable content, leading people to unwittingly download suspicious files to their computer, which can be exploited either immediately or at a later date by hackers.

If a young person's computer or mobile device is compromised their personal data could be obtained and potentially be used in an attempt at grooming them for the purposes of sexual exploitation.

Some simple rules can be followed to minimise the risk of attack and should be considered by professionals and parents alike who have protection of children and young people within their day-to-day lives:

- Switch on automatic operating system updates in either Windows or Mac OS. This will ensure that known vulnerabilities to operating systems and software are fixed at the earliest opportunity.

- Install reputable anti-virus (AV) software and update it regularly so that newly discovered virus signatures can be updated.

- Ensure that this AV software is allowed to scan the computer regularly so that any malware can be healed or deleted.

- Avoid opening any files that are received via email or social media/messaging clients unless they are from a known and trusted source.

- Change system passwords regularly and use secure and strong replacements.

- Ensure Wi-Fi systems have a strong access password, both to join the network or access the router (details of these can normally be located on your internet service provider's website).

- Avoid visiting supposed free music download sites as these are often havens for malware. There are many free and reasonably priced music and media client sites available in the UK. Visit www.thecontentmap.com for details of all the places where media can be obtained legally in the UK.

- If you feel that your computer's security has been compromised, disconnect the affected computer from the internet immediately and investigate yourself by using a search engine on another, uncompromised device, or seek professional help.

- Ensure that all family members are conversant with these tips.

Professional boundaries in relation to your personal internet use and social networking online

Anyone who works with children, young people, adults or their families, whether it is in a paid or voluntary capacity, must always have their professional role in mind when using social networking sites and should always consider how their behaviour could affect their professional reputation and employment, for instance inadvertently posting inappropriate comments about work on your profile. Remember, it's very difficult to control exactly who will end up seeing comments posted on social networking sites. **All digital records should be considered to be permanent**.

Professionals should also be cautious in their communications with children so as to avoid any possible misinterpretation of their motives or any behaviour that could be construed as grooming. Do not put yourself at risk by communicating with children outside of your organisation's boundaries. Communication with children you work with should always be via your organisation's networks.

Remember, professionals working with children and young people, or their families, may be vulnerable to having an allegation made against them or being the victim of cyberbullying. Sometimes this is a result of a communication or a situation being misconstrued, and this can also relate to communications with adults, friends and colleagues. At other times it may also be that someone, through having complex needs, may develop an unhealthy interest in the professional as a person.

Good practice guidelines

- DO NOT behave in a way that could suggest that you are trying to develop a personal relationship with a child, young person or vulnerable adult.

- DO NOT post any content that could be deemed defamatory, obscene or libellous.

- DO NOT post comments that exhibit or appear to endorse grossly irresponsible behaviour or law breaking of any kind.

- DO NOT use your personal social network profile/email to communicate with or share images or take images of children/young people and their parents/carers.

- DO NOT give out your personal contact details to children or parents/carers; professional communication should always be through a work provided email or work phone number.

Appropriate behaviour

- Set the privacy settings for any social networking site you use to ensure that only the people you want to have sight/access can see the contents. Keep these updated. The default settings for most social networking sites are set to public, whereby anyone can see everything.

- Ensure your mobile devices is password/PIN protected. This will ensure that other people can't use your equipment and get you into trouble.

- If you need to contact service users (i.e. children, young people, adults or their parents or carers) or their families through social networking sites, have a separate professional online identity/account. Ensure that your manager is aware of your professional online persona.

- Make sure that all publicly available information about you is accurate and appropriate – think particularly about whether images/stories that you may have posted in your personal life are appropriate for a person with a professional life and a reputation to lose. If you don't want it to be public, don't put it online.

- Be mindful about how you present yourself when you are publishing information about yourself or having 'conversations' online.

- If you are unsure who can view online material, assume that it is publicly available. Remember – once information is online you no longer have control over it. Other people may choose to copy it, to edit it, to pass it on and to save it.

- When you receive any new equipment (personal or private) make sure that you know what features it has as standard and take appropriate action to disable/protect.

Inappropriate behaviour

- Giving out your personal information to service users i.e. children, young people, adults or their parents or carers. This includes personal mobile phone numbers, social networking accounts, personal website/blog URLs, online image storage sites, passwords/PIN numbers etc.

- Using your personal mobile phone to communicate with service users i.e. children, young people, adults or their parents or carers either by phone call, text, email, social networking site.

- Using the internet or web-based communication to send personal messages to service users.

- Sharing your personal details on a social network site with service users. This includes accepting them as friends. Be aware that belonging to a 'group' may give 'back door' access to your page even though you have set your privacy settings to family and friends only.

- Adding or allowing service users to join your contacts/friends list on personal social networking profiles.

- Using your own digital camera/video for work. This includes cameras on mobile phones.

- Playing online games with service users. This can be difficult when the culture is to play with 'randoms'. Check out before you play online with someone you don't know.

The best way to test your privacy settings is to search for yourself regularly on a search engine (i.e. Google or Bing). If you do find anything that may have an impact on your professional reputation then save the evidence by taking a photo or screenshot then use the reporting procedures on the sites involved. Professionals can also contact the Professionals Online Safety Helpline for advice.

Further reading

While many modern problems are caused by the internet, very often the solutions are to be found online as well. Below are some points of reference that may be valuable for further reference.

The Child Exploitation and Online Protection Centre (CEOP)
CEOP works with child protection partners across the UK and overseas to identify the main threats to children and co-ordinates activity against these threats to bring offenders to account. They protect children from harm online and offline, directly through National Crime Agency (NCA) led operations and in partnership with local and international agencies.

Their approach seeks to be holistic. Officers in CEOP and across the NCA who specialise in this area of criminality work side by side with professionals from the wider child protection community and industry.

Their website (www.ceop.police.uk) contains a lot of useful advice for parents, carers and young people alike.

Get Safe Online
Get Safe Online (www.getsafeonline.org) is an extremely useful resource for concerns people may have around many aspects of the internet. There are specific areas on the website concerning safeguarding children online.

National Society for the Prevention of Cruelty to Children (NSPCC)
The NSPCC is a registered charity which, as the names suggest, has an aim to reduce harm to children. There are many facets to the NSPCC, including Childline, reporting facilities for adults who are concerned about a young person, community projects and some excellent resources for children, parents and carers alike.

Their website (www.nspcc.org.uk) contains a section providing advice for parents on keeping children safe online.

UK Council for Child Internet Safety (UKCIS)
The UK Council for Child Internet Safety is a group of more than 200 organisations drawn from across government, industry, law, academia and charity sectors that work in partnership to help keep children safe online.

There are many helpful documents on their website: www.gov.uk/government/groups/uk-council-for-child-internet-safety-ukccis

Internet Watch Foundation

The Internet Watch Foundation (www.iwf.org.uk) work internationally to identify and remove online images and videos of child sexual abuse.

Professionals Online Safety Helpline

The Professionals Online Safety Helpline (www.saferinternet.org.uk/professionals-online-safety-helpline) – Supporting all professionals working with children and young people including teachers, social workers, doctors, police, coaches, foster carers, youth workers with concerns regarding online safety issues. Telephone 0344 381 4772.

References

ACPO (2012) *Good Practice Guide for Digital Evidence* [online]. Available at: http://library.college.police.uk/docs/acpo/digital-evidence-2012.pdf (accessed September 2019).

Crown Prosecution Service (2018) *Guidelines on Prosecuting Cases Involving Communications Sent Via Social Media* [online] Available at: www.cps.gov.uk/legal-guidance/social-media-guidelines-prosecuting-cases-involving-communications-sent-social-media (accessed September 2019).

Sentencing Council (2014) *Sexual Offences: Definitive guidelines* [online]. London: Sentencing Council. Available at: www.sentencingcouncil.org.uk/wp-content/uploads/Sexual-offences-definitive-guideline-Web.pdf (accessed September 2019).

The College of Policing (2016) *Briefing Note: Police action in response to youth produced sexual imagery ('Sexting')* [online]. Available at: www.college.police.uk/News/College-news/Documents/Police_action_in_response_to_sexting_-_briefing_(003).pdf (accessed September 2019).

DCMS (2016) *Child Safety Online: A practical guide for providers of social media and interactive services* [online] Available at: www.gov.uk/government/publications/child-safety-online-a-practical-guide-for-providers-of-social-media-and-interactive-services/ (accessed September 2019).

Chapter 8: Multi Agency Public Protection Arrangements (MAPPA)

By Sally Lester and Duncan Sheppard (edited by Nigel Boulton)

Chapter overview

- Background to MAPPA.

- Roles and responsibilities of component bodies.

- MAPPA categories.

- Levels of MAPPA management.

- MAPP meetings.

- Information sharing and ViSOR.

- Liaison with victims.

- Serious case reviews.

- National oversight of MAPPA.

- Active Risk Management System (ARMS).

Background

Multi Agency Public Protection Arrangements (MAPPA) is the name given to the framework under which organisations work together in partnership to assess and manage sexual and violent offenders, and individuals deemed to present a risk of harm to other people. The arrangements are designed to protect the public, including previous victims of crime, from serious harm.

MAPPA was initially introduced by the Criminal Justice and Court Services Act (2000) (CJCSA) and was strengthened by the Criminal Justice Act (2003) (CJA). This legislation placed on a statutory basis what had previously been a series of ad hoc arrangements that criminal justice agencies and others used to work effectively together to manage these individuals and the attendant risks.

Under these arrangements, MAPPA panels and Strategic Management Boards were established in each of the 42 criminal justice areas in England and Wales. MAPPA is supported nationally by the Public Protection Group (PPG) in HM Prison and Probation Service (HMPPS). MAPPA guidance was issued by the Secretary of State for Justice (Ministry of Justice et al, 2014) under the CJA in order to help the relevant agencies in dealing with MAPPA offenders, and has been periodically updated[12]. All relevant agencies are required to have regard to this guidance.

MAPPA is not a statutory body in itself but is rather a mechanism through which agencies can better discharge their statutory responsibilities and protect the public in a co-ordinated manner. It consists of a set of procedures and, most importantly, meetings at which individual cases can be discussed with input and intelligence from a range of relevant organisations and sources.

It is an important principle of the arrangements that MAPPA itself cannot make decisions, but it is the collective responsibility of the agencies involved and present to make decisions and be held accountable. Agencies at all times retain their normal statutory responsibilities and obligations. They need to ensure that these are not compromised by MAPPA. In particular, no agency should ever feel pressured to agree to a course of action that they consider is in conflict with their statutory obligations and their wider responsibility for public protection.

Composition of MAPPA

A number of 'component bodies' are legally required to support MAPPA and the day-to-day running of the arrangements. For more detail of the precise bodies see p258

Responsible Authority

The Responsible Authority is the primary agency for MAPPA and consists of the police, the prison service and National Probation Service (NPS), working together. The Responsible Authority has a duty to ensure that the risks posed by specified sexual and violent offenders are assessed and managed appropriately.

---

12 The most recent update was published in April 2019.

In 2014, under the Transforming Rehabilitation Programme, Probation Trusts were replaced by the NPS and 21 Community Rehabilitation Companies (CRCs)[13]. Currently, all MAPPA-eligible offenders who require 'probation services' are managed by the NPS (or the Youth Offending Service (YOS) if they are aged under 18).

Lead Agency

The lead agency is the agency with the main statutory authority and responsibility to manage a MAPPA-qualifying offender in the community. The lead agency will not always be a member of the Responsible Authority i.e. the police, prison service or NPS. All agencies must support the lead agency in the management of a MAPPA-qualifying offender.

'Duty-to-co-operate agencies'

Other bodies have a statutory duty to co-operate with the Responsible Authority in their task, known as 'duty-to-co-operate agencies' (DTC agencies). These include: housing, Youth Offending Services, education, health, Children's Services, providers of electronic monitoring and the UK Border Agency. Their contribution plays an important role in protecting the public by sharing information that improves the assessment and management of the risk of harm presented by individual offenders. Additionally, helping offenders to resettle in the community and reduce offending-related issues contributes to the work to help them avoid reoffending. Co-operation also ensures that all agencies involved know what others are doing and can avoid duplicating or unintentionally compromising the work of others.

Strategic Management Board

The supervision of the work of the MAPPA is carried out by the Strategic Management Board (SMB) in each MAPPA area, which are coterminous with police force areas. It has a range of governance related functions, including monitoring performance, ensuring anti-discriminatory practice, measuring compliance with the MAPPA key performance indicators (KPIs), and producing the annual MAPPA report. The SMB should include senior representatives from each of the DTCs in the area. This is not a statutory requirement, but it is highly recommended.

Lay advisers

The Criminal Justice Act (2003) also provides for an independent perspective on the work of these groups by lay advisers, who are members of the public. The Secretary of State has a statutory duty to appoint two lay advisers to each MAPPA area.

---

13 At the time of writing, the re-nationalisation of probation has just been announced.

Identification and notification of MAPPA offenders

When a person has been cautioned or convicted of a violent or sexual crime, the first responsibility of the relevant bodies is to identify whether the individual may be liable to management under MAPPA. The agencies responsible for this assessment are probation, police, prisons, youth offending services (YOSs) and mental health services.

If a case meets the relevant criteria, the local MAPPA co-ordinator is notified of the offender's forthcoming release into the community, or the commencement of a community order or suspended sentence. It is the agency that has the leading statutory responsibility for the case that will notify the MAPPA co-ordinator. Offenders are then placed into one of three MAPPA categories, according to the seriousness of the offence and sentence.

MAPPA categories

Category 1 offenders: registered sexual offenders (RSOs)

This category includes offenders required to comply with the notification requirements set out in Part 2 of the Sexual Offences Act (2003) (SOA (2003)). These offenders are often referred to as being on the 'sexual offender's register'.

A person will become subject to the notification requirements of Part 2 of the SOA (2003) if, for an offence listed in schedule 3 of the SOA (2003), they are:

■ convicted of an offence

■ found not guilty by reason of insanity

■ found to be under a disability and to have done the act charged

■ cautioned in respect of such an offence (in England, Wales or Northern Ireland).

The police are notified in advance of the release or discharge of offenders who will be subject to the notification requirements in the community. National arrangements are in place to make sure this happens for offenders leaving prison or youth custody. The MAPPA Co-ordination Unit informs the police of any notifications from the mental health services of offenders who are about to be discharged from hospital and who will be in Category 1.

Category 2 offenders: violent offenders and other sexual offenders

It is important to note that a conviction for a violent offence in Part 1, or a sexual offence in Part 2, of Schedule 15 of the Criminal Justice Act (2003), does not make the offender subject to MAPPA Category 2 unless he or she also receives one of the sentences listed below at A.

The following offenders are included in Category 2:

A. Those convicted of a relevant offence (murder or any of the offences in Schedule 15 of the Criminal Justice Act (2003)) who receive one of the following sentences:

- Imprisonment for a term of 12 months or more (note that this includes a sentence of an indeterminate term and cases where the sentence is suspended).

- Detention in youth detention accommodation for a term of 12 months or more (note that this includes a sentence of an indeterminate term and cases where the sentence is suspended).

- A hospital order (with or without restrictions) or guardianship order.

B. Those found not guilty of a relevant offence (murder or any of the offences in Schedule 15 to the CJA (2003)) by reason of insanity or to be under a disability (unfit to stand trial) and to have done the act charged who receive a hospital order (with or without restrictions).

In the majority of cases where sexual offenders attract the serious penalties described above, they will also be liable to registration as a sexual offender and therefore listed as Category 1. There are a small number of cases where either the sexual offence itself does not attract registration or the sentence does not cross the above thresholds for registration. In these cases, the offender may be listed in Category 2.

The legislation is not retrospective and therefore only includes those offenders who have been sentenced (or received a Disqualification Order) since April 2001, or who were serving a sentence for a relevant offence on that date. They remain in Category 2 only for so long as the sentence for that offence or the Disqualification Order is current.

Those convicted of sexual offences who served their sentence before the introduction of the sex offender registration in 1997 are not listed under Category 2 on this basis, nor are those offenders who have completed their period of registration (unless they also have a Disqualification Order). If there are concerns about the risk an offender presents, options for consideration are:

- applying for a civil order
- considering whether they meet the criteria for Category 3.

Category 3 offenders: other dangerous offenders

This category contains offenders who do not meet the criteria for either Category 1 or Category 2 but who have committed an offence and are considered by the Responsible Authority to pose a risk of serious harm to the public which requires active multi-agency management. For example, it could include offenders under the supervision of probation services or youth offending services on a community sentence or order.

To register a Category 3 offender, the Responsible Authority must establish that a person has either:

- a conviction for any offence (current or historic, within the UK or abroad)
- received a formal caution (adult or young person) or reprimand/warning (young person) for any offence
- been found not guilty of any offence by reason of insanity
- been found to be under a disability (unfit to stand trial) and to have committed any act charged against him or her.

And:

- the offence for which they qualify indicates that the person may be capable of causing serious harm to the public.

Offenders should not be registered as Category 3 unless a multi-agency approach at Level 2 or 3 (see below) is necessary to manage the risks they present.

Offenders can only be identified in one of the three categories at a time. They can only be considered for Category 3 if they do not meet the criteria for Category 1 or Category 2, and they can only fall into Category 2 if they do not meet the criteria for Category 1. However, an offender who ceases to meet the criteria of one category can still be identified in a different category if they meet the relevant criteria.

Levels of MAPPA management

Within each of the categories there are three different levels of management i.e. an offender can be Category 1 and under Level 2 management.

The three levels of MAPPA management are:

- Level 1: ordinary agency management.

- Level 2: active multi-agency management.

- Level 3: active enhanced multi-agency management.

Level 1 case

Ordinary agency management at Level 1 is where the risks posed by the offender can be managed by the agency responsible for the supervision or case management of the offender. This does not mean that other agencies will not be involved, only that it is not considered necessary to refer the case to a Level 2 or 3 MAPPA meeting.

It is essential that information sharing takes place, disclosure is considered, and there are discussions between agencies as necessary.

The relevant Responsible Authority agency must have arrangements in place to review cases managed at Level 1 in line with their own policies and procedures.

Level 2 case

Cases should be managed at Level 2 where:

- the offender is assessed as posing a high or very high risk of serious harm, or

- the risk level is lower, but the case requires the active involvement and co-ordination of interventions from other agencies to manage the presenting risks of serious harm, or

- the case has been previously managed at Level 3 but no longer meets the criteria for Level 3, or

- multi-agency management adds value to the lead agency's management of the risk of serious harm posed.

Level 3 case

Level 3 management should be used for cases that meet the criteria for Level 2 but where it is determined that the management issues require senior representation from the Responsible Authority and DTC agencies. This may be when there is a perceived need to commit significant resources at short notice or where, although not assessed as high or very high risk of serious harm, there is a high likelihood of media scrutiny or public interest in the management of the case and there is a need to ensure that public confidence in the criminal justice system is maintained.

Categories and levels

It is important to stress that the level of management is not directly related to the level of risk; in other words, a Level 3 case is not necessarily riskier than a Level 2. The management level is about the *extra value* a MAPPA meeting can provide. So, if the case is being managed at Level 1, but due to a change in circumstances extra resources from other agencies are required (for example, housing or a mental health assessment) then consideration can be given to raising the level of management to Level 2, when a formal meeting will take place, even though the level of risk may not have increased. However, there will be other times when there is a clear link between the level of management and degree of risk and the more resources required will increase in line with an increased level of risk.

There is a central question in determining the correct MAPPA level: what is the lowest level of case management that provides a defensible risk management plan (RMP)?

The majority of MAPPA-eligible offenders are managed at Level 1 i.e. through the ordinary management of one agency, although this will often involve sharing information with other relevant agencies. The figures below are for 2017/18.

Table 8.1: MAPPA category figures

	Category 1	Category 2	Category 3	Total
Management levels	Registered sexual offenders	Violent offenders	Other dangerous offenders	
Level 1	57,989	21,570	–	79,559
Level 2	601	426	249	1276
Level 3	47	60	41	148
Total	58,637	22,056	290	80,983

Note: Category 3 offenders are managed only at Level 2 and Level 3.
(Ministry of Justice, 2018)

Key learning: Examples of category management

Samuel, a UK national, was convicted abroad of rape of an adult woman and sentenced to five years imprisonment. Following his sentence, he was deported back to the UK where police applied for a Notification Order (NO) to have him placed on the sex offenders' register. Once the NO had been granted by the court, he was subject to all the requirements of sex offender management as if he had been convicted in the UK. He qualified for MAPPA as a Category 1 registered sex offender and was subject to indefinite notification requirements. The lead agency was the police.

Hassan was convicted of Section 18 of the Offences Against the Persons Act (1861) of grievous bodily harm on his partner and sentenced to three years' imprisonment. This offender then qualified as a MAPPA Category 2 offender as he had been convicted of a relevant violent offence and had been sentenced to 12 months or more imprisonment. Due to the concerns about his ex-partner, the offender was managed at Level 2, requiring formal MAPPA meetings to discuss the management in the community. The lead agency was the National Probation Service (NPS). Following the end of this offender's licence, management by the NPS ceased, however due to the continuing concerns he was kept at Level 2 management but moved from Category 2 to Category 3, with the lead agency being the police.

Sharon was convicted of a minor assault and harassment of her ex-partner and received a community sentence. There were a number of concerning elements to the case, which the offender manager wanted to discuss at a MAPPA Level 2 meeting. The offender will not qualify as a Category 2 due to not receiving a 12-month or more custodial sentence, however she qualified as a Category 3 offender and can be managed at either Level 2 or 3.

Lead agency

The lead agency is the organisation with the statutory authority and responsibility to manage a MAPPA offender in the community.

The police are responsible for managing MAPPA offenders in Category 1 (registered sexual offenders), although in practice they will often share the management with the NPS or YOS because many offenders will be subject to supervision on licence or a community order.

The NPS is responsible for the management of Category 2 offenders aged 18 and over who are released on licence from a sentence of 12 months' custody or more. Those aged under 18 will be managed by the YOS.

The NPS may be the lead agency for Category 3 offenders.

All MAPPA offenders must be managed by the lead agency in the relevant MAPPA area. Where an offender is serving a prison sentence, the Responsible Authority will be identified by the agency managing the case. If there is any dispute over the location of the Responsible Authority, this will be determined by the original committing magistrate's court. The Violent and Sex Offender Register (ViSOR) national data system (see p257) will indicate the officer, agency and area managing the offender. When an offender is released on licence or discharged from hospital, the Responsible Authority will be identified by the agency managing the case. If the offender is not returning to live in the original area post-release, the location will be determined by either:

■ the transfer policy of the National Probation Service

■ the Young Offender Service transfer process

■ registration requirements for sexual offenders

■ discharge arrangements from hospital.

Information sharing

The purpose of sharing information about individuals (known as data subjects) is to enable the relevant agencies to work more effectively together in assessing risks and considering how to manage them. The sharing of information must be in accordance with the law, and any information shared must be relevant, proportionate and necessary. Agencies need to strike the right balance between a desire to share all relevant information so that nothing is overlooked and public protection is not compromised on the one hand, and the importance of respecting the rights of data subjects on the other, which will limit what can be shared in terms of relevance and proportionality. This decision needs to be informed by an understanding of the General Data Protection Regulation (GDPR), Data Protection Act (2018) and the Human Rights Act (1998) (HRA (1998)). The Criminal Justice Act (2003) expressly permits the sharing of information between the Responsible Authority agencies for MAPPA purposes.

Chapter 9 provides further details concerning information sharing and the law.

ViSOR

ViSOR is a national, secure, confidential database that supports MAPPA. It provides a central store for sharing up-to-date information and intelligence between the three Responsible Authority agencies (probation, police and prisons) as well as the recording of risk assessments, risk management plans and the minutes of MAPP meetings.

ViSOR improves the safe transfer of key information when MAPPA offenders move between areas, including to other UK jurisdictions. It also provides consistent management information to support the SMB in performance analysis and improvement.

A ViSOR record must be created for all MAPPA offenders, including those currently serving custodial sentences.

The responsibility for creating and managing ViSOR records is as follows:

- Category 1 offenders – the police.

- Category 2 offenders – the National Probation Service is responsible for Category 2 cases managed at Level 2 and 3.

- Category 3 offenders – where the case was actively managed by the National Probation Service on licence and, at its expiry, the management has been transferred to Category 3, or the offender is currently being managed on a community order, the National Probation Service is responsible for the management of the case on ViSOR.

- For all other Category 3 cases, the police are responsible for the creation and management of records.

MAPP meetings

The structural basis for the discussion of MAPPA offenders who need active inter-agency management is the MAPP meeting. The Responsible Authority agencies and the MAPPA co-ordinator are permanent members of these meetings; DTC agencies are then invited to attend as necessary for any offender for whom they can provide additional support and management. The frequency of meetings depends on the level of management deemed appropriate for the individual.

Neither offenders nor their representatives are permitted to attend MAPP meetings.

The structure of MAPP meetings

The purpose of a MAPP meeting is for agencies to share information that informs a multi-agency assessment of the likelihood of reoffending and of the risk of serious harm to other people. The accuracy and completeness of this assessment is critical to inform an effective MAPPA risk management plan (RMP) – a plan of work with the offender that addresses all the risks identified in the assessment. Actions may be allocated to the constituent agencies, who are responsible for delivering these and for reporting back on progress.

Attendance at MAPP meetings: roles and responsibilities for professionals

Because Level 1 management is the sole responsibility of one agency, formal MAPP meetings do not have to take place for these offenders. While other agencies may be involved in their management from time to time, this is dealt with in a less formalised manner.

An effective Level 2 or Level 3 meeting requires representatives from agencies to be able to make decisions that commit those agencies' resources. Therefore, at Level 2 and Level 3 MAPP meetings, all agencies must either be represented by the SMB agreed level of personnel or have delegated their authority to a representative.

Continuity of personnel enhances the effectiveness of Level 2 and Level 3 MAPP meetings by establishing good working relationships across agencies. Some areas establish a standing membership from key agencies for their Level 2 and 3 MAPP meetings. These representatives ensure that all relevant information from their area of work is made available to the meeting and sometimes suggest who should additionally be invited to assist in the management of a specific case.

The meeting is chaired by a police or probation representative of senior rank.

Police

The police attend or chair all Level 2 and 3 meetings. The officer attending the meetings should be of high enough rank to allocate police resources. This will usually be an Inspector for Level 2 and Chief Inspector for Level 3.

In addition, where the case being discussed concerns a registered sexual offender, a police officer from the MOSOVO (Managing Sexual Offenders and Violent Offenders) team who has detailed knowledge of the offender also attends the meeting. In other cases, meetings are attended by police from specialist units e.g. child protection or domestic violence, or by an officer from a Basic Command Unit who is able to provide local intelligence where required.

National Probation Service

Managers from the National Probation Service attend or chair all Level 2 and 3 meetings, usually at the grade of middle manager for Level 2 and senior manager for Level 3.

Where the case is managed by the National Probation Service, the offender manager responsible for the case attends along with other NPS staff who are actively engaged with the offender and can contribute to the risk assessment and management e.g. staff from approved premises where the individual is residing.

Victim liaison officers attend or provide reports where they are actively engaged with the victim or the victim's family, either under the statutory Victim Contact Scheme or on a discretionary basis.

Prisons

In cases where the offender is in custody, the Prison Service or private sector contracted prison management should provide an intelligence report (MAPPA F form). Where appropriate, a prison representative should attend the meeting in person or by video or telephone conferencing, as they may be able to provide information that is crucial to the effective assessment and management of the offender's risk of harm to others both during the sentence and on release. In some cases, there are specific actions that the prison service may take to assist in the delivery of the risk management plan.

Other agencies

Where the referral has come from another agency, the case manager from that agency must attend with any other colleagues who are required to assist in the risk assessment and management of the offender.

The general responsibilities of the DTC agencies should inform the contributions that representatives make to MAPP meetings.

- **Youth Offending Services** refer to MAPPA all young people for whom they are responsible who meet the MAPPA eligibility criteria, for undertaking a comprehensive risk assessment. A representative from the YOS and Children's Services should attend relevant meetings.

- **Jobcentre Plus**[14] should assist with and restrict employment and training in order to protect the public.

- **The local education authority** can make a helpful contribution to the work of MAPPA by providing child protection awareness training for pupils, and by

---

14 Technically referred to as 'Ministers of the Crown exercising functions in relation to social security, child support, war pensions' employment and training'.

being alert to local activities that could provide a threat to pupils, and taking appropriate action.

- **The local housing provider** can provide helpful advice about accommodation, the procedures by which it is allocated and the suitability of housing stock. They do not have a specific duty to accommodate an offender unless the individual is in a defined priority needs category.

- **Registered social landlords** are a diverse sector. Where they accommodate MAPPA offenders, an information sharing protocol should be in place.

- **The local authority** has a statutory duty under section 47 of the Children Act (1989) to safeguard a child's welfare where they have reasonable cause to suspect that the child is suffering, or may suffer, from significant harm. This may include working with MAPPA agencies to manage the risk that a known dangerous offender poses to children in the area. The Local Safeguarding Children Board should link to the local MAPPA and ensure that policies and procedures are compatible. Similarly, the Safeguarding Adults Boards require local agencies to collaborate to protect an adult at risk.

- **Health services**, including a range of health practitioners and administrators, may be involved with MAPPA – for example, some MAPPA cases may be offenders with a history of mental ill-health. Mental Health Trusts also have a statutory role in relation to certain MAPPA offenders. Responsible Authority agencies may be involved with the management of a patient through the Care Programme Approach (CPA), which is consistent with management at Level 1. Referral to MAPPA Levels 2 or 3 should only be made when it is clear that the CPA is not equipped to deal with the risks identified.

- **Providers of electronic monitoring (EM)** are responsible for 'tagging' offenders using either radio frequency tags, which monitor breach of curfew requirements, or, more recently, tags which use Global Positioning System (GPS). The latter, rolled out nationally in 2019, provide location monitoring and can be used to monitor adherence to both inclusion and exclusion zones. They can be used to support the management of offenders on Home Detention Curfew (HDC), or those on parole or community orders, which may include some MAPPA offenders. The EM provider may be able to contribute to the assessment and further management of the risks presented by an individual.

- **Immigration Enforcement** was added to the DTCs in 2011 in the light of informal co-operation that had developed between the agency and local criminal justice agencies. The aim is to ensure that Immigration Enforcement can prioritise the most dangerous sexual and violent offenders and improve the information flow to immigration removal centres (IRCs) to manage the risk from individuals and safeguard vulnerable adults and children.

Specialist police forces

- **The British Transport Police (BTP)** serves the community through actively managing offending and anti-social behaviour on the railway network. It is part of the ViSOR community and, where appropriate, should be involved in the risk management of MAPPA offenders.

- **The Royal Military Police** is the military specialist for all three branches of the armed forces and is responsible for policing the military community worldwide. They work closely with local police to ensure that the requirements of the Sexual Offences Act (2003) are met in relevant cases. The Royal Military Police is part of the ViSOR community.

- **The Civil Nuclear Constabulary (CNC)** provides protection for nuclear sites and materials. Where appropriate, the local police will share information with the CNC.

Content of the meeting

The MAPPA Guidance (Ministry of Justice *et al*, 2014) recommends standard documents known as the MAPPA Document Set. These were introduced in order to establish national consistency, particularly with regard to referral and minute-taking for Level 2 and 3 cases. The meeting agenda is laid out in the document set. Attendees at a Level 2 MAPP meeting should be provided with the original referral information on all occasions when the case is discussed. Additional information from other agencies will be provided at the meeting.

The meeting must include:

- a statement about confidentiality
- current assessment of risks
- an agreed a risk management plan based on the risks including any potential victim safety plan
- consideration of any diversity issues that may affect the offender or have a bearing on the risks he or she may present, and how these will be managed
- a decision as to whether disclosure of information to a third party should take place (Level 2 and 3 meetings)
- consideration of how to handle any press or media interest, where this may be relevant
- identification of the ViSOR record owner who will be responsible for updating the record.

The chair draws together all available information to inform the MAPPA Risk Management Plan (RMP). A date will be set for a review meeting, unless a decision has been taken to manage the case at Level 1. Where the offender is managed in the community, this review should be at least every 16 weeks for a Level 2 case, and at least every eight weeks for a Level 3 case.

Reducing, or where appropriate increasing, the level of MAPPA management should be considered at the end of every meeting. The decision should be based on the most appropriate management level for the case rather than the level of assessed risk. There is always the option of re-referring any case that warrants the higher MAPPA level management because of changing circumstances.

MAPP meeting minutes

In working with offenders, victims and other members of the public, all agencies have agreed boundaries of confidentiality. The information contained in the MAPP meeting minutes must respect those boundaries of confidentiality and be distributed under a shared understanding that the meeting is called in circumstances where it is felt that the risk presented by the offender is so great that issues of public or individual safety outweigh those rights of confidentiality.

MAPPA is not an official body in itself but a set of arrangements that exist to assess and manage the risks posed by offenders. No individual MAPPA agency has the authority to release confidential information shared at the meetings without the express permission of the chair, who may consider whether an executive summary of the minutes might be appropriate.

This summary would include: the reason for referral to a MAPP meeting; the referring agency but not the name of the referring officer; a summary of the risks identified; the agreed risk assessment and the level of MAPPA management required; an outline of the RMP; dates of recent meetings and details of the chair. General victim issues can be included but care must be taken not to include any sensitive victim information, or anything that may identify a victim or place them at risk.

Terrorists and domestic extremists

Some extremist offenders will be identified by the nature of their conviction. Terrorist legislation offences are listed in Schedule 15 to the CJA (2003). However, for others, the court will determine the nature of the link to terrorism or domestic extremism, for example those where the circumstances of the offence demonstrate a terrorist motive, or those convicted of offences committed in the name of a cause. Given the nature of their offending, these offenders should be considered for active multi-agency management at MAPPA Level 2 or 3, even though some may have committed what appears to be a low-level offence. Some may be subject to electronic monitoring using special case protocols.

Given the potential risks associated with this group of offenders, the Responsible Authority maintains an interest in their management and has specialists who can provide advice and support.

Foreign national offenders

The MAPPA processes for foreign national offenders (FNOs) who are living in the community are the same as for UK citizens. It is important to remember that MAPPA Category 1 offenders are subject to the same notification requirements as UK nationals – this is particularly relevant for foreign travel.

Prisons are required to notify Immigration Enforcement of certain categories of FNOs once convicted and sentenced. The notification form includes a question to identify if the FNO is a MAPPA nominal. The Offender Manager will liaise with Immigration Enforcement about release arrangements and licence conditions and will advise Immigration Enforcement regarding risk of serious harm, to enable consideration of whether the FNO should be detained further in prison or an immigration removal centre (IRC). In some cases, this will require referral to a Level 2 or Level 3 MAPP meeting.

Offenders with mental health issues and MAPPA

There are a number of provisions of the Criminal Justice Act (2003) under which offenders with mental health issues may become subject to MAPPA. These may be summarised as follows:

The offender is subject to the notification requirements of the SOA (2003) if:

- The offender is convicted of a relevant offence and receives a custodial sentence of 12 months or more, or a hospital or guardianship order under the Mental Health Act (1983) (MHA (1983)).

- The offender is charged with a relevant offence but is found not guilty by reason of insanity or to be under a disability (unfit to stand trial), but the court finds that the offender has committed the crime and as a result gives them a hospital order or guardianship order.

- The Responsible Authority considers that an offender with mental health issues, by reason of his or her offences, presents a risk of serious harm to the public.

Offenders with mental health issues who are subject to MAPPA may be detained in hospital having either been sent there directly by the court making a hospital or guardianship order, or by the Secretary of State while in prison or in immigration detention. Those living in the community may have been conditionally discharged under the MHA (1983) or may be subject to a community treatment order.

The MAPPA co-ordinator does not have routine access to case records held by mental health services, so the appropriate notification will need to be completed. The management of the case remains the responsibility of the hospital. The responsible clinician has the discretion to communicate significant events to the MAPPA co-ordinator, for example when the patient may be granted leave out of the hospital grounds, or transfers to another hospital.

More details about the management of MAPPA-eligible offenders who have mental health issues are available in the *MAPPA Guidance* (Ministry of Justice, 2012, V4.4, updated March 2019).

Critical public protection cases

A critical public protection case (CPPC) is an offender who is already a Level 3 case, but it is deemed that extra resources are required in order to manage and mitigate risk. These may include temporary additional staff cover or upgrading facilities in an approved premise, escort duties, or specific interventions that will contribute to public protection. The management of a very small number of registered CPPCs requires national oversight, which is provided by a dedicated team. National CPPC arrangements are reserved for genuinely exceptional cases where areas require additional support to manage the ongoing risk to individuals (public, victims, staff or offender), or where ministers may have an interest in the case due to the national profile of the offence, the offenders and their victims.

Liaison with victims

Victim safety, preventing re-victimisation and avoiding the creation of new victims is fundamental to the MAPPA agencies' public protection role. It is essential that MAPPA agencies' decision-making is informed by effective engagement with previous and current victims, and where practicable and appropriate, with potential victims as well. Only by doing this can the Responsible Authority be satisfied that the risk assessment and the RMP reflect concerns about victims and provide appropriate measures to protect them.

Under the CJCSA (2000), as amended by the Domestic Violence, Crime and Victims Act (2004), where the offender has been sentenced to 12 months or more in custody, or has been made the subject of certain mental health disposals, a Victim Liaison Officer (VLO) employed by the National Probation Service is required to contact victims of serious sexual and violent offences and offer the services of the Victim Contact Scheme. The aim of this contact is to provide specified information to the victim, such as the month of release, and to allow the victim to make representation about which conditions they would wish to see on any release licence to reassure and protect them, and also to represent their views at each appropriate MAPP meeting. Victims may not attend MAPP meetings in person.

Victims can make an important contribution to risk assessment and they may have a critical interest in the management of risk, but, while active and important, it is not an executive role. The victim is central to the offence and may understand the risk the offender presents, but he or she informs rather than decides the RMP because ultimately he or she is not responsible for delivering it.

Links with a Multi-Agency Risk Assessment Conference (MARAC)

The focus of a MARAC is the protection of those victims who are at a high risk of serious harm from domestic abuse. A meeting is convened to share information to enable an effective RMP to be developed. To avoid duplicating effort and resources, the work of a MARAC and MAPPA should be co-ordinated in such a way as to provide the most effective response to the victim. The MAPP meeting should take precedence over the MARAC as it is a statutory set of arrangements. Where an offender is managed at Level 2 or 3 of MAPPA, and the victim has been referred to the local MARAC, the Independent Domestic Violence Advisers (IDVA) are invited to the MAPP meeting. The quality of the MAPPA RMP will be enhanced by the additional information that the IDVA and others can provide.

MAPPA Serious Case Reviews (SCR)

Although the risk of serious harm can be managed, it cannot be eliminated. The Responsible Authority and DTC agencies are expected to do all they reasonably can to protect the public from serious harm, but there will be occasions when an offender who is subject to MAPPA commits a Serious Further Offence (SFO). In these circumstances, a MAPPA Serious Case Review (MAPPA SCR) may be undertaken to examine whether the arrangements were effectively applied and whether the agencies worked together to do all they reasonably could to manage effectively the risk of further offending in the community.

The aims of the MAPPA SCR will be to establish whether there are lessons to be learned, to identify them clearly, to decide how they will be acted upon, and, as a result, to inform the future development of MAPPA policies and procedures in order to protect the public better. It may also identify areas of good practice.

Mandatory SCRs

The Strategic Management Board must commission a MAPPA SCR if both of the following conditions apply:

- The MAPPA offender (in any category) was being managed at Level 2 or 3 when the offence was committed or at any time in the 28 days before the offence was committed.

- The offence is murder, attempted murder, manslaughter, rape or attempted rape.

Discretionary SCR

There will be other SFOs which may trigger a MAPPA SCR. This will depend on the circumstances of the particular case and whether there has been a significant breach of the MAPPA Guidance, but MAPPA SCRs might be commissioned when:

- a Level 1 offender is charged with murder, manslaughter, rape or an attempt to commit murder or rape

- an offender being managed at any level is charged with a serious offence

- it would otherwise be in the public interest to undertake a review e.g. following an offence which results in serious physical or psychological harm to a child or vulnerable adult.

Responsible Authority National Steering Group (RANSG)

This is the national co-ordinating body tasked with exercising oversight of MAPPA and ensuring its continued development. It is chaired by the Head of the OMPPG in HMPPS. The RANSG produces a national MAPPA business plan annually, which the Responsible Authority will be required to mirror in the Strategic Management Board (SMB) business plan.

National MAPPA team

This is a team based within the PPG, consisting of civil servants and seconded staff from police and from across HMPPS. Its functions include:

- issuing MAPPA guidance on behalf of the Secretary of State
- producing the national MAPPA annual statistics
- managing the appointment of lay advisors
- collecting and disseminating good MAPPA and public protection practice
- supporting local areas with training
- advising and supporting local MAPPA on the management of complex cases and on public protection issues
- providing advice, support and quality assurance for MAPPA Serious Case Reviews
- working with other government departments and agencies to consider the implications of related policy on MAPPA, public protection and other partnership working.

For more detailed information about MAPPA, you are advised to refer to the full MAPPA guidance (Ministry of Justice, 2012, V4.4, updated March 2019).

Key learning

- Multi Agency Public Protection Arrangements (MAPPA) is a statutory framework under which organisations work together to assess and manage sexual and violent offenders and others who present a risk of harm to other people.

- Police, probation and prisons are the 'Responsible Authority' for MAPPA. Other organisations have a statutory 'Duty to Co-operate'.

- Offenders eligible for MAPPA management are described as Category 1, 2 or 3. They are managed at Levels 1, 2 or 3, depending on the level of management and resources they require.

- The purpose of MAPP meetings is to share information about an individual in order to make an accurate assessment of the risks they present and to put in place a plan to manage their risks. All agencies are responsible for carrying out the actions agreed as part of the plan.

Active Risk Management System (ARMS)[15]

ARMS is a Dynamic Risk Assessment framework that draws together assessment outcomes into a risk management plan. It focuses on the 'here and now' using a range of dynamic factors found to be predictive of reoffending or desistance from offending. The ARMS assessment is designed for use with sex offenders who are male, aged 18 years of age and over. It is designed for use by police officers, probation officers and eventually prison staff who manage sex offenders.

ARMS has been jointly developed by the National Police Chiefs' Council (NPCC) and HMPPS and is owned by these two agencies. The development of ARMS arose from a detailed review undertaken by the Ministry of Justice Multi Agency Risk Assessment Advisory Group (MARAAG) into the current effectiveness of existing risk assessment frameworks for sexual offenders. The framework is compatible with the needs of the three primary agencies charged with managing the risk posed by sexual offenders – the police, the National Probation Service and the prison service. It not only identifies significant risk factors but also takes account of the role of protective factors in encouraging offenders to desist from offending. It then draws these conclusions into a risk management plan.

ARMS is a framework that aims to identify and track current behaviours related to both the risk of recidivism of sexual offending and desistance (termed 'risk and protective factors' in ARMS) and guiding the practitioner in determining the priority of work to be afforded to each factor in terms of risk management planning.

It is a framework that guides the provision of interventions, management strategies and controls based on the strengths and risks of individual offenders. It does not make a conclusion about a dynamic risk level or score. Rather, the framework is designed to arrive at a general level of risk management through which an effective plan is identified and reviewed. It is this emphasis on identifying an action-orientated approach to offender management through which progress can be actively measured that makes ARMS particularly unique.

It is intended to be used from the point of conviction through to case closure, guiding clinical judgment to ensure effective case management. It is in the integration of assessment with risk management planning that allows ARMS to be particularly helpful for structuring effective offender management.

Since development, ARMS has undergone a rigorous evaluation (Donathy & Woodhams, 2014). The findings from three pilot studies were encouraging and saw the project shift from development into implementation and national roll out.

---

15 The remainder of this chapter was written by Duncan Sheppard and Mark Blandford.

ARMS is now expected to be used by the police to assess the risk posed by sexual offenders across England and Wales.

From June 2015, it will be used within the Police Service of England and Wales by all the police offender managers to assess police-managed registered sex offenders in the community.

Rather than replacing existing core arrangements for the risk assessment of sexual offenders, ARMS was developed to be integrated with Risk Matrix 2000 (Hanson & Thornton, 2000; Thornton, 2002) and OASYs (National Offender Management Service, 2002). It was also aligned to factors within Sex Offender Treatment Programmes (Thornton, 2002) and (Mann & Marshall, 2009) and incorporated research derived from strength-based models of offender rehabilitation such as the Good Lives Model (Ward & Stewart, 2003).

ARMS consist of five key stages

- The assessment of a range of risk factors.
- Assessment of a range of protective factors, an overall priority assessment of the case.
- A Risk Matrix 2000 assessment.
- A combination assessment of RM2000 and ARMS priority assessment.
- The assessment of a general level of risk management and finally a risk management plan.

ARMS provide a number of benefits and uses:

- Consistency across police areas in England and Wales.
- A more holistic and balanced approach to the assessment of risk.
- Identifying evidence-based actions aimed at reducing risk or increasing strengths in offenders.
- Can be used as an aid to prioritise actions for the management of risk.
- Can be used as a guide to establishing a visiting timetable in line with national standards.
- Can be used in support of decision making within a multi-agency approach, particularly within the MAPPA framework.

- They provide consistency in defining risk levels that are more linked to the risk associated with the case in question.

- Used in support of applications for civil orders where a more evidence-based assessment of risk is required.

- Where there is an application by the offender to be removed from the register under the Sexual Offences Act (2003) (Remedial) Order 2011.

- Can be used as a national standard for risk management planning.

- Provide supervision with a clear and precise rationale for why certain activity and actions are being undertaken that can be reviewed and measured over time.

ARMS risk factors

ARMS focus is only on those risk factors that have strong empirical support and, importantly, those which are observable to the assessor. These are as follows:

Opportunity

Sexual offending cannot occur unless the opportunity to do so presents itself. This opportunity stage will often be the manifestation of the thought processes undertaken by the offender aimed at engineering the circumstances where an offence can be carried out.

Sexual pre-occupation

This factor has been identified as a significant risk factor and refers to the degree to which an individual's life is dominated by the pursuit of sex. Sexual pre-occupation has long been recognised as having a link with sexual offending and has been found to be a significant predictor of sexual recidivism (Mann *et al*, 2010). The assessor should determine whether the pursuit of sex is the offender's main or sole interest, or whether he has other interests and activities.

Offence-related sexual interests

This risk factor involves sexual interests that are more easily gratified through offending than through legal consensual sexual activities.

Emotional congruence with children

The individual finds it easier to satisfy their needs for friendship, emotional intimacy and romance with children under 14 rather than with adults. It may involve feeling 'in love' with a child, wanting to spend large amounts of time with children, developing interests that would be shared by children.

Hostile orientation

The individual has a negative orientation to others. Grievance thinking, callousness and hostility towards others are recorded under this heading.

Poor self-management

This risk factor involves a chaotic and impulsive lifestyle resulting in stress, boredom, reckless choices and exposure to negative influences, poor regulation of feelings and lack of ability to cope with life's problems.

ARMS protective factors

While much has been written regarding the role of risk factors in predicting future recidivism, less is known about the role of protective factors. Current research appears to indicate that these factors play a significant role in encouraging the offender to desist from offending – something that practitioners can influence and play an active role in encouraging.

ARMs have adopted the following definition for desistance:

'...the process of abstaining from crime among those who previously had engaged in a sustained pattern of offending.' (Maruna, 2001)

Social influences

This factor has two separate and opposing strands to it: anti-social influences and pro-social influences.

Anti-social influences can be described as people that are predominately of a criminal or anti-social nature and whose lives have a negative influence on an individual.

A pro-social network includes those people who the individual has significant contact with, who he values and/or respects, who provide him with social or practical support when they are not paid to. It may include family members, friends and acquaintances that he regularly spends time with.

A commitment to desist

This protective factor involves an individual having identified a pro-social (non-offender) sense of who he is (or is becoming), and he likes that identity. It has been described as creating a new 'self-narrative' where offenders talk about going straight or becoming a new person (Maruna, 2001). This has been described as an ongoing process and one in which practitioners can actively assist.

An intimate relationship

Having a close and valued relationship with a pro-social other person who really knows them and provides healthy emotional support is a valuable protective factor. This should be a relationship that is more than a social acquaintance, and which includes a significant degree of intimacy. While the protective nature of this factor generally relates to spouses and partners, it is possible to have an intimate relationship with a close family member and such relationships should be rated here if contact with the family member is so regular and significant that it breaks up the routine of pro-offending environments or thoughts.

Employment/positive routine

The protective nature of this factor involves a commitment to appropriate, stable employment. In order to act as a protective factor, the employment needs to have a meaning for the offender beyond simply being a means of making a living. For example, if the individual finds their work satisfying, if it gives them a purpose and meaning in their lives, or if it provides a new set of routines that takes the individual out of their old criminal routines, then it is more likely to be protective.

Social investment – 'giving something back'

Offenders who find ways to contribute to society, their community or their families, appear to be more successful at giving up crime, for example the opportunity to mentor, assist or enhance the life of other people. If these achievements are formally recognised, the effect may be even stronger.

Rating ARMS risk and protective factors

It is worth noting that ARMS differ from a number of other frameworks in that, when rating the factor, the assessor is not required to 'score' the existence of the factor. This is because the ARMS framework does not rely upon a percentile ranking to evaluate future risk but rather relies on the assessor to make a subjective evaluation on the extent the factor exists and then to make a determination as to what level of priority should be given to address the particular item rated.

The rating scale is either high, medium or low priority, or unable to rate.

General level of risk management

Arriving at the general level of risk involves the assessor having to consider the Risk Matrix 2000 (Hanson & Thornton, 2000) actuarial assessment of risk against the ARMS overall priority level.

Risk Matrix 2000 is a statistically derived risk classification process for males aged at least 18 years of age who have been convicted of a sexual offence. Developed for use in the UK it uses simple factual information about an offender's past history to divide them into categories of very high, high, medium or low risk that differ substantially in their rates of reconviction for sexual or violent offending.

There is no set formula identified for how the assessor combines the ARMS assessment with the Risk Matrix 2000 assessment, rather the assessor is required to use professional judgment in their consideration using the defined levels of risk management provided to guide their decision. In doing so, the assessor at this point provides a narrative that sets out their conclusions in support of their final assessment.

Further reading

Home Office (2010) *Guidance on Part 2 of the Sexual Offences Act 2003*.

Home Office (2010) *Guidance on Review of Indefinite Notification Requirements Issued Under Section 91F of the Sexual Offences Act 2003*.

Wood J & Kemshall H (2007) *The Operation and Experience of Multi-Agency Public Protection Arrangements (MAPPA)* [online]. London: Home Office. Available at: www.dmu.ac.uk/documents/health-and-life-sciences-documents/research/rdsolr1207. pdf (accessed September 2019).

HMI Probation (2011) *Putting the Pieces Together: An inspection of multi-agency public protection arrangements* [online]. Available at: https://webarchive. nationalarchives.gov.uk/20130206123831/https://www.justice.gov.uk/downloads/ publications/inspectorate-reports/hmiprobation/joint-thematic/mappa-thematic-report.pdf (accessed September 2019).

HMI Probation (2015) *A Follow-Up Inspection of Multi-Agency Public Protection Arrangements* [online]. Available at: www.justiceinspectorates.gov.uk/cjji/wp-content/uploads/sites/2/2015/10/MAPPA-follow-up-thematic-report.pdf (accessed September 2019).

National Policing Improvement Agency on behalf of Association of Chief Police Officers (2010) *Guidance on Protecting the Public Managing Sexual Offenders and Violent Offenders*. Second Edition, Version 2.

National Offender Management Service/de Montfort University (2014) *Risk of Harm Guidance and Training Resources* (available at: http://nomsintranet.org.uk/roh/).

National Offender Management Service (2016) *NOMS Guidance for Working with Domestic Abuse*.

HMI Probation (July 2017) *Probation Hostels' (Approved Premises) Contribution to Public Protection, Rehabilitation and Resettlement* [online]. Available at: www.justiceinspectorates.gov.uk/hmiprobation/wp-content/uploads/sites/5/2017/07/Probation-Hostels-2017-report.pdf (accessed September 2019).

HM Government (July 2018) *Working Together to Safeguard Children*.

HMI Probation (January 2019) *Management and Supervision of Men Convicted of Sexual Offences*. Available at: https://www.justiceinspectorates.gov.uk/hmiprobation/inspections/sexualoffencesthematic/ (accessed September 2019).

Probation Instructions (PIs) are available at: www.justice.gov.uk/offenders/probation-instructions (accessed September 2019). Some also function as Prison Service Instruction (PSIs). The following instructions are of particular relevance to MAPPA:

- PI 02 2014 – Safeguarding of children and vulnerable adults

- PI 05 2014 - PSI 14 2014 Case allocation

- PI 07 2014 Case transfers: For offender's subject to statutory supervision either pre-release from custody or whilst completing an order or licence

- PI 08 2014 – Process for Community Rehabilitation Companies to refer cases in the Community to NPS for review – risk escalation review

- PI 10 2014 – Managing Terrorist and Extremist Offenders in the Community

- PI 15 2014 – Notification and review procedures for Serious Further Offences

- PI 32 2014 Approved Premises

- PI 48/2014 Victim Contact Scheme Guidance Manual (Chapter 3 subsequently amended by PI 03/2017)

- PI 52 2014 – Provision of Offender Risk Information to Home Office Immigration Enforcement Regarding Foreign National Offenders who are being considered for Deportation

- PI 53 2014 - PSI 36 2014 Polygraph Examinations: Instructions for Imposing Licence Conditions for the Polygraph on Sexual Offenders

- PI 56 2014 - PSI 40 2014 Mandatory use of ViSOR

- PI 57 2014 - PSI 41 2014 Process for Community Rehabilitation Companies to refer cases in custody or the community to National Probation Service for risk review, including escalation

- PI 10 2015 - PSI 13 2015 Release on Temporary Licence

- PI 14 2015 - PSI 22 2015 - AI 11 2015 Generic Parole Process for Indeterminate and Determinate Sentenced Prisoners

- PI 15 2015 - AI 16 2015 Implementation of the Active Risk Management System (ARMS)

- PI 06 2016 - PSI 03 2016 - AI 06 2016 Adult Social Care

- PI 14 2016 - PSI 15 2016 Handling of sensitive information, including information provided by victims for the purpose of Parole Board Reviews

- PI 17 2016 - PSI 18 2016 Public Protection Manual

- PI 03 2017 Probation Victim Contact Service – Non-statutory cases

- PI 04 2018 - AI 04 2018 Critical Public Protection Cases MP Notification Scheme

- PI 06 2018 Notification and Review Procedures for Serious Further Offences

- PI 07 2018 - AI 05 2018 Through the Gate (TTG) Instructions and Guidance on Schedule 7

- PI 01 2019 Information Sharing and the Effective Management of the Electronic Monitoring Requirement (Community Sentences)

Some Probation Instructions and Prison Service Instructions have been replaced by Policy Frameworks. The following are relevant to MAPPA and are available at: www.gov.uk/government/collections/prison-probation-policy-frameworks

- Manage the Custodial Sentence Policy Framework (28 November 2018 - reissue date)

- Intelligence Collection, Analysis and Dissemination Policy Framework (11 March 2019)

- Home Detention Curfew (HDC) Policy Framework (28 March 2019)

- Recall, Review and Re-release of Recalled Prisoners Policy Framework (1 April 2019)

- Multi Agency Lifer Risk Assessment Panel (MALRAP) Policy Framework (4 April 2019)

The legislation relevant to this chapter is:

- Mental Health Act (1983)
- Children Act (1989)
- General Data Protection Regulation (2018)
- Data Protection Act (2018)
- Human Rights Act (1998)
- Criminal Justice and Court Services Act (2000)
- Criminal Justice Act (2003)
- Sexual Offences Act (2003)
- Domestic Violence, Crime and Victims Act (2004)
- Safeguarding Vulnerable Groups Act (2006)
- Care Act (2014)
- Social Services and Wellbeing (Wales) Act (2014)
- Violence against Women, Domestic Abuse and Sexual Violence (Wales) Act (2015)

References

Donathy R & Woodhams J (2014) *Active Risk Management System (ARMS): Initial findings from the pilot study.*

Hanson RK & Thornton D (2000) Improving risk assessments for sex offenders: a comparison of three actuarial scales. *Law and Human Behavior* **24** 119–136.

Maruna S (2001) *Making Good: How ex-convicts reform and rebuild their lives.* Washington, DC: American Psychological Association.

Mann RE, Hanson RK & Thornton D (2010) Assessing risk for sexual recidivism: some proposals on the nature of psychologically meaningful risk factors. *Sexual Abuse: A journal of research and treatment* **22** (2) 191–217.

Mann RE & Marshall WL (2009) Advances in the treatment of adult incarcerated sex offenders. In: AR Beech, LA Craig & KD Browne (Eds) *Assessment and Treatment of Sex Offenders: A handbook.* Chichester: John Wiley & Sons.

Ministry of Justice (2012) *MAPPA Guidance 2012 V4.4 updated March 2019* [online]. London: Ministry of Justice. Available at: https://mappa.justice.gov.uk/connect.ti/MAPPA/view?objectId=41211397 (accessed September 2019).

Ministry of Justice (2018) *Multi-Agency Public Protection Arrangements (MAPPA) Annual Report 2017/18* [online]. London: Ministry of Justice. Available at: https://assets.publishing.service.gov.uk/government/uploads/system/uploads/attachment_data/file/751006/mappa-annual-report-2017-18.pdf (accessed September 2019).

Thornton D (2002) Constructing and testing a framework for dynamic risk assessment. *Sexual Abuse: A journal of research and treatment* **14** 139–154.

Thornton D (2007) *Scoring Guide for Risk Matrix 2000* [online]. Available at: www.birmingham.ac.uk/Documents/college-les/psych/RM2000scoringinstructions.pdf (accessed September 2019).

Ward T & CA Stewart (2003) The treatment of sex offenders: risk management and good lives. *Professional Psychology: Research and Practice* **34** 353–360.

Chapter 9: Information sharing and intelligence-led safeguarding

By Nigel Boulton

Chapter overview

- Context.
- Duty to co-operate (work together).
- Understanding need, harm and risk.
- Information sharing and communication.
- Information sharing – the law.
- Consent.
- Necessity, proportionality and relevance.
- Seven golden rules.
- Multi Agency Safeguarding Hubs (MASH).
- Five core elements.
- Basic rules of the MASH model.
- Researching information and intelligence.

Introduction

'Information: Facts provided or learned about something or someone.'

'Intelligence: The collection of information of … value.'
Oxford Dictionary Online (2019)

Many professionals from a range of organisations who are involved with the protection of children and adults at risk have to make difficult decisions about the assessment of need, harm and risk on a daily basis, sometimes alone and with little support or advice. Very often these decisions have a significant impact on the individuals, families and communities involved, and on occasions they have to be made quickly in order to protect the vulnerable. These critical decisions are very often made with little information, sometimes only that available to the professional at the time, and can very often be limited to one agency's knowledge and understanding. There are several well-recognised risk assessment models in existence to help and guide professionals' thinking and decision making (see Chapter 1 (child protection), Chapter 4 (domestic violence) and Chapter 8 (MAPPA) for examples).

However, many important decisions concerning children and adults at risk can and are made in a more controlled environment, where urgency is not the main driver. All local authorities who hold the legal duty to make these decisions do so through a referral and assessment process that will have evolved within the local context.

Seeing the true levels of need, harm and risk within individuals or families is not easy in a society where there are many professionals working within numerous, separate organisations, all of whom may have different levels of knowledge and contact with families and individuals. All these professions have developed over many years and as a result there is no single view of professional involvement and knowledge across the professions.

It is still the case that all statutory organisations at this time use different databases to store their case records and personal data relating to children, adults and families. Some use separate systems within different departments within the same organisation, which may or may not connect with each other, and some are still held as paper records.

It is widely accepted by all the safeguarding professions, therefore, that decisions are better if they are based on the best information and intelligence available at a given time, and yet in the vast majority of cases a complete picture of the information is not held by any single organisation, and rarely by the organisation charged with making a particular decision. Achieving a more complete picture of a case requires organisations to work together closer than ever before, and if this can be achieved then the actions that follow can be more proportionate and relevant to the need, harm and risk being presented at the time.

This chapter discusses the legal and professional context within which decisions are being made. It then identifies the benefits of making some of the more difficult of these decisions from a much stronger foundation of information and intelligence, where knowledge is pooled from across many organisations and professions.

Decisions are not necessarily difficult just because they are critical or urgent in the protection of children. Professionals should always consider the 'No delay' principle within children's social work as a key foundation in their practice. It is fundamental even in the world of multi-agency working and information sharing, that when it is clear an urgent intervention is required on the basic initial information then this is a decision that is not difficult (it will be critical and important) and should be made with no delay.

Finally, it examines the Multi Agency Safeguarding Hub (MASH) style of working, designed to improve information flow between the safeguarding professions in order to aid decision making. This type of knowledge-based decision making is described as intelligence-led safeguarding. It can only occur, however, if multiple organisations and agencies who hold knowledge (information and intelligence) about individuals, children and families share it (within the law) and effectively communicate with each other at the earliest stage when harm or risk is identified, considered or suspected. Where organisations who hold the various pieces of information can work in close partnership to consider concerns about children and adults as soon as they are first raised, then need, harm and risk can be identified much earlier. This early identification can then inform preventative, diversion and intervention strategies.

Sharing information to support decision making is appropriate to all levels of need, harm and risk, not just the highest. In fact, it is fair to say that it is the lower levels of need, harm and risk, for instance where children may be suffering ongoing low levels of neglect, that are among the hardest to identify and understand, and these lower-risk cases can benefit enormously from information sharing at an early stage.

In her review of child protection, Professor Munro (2011) identified the difficulty for professionals when assessing harm and understanding the appropriate support or intervention:

'Statutory guidance tells those working with children and families to refer such children to children's social care but making this decision is not straightforward. Abuse and neglect rarely present with a clear, unequivocal picture. It is often the totality of information, the overall pattern of the child's story that raises suspicions of possible abuse or neglect.'

It is for this reason that this chapter promotes the legal sharing of partnership information at the earliest stage possible, regarding all levels of concern in relation to children and adults with additional needs, suffering harm or at risk.

Context

A local authority has the general duty to safeguard and promote the welfare of children within their area who are in need, and so far as is consistent with that duty, to promote the upbringing of such children by their families by providing a range and level of services appropriate to those children's needs. Where there is reasonable cause to suspect that a child is suffering, or likely to suffer, significant harm, the local authority is required under Section 47 of the Children Act (1989) to make enquiries to enable it to decide whether it should take any action to safeguard and promote the welfare of the child.

For many years the Department of Health guidance *No Secrets* (2000a) provided the driver for adult safeguarding, stating that, 'Local authority social services departments should play a co-ordinating role in developing the local policies and procedures for the protection of vulnerable adults from abuse'.

The Care Act (2014) put this on a statutory footing for the first time, stating under Sections 42 (1-3):

'Where a local authority has reasonable cause to suspect that an adult in its area (whether or not ordinarily resident there);

has needs for care and support (whether or not the authority is meeting any of those needs)

is experiencing, or is at risk of, abuse or neglect, and

as a result of those needs is unable to protect himself or herself against the abuse or neglect or the risk of it.

The local authority must make (or cause to be made) whatever enquiries it thinks necessary to enable it to decide whether any action should be taken in the adult's case and, if so, what and by whom.'

Abuse includes financial abuse, which is further defined in the Act (see Chapter 4).

Duty to co-operate/work together

The Children Act (2004) (as amended by the Social Work Act (2017)) defines safeguarding partners and their duty to co-operate to safeguard and promote the welfare of children.

Section 16 E (1) states:

'The safeguarding partners for a local authority area in England must make arrangements for:

the safeguarding partners, and

any relevant agencies that they consider appropriate

to work together … to safeguard and promote the welfare of children in the area.'

Section 16 E (3) identifies the safeguarding partners as the local authority, the police and a Clinical Commissioning Group for the area.

It also describes relevant agencies being any person who is either specified in a regulation as such by the secretary of state or exercises the functions in relation to children. This enshrines in law the requirement for all organisations who work to safeguard or promote the welfare of children in a local authority area to work together.

Working Together to Safeguard Children: A guide to inter-agency working to safeguard and promote the welfare of children (Department for Education, 2018) reinforces the working together responsibility stating:

'The three safeguarding partners should agree on ways to co-ordinate their safeguarding services; act as a strategic leadership group in supporting and engaging others; and implement local and national learning including from serious child safeguarding incidents.'

Section 6 of The Care Act (2014) identifies a list of statutory organisations with whom the local authority must co-operate to deliver their respective functions to safeguard adults at risk. The section also identifies what form this co-operation may take and exemptions to it (see Chapter 4).

Understanding need, harm and risk

Levels of need, harm and risk can vary depending on the circumstances and context an individual or family may be in at any given time. Need, harm and risk also alter, sometimes rapidly, as circumstances change.

To protect children and adults or to provide support firstly requires the authorities charged with delivering the services to be able to see the need, harm or risk as early as possible. They need to assess it as best they can and, based on this understanding, make the best decision they can concerning support as well as prevention, diversion or intervention. This understanding of the need, harm and risk can be used to make proportionate decisions concerning the levels of prevention and intervention.

In simplified terms, the law and professional practice at present describe various levels of need, harm and risk in two distinct ways: harm and risk that require a statutory response, commonly referred to as 'being above the threshold' (referring to a statutory threshold above which a local authority is required to intervene through social work practice), and need, harm and risk that falls below that threshold.

Working Together (2018) states:

'The safeguarding partners should publish a threshold document, which sets out the local criteria for action in a way that is transparent, accessible and easily understood. This should include:

- *the process for the early help assessment and the type and level of early help services to be provided*
- *the criteria, including the level of need, for when a case should be referred to local authority children's social care for assessment and for statutory services under:*
    - *section 17 of the Children Act (1989) (children in need)*
    - *section 47 of the Children Act (1989) (reasonable cause to suspect a child is suffering or likely to suffer significant harm)*
    - *section 31 of the Children Act (1989) (care and supervision orders)*
    - *section 20 of the Children Act (1989) (duty to accommodate a child)*
- *Also clear procedures and processes for cases relating to:*
    - *the abuse, neglect and exploitation of children*
    - *children managed within the youth secure estate*
    - *disabled children.*

This should be readily available in all local areas.'

All children and young people resident within England and Wales are entitled to the range of services that sit on a continuum, including universal services, targeted services for vulnerable children, and safeguarding and specialist services if their needs are assessed as being complex or acute.

The levels are:

Universal: Level 1. All children and young people require universal services at some point at Level 1. Parent(s)/carer(s) plan for example how their children will access these services e.g. choosing a school, appointment at a dentist etc.

Universal Plus: Level 2. Many children and young people require some additional support – this can be provided within a universal setting or by additional services e.g. School Learning Mentor or additional support from a health visitor. Parent(s)/carer(s) usually access these services for their children by applying directly to them or by asking the relevant universal service to help them. Young people can directly access some services. Where two or more additional services are needed, it is advisable for the parent to be offered help to get the right help for their child by assessing the child or young person's needs using an Early Help Assessment (EHA).

Targeted support: Level 3. If the EHA recommends the provision of services, a lead professional to support the child, young person, and parent(s) will co-ordinate the plan through a Team Around the Family (TAF) meeting. A smaller number of children and young people have higher levels of need and require a co-ordinated multi-agency plan and partnership decision making.

Specialist/ Acute: Level 4. Some children and young people and their families have more complex needs requiring a Social Work assessment. Where Social Care is involved, the social worker will co-ordinate the multi-agency plan to support the parent(s)/carer(s), and ensure that children and young people are receiving the services they need. This will be through a Child in Need, Child Protection or a Looked After Care Plan for example, as appropriate.

For cases within level 4, services are delivered under the Children Act (1989) by a local authority in two ways:

- Under Section 47(1) of the Act, where a local authority is informed that a child who lives, or is found, in its area and it has reasonable cause to suspect is suffering, or is likely to suffer, significant harm, the authority shall make, or cause to be made, enquiries which it considers necessary to enable it to decide if it should take any action to safeguard or promote the child's welfare.

- Under Section 17 of the same Act the local authority is empowered to provide services for children in need, their families and others.

As identified above, Section 42 of the Care Act (2014) states that a local authority must make an enquiry if it suspects that an adult in its area who needs care and support is experiencing, or is at risk of, abuse or neglect, and as a result of those needs is unable to protect himself or herself against the abuse or neglect or the risk of it.

Establishing whether cases are below or above the threshold is therefore critical if the appropriate intervention or support is to be provided. On occasions, the decision will be made to use a statutory power to ensure services are provided for children, sometimes without the consent and agreement of the individual or, if appropriate, the parents. These decisions are therefore hugely important and should be based on the best information picture at the time, as described above.

These decisions, which due to their legal standing can be challenged in court, need to be recorded with both the reasons and rationale as well as the information underpinning them.

Cases for children and young people that do not require the statutory intervention of the local authority may attract support and interventions with the consent of the individual or family, from a wide range of different organisations and services. This early intervention for children and young people is known across England and Wales as Early Help. In order for this support and challenge to be enabled, the children and families need to be identified as early as possible.

Munro (2011) states:

'That there is a strong case for providing early help is relatively easy to understand. More difficulty is introduced when considerations about abuse and neglect are added. It is easy to offer a definition of which families or problems can be helped through a range of preventative services, but in practice, there are many difficulties in assigning children and families to appropriate services that meet their needs. However, making decisions about when a child is or may be suffering harm and needs a child protection response is, in many cases, complex.' (p79)

Working Together (2018) identifies the need for assessing and providing Early Help. It states:

'Providing early help is more effective in promoting the welfare of children than reacting later. Early help means providing support as soon as a problem emerges, at any point in a child's life, from the foundation years through to the teenage years. Early help can also prevent further problems arising; for example, if it is provided as part of a support plan where a child has returned home to their family from care, or in families where there are emerging parental mental health issues or drug and alcohol misuse.'

Effective early help relies upon local organisations and agencies working together to:

- identify children and families who would benefit from early help

- undertake an assessment of the need for early help

- provide targeted early help services to address the assessed needs of a child and their family which focuses on activity to improve the outcomes for the child.

Local authorities, under section 10 of the Children Act (2004) (as amended by the Social Work Act (2017)), have a responsibility to promote inter-agency co-operation to improve the welfare of all children.

These cases are managed using The Early Help Assessment (EHA), which replaced the Common Assessment Framework (CAF). They have been designed specifically to help professionals assess needs at an earlier stage and then work with families, alongside other professionals and agencies, to meet them.
It is widely recognised that early intervention, which may include support and challenge to some parents and families, is essential to ensure the best possible outcomes for children. This support or intervention is not needed by the majority of parents and families but only by those who may be struggling for a variety of reasons to deliver 'good enough' parenting, and this in turn is causing harm or the potential for harm to their children.

Information sharing and communication

As has been identified, one vital area of co-operation in respect of safeguarding and the early understanding of need, harm and risk in both children and adults is the sharing of information. Another is the communication between professionals and directly with the local authority in respect of concerns and requests for support in some way.

It is this initial sharing and communication that is the starting point for all services to be able to identify need, harm and risk, and this identification underpins the decision as to which diversion, prevention or intervention services or actions should be delivered in support of vulnerable people and families.

Sharing information and communication between professionals remains essential after the initial identification of need, harm and risk when support and interventions may be being provided by more than one organisation.

It is accepted without question that communication between organisations, or partners as they are known, and the sharing of information are two key requirements that fall within the co-operation banner under Section 10 of the Children Act (2004) (as amended by the Social Work Act (2017)) and Section 6 of the Care Act (2014)

Section 16 E (4) the Children Act (2004) (as amended by the Social Work Act (2017)) makes the following provision concerning the sharing of information:

'(1) Any of the safeguarding partners for a local authority area in England may, for the purpose of enabling or assisting the performance of functions conferred by section 16E or 16F, request a person or body to provide information specified in the request to:

    a. *the safeguarding partner or any other safeguarding partner for the area,*

    b. *any of the relevant agencies for the area,*

    c. *a reviewer, or*

    d. *another person or body specified in the request.*

(2) The person or body to whom a request under this section is made must comply with the request.

(3) The safeguarding partner that made the request may enforce the duty under subsection (2) against the person or body by making an application to the High Court or the county court for an injunction.

(4) The information may be used by the person or body to whom it is provided only for the purpose mentioned in subsection (1).'

Section 16 E, as has been identified above, identifies a statutory requirement for safeguarding partners to safeguard and promote the welfare of children.

Information Sharing: Advice for practitioners providing safeguarding services to children, young people, parents and carers (HM Government, 2018) supports frontline practitioners working within either child or adult services who have to make decisions about sharing personal information on a case-by-case basis. The guidance can be used to supplement local guidance and encourage good practice in information sharing.

Information sharing and the law

There are many pieces of legislation in England and Wales that provide legal justification for the sharing of personal information. In respect of safeguarding and promoting the welfare of children, the relevant acts of Parliament are:

■ The Data Protection Act (2018)

■ The Children Act (1989)

■ The Children Act 2004 (as amended by the Social Work Act (2017)).

In relation to sharing information to safeguard adults at risk, the relevant legislation is:

■ The Data Protection Act (2018)

■ The Care Act (2014).

The first principle of the Data Protection Act (2018), identified in Section 35 (1), states that the processing of personal data must be lawful and fair.

The Data Protection Act together with the GDPR should be considered at all times in terms of processing of personal data, however the Children Act (1989) and the Children Act (2004) (as amended by the Social Work Act (2017)) should be considered the legal gateways for information sharing in relation to children for cases that are initially assessed as being above the statutory threshold that requires a statutory response.

Sections 10 and 16E of the Children Act (2004) (as amended by the Social Work Act (2017)), however, placed further obligations upon local authorities and their safeguarding partners to co-operate, including the sharing of information in order to ensure they both safeguard and promote the welfare of children. Some concerns regarding the welfare of children where information will need to be shared will often fall below the threshold that requires a statutory response.

These cases may still contain need, harm and risk that will be better understood through the sharing of information held by different partners. This type of information sharing will require the consent of a parent or other relevant individual.

The duty to co-operate under the Care Act (2014), meanwhile, can be considered the main legal framework in relation to adults at risk.

Information sharing must take place in accordance with statutory requirements pertaining to the disclosure of information, namely the Data Protection Act (2018), the Human Rights Act (1998) and the Common Law duty of confidentiality.

All decisions to share or not share information must be made on a case-by-case basis and recorded – the well-known phrase 'if it isn't written down it didn't happen' is very true and always worth remembering.

Article 8 of The Human Rights Act (1998) states that 'Everyone has the right to respect for his private and family life, his home and his correspondence'.

However, because this is not an absolute right, there are occasions when it is lawful for the state to interfere with this right and share information. The sharing of information in relation to safeguarding and promoting the welfare of children and adults at risk is such an occasion. Furthermore, sharing information may in fact be in line with Articles 2 and 3 of the Human Rights Act, namely the right to life and the right to prohibition of torture or inhuman or degrading treatment. These articles of the Human Rights Act are absolute rights for all individuals. If either of these are engaged (ie. a person's rights to these are at risk) then the right to privacy can clearly be degraded by sharing information with or without the consent of an individual.

Duty of confidence

Information held by agencies may have been gathered where a duty of confidence is owed to both the holder of the information and to the person who is the subject of that information (ie. the common law presumption that certain information will be confidential). However, duty of confidence is not an absolute bar to disclosure, as information can be shared where consent has been provided or where there is a strong enough public interest to do so. The Data Protection Act (2018) identifies:

'…processing of personal data that is necessary for the performance of a task carried out in the public interest or in the exercise of the controller's official authority includes processing of personal data that is necessary for the administration of justice.'

While a professional should always ensure they consider the proportionality and necessity of sharing any item of personal information, doing so for the protection of children or other vulnerable persons clearly fulfils the public interest test. All information shared with a partner agency must also be relevant to the concern under review.

Consent

The starting point for any sharing of information is that practitioners should be open and honest with individuals and families from the outset about why, what, how and with whom information will or could be shared.

Consent should be obtained from a person who is legally competent to do so. The Data Protection Act (2018) together with the GDPR identifies that a child of 16 years and over can consent to their information being shared. In very broad terms, therefore, a person who is 16 years old or over in England and Wales is competent to make a decision concerning consent to share their personal information. Consent should be written, informed and explicit, clearly explaining the process, the information that will be shared and with whom, together with a person's rights to refuse, limit or withdraw consent and any implication that may have on service delivery.

The local authority is responsible for clarifying that the partnership has received consent for relevant cases before any action is decided.

Children and young people

In most circumstances for those under 16, specific consent must come from a parent who holds parental responsibility or a carer who has obtained this from a court. It is possible, however, for children aged 13 and over to give consent concerning their personal data but this is in relation to the provision of an Information Society Service (ISS). ISS examples are online shops, live or on-demand streaming services or companies providing online communication services. A young person may also consent if they are assessed as mature enough to make such decisions. The 'Gillick' competency test and Fraser Guidelines, which originate from a sexual health case in 1982, are widely used by professionals to help in this regard, although they do not relate directly to the issues of information sharing consent.

Consent must be obtained from the parent/carer before any referral is made to the local authority. There are however a few exceptions in the following circumstances:

- Where there are child protection concerns.

- When it is suspected that attempts to seek consent will place the child at risk of significant harm (the referrer must stipulate safeguarding concerns in writing and indicate the escalation of need, risk, or harm to the child for a decision to be made to override consent based on the concerns raised).

- When the referrer has sought consent and the parent has refused permission – if this is the case and the referrer believes that not referring the concerns is likely to escalate a situation and may place the child at risk of significant harm/potential harm (the referrer must consider and record the overriding of consent).

If the rationale for a refusal to consent is unclear to the local authority, the case should be immediately discussed with the referrer and a decision should be made as to whether to proceed or not. Decisions to overrule consent must be recorded and clarified based on safeguarding concerns. Consent from the parent or carer must be obtained (except for police notifications) or indicated, recorded, and justified on all incoming referrals from professionals.

A local authority will always accept a referral about a child regardless of whether consent has been given, but before any support or advice is given the parent will be contacted and consent obtained. Consent is required for a service to be offered. Where a child is in need of a service (under Section 17 of the Children Act (1998)) then the first action for the local authority will be to obtain consent, unless already obtained.

If there is a significant change in the way the information is to be used at any time, or there is a change in the relationship between the agency and the individual, consent should be sought again. It is also important to remember that individuals have a right to withdraw or limit consent at any time.

When a child is assessed as in need of protection, then consent to share information between agencies should be considered but is not essential. The safety of the child is paramount: the no-delay principle must be adhered to. However, there must be a proportionate reason for not seeking consent and the person making this decision must try to weigh up the important legal duty to seek consent and the damage that might be caused by the proposed information sharing on the one hand, against whether any damage might be caused by seeking consent, and if so what type and amount of harm might be caused (or not prevented).

There is no absolute requirement for agencies to obtain consent before sharing information, nor should there be a blanket policy of never doing so. There is, however, an obligation to consider on all occasions and on a case-by-case basis, whether information will be shared with or without consent. This determination by a practitioner should always be reasonable, necessary and proportionate. It should always be recorded together with the rationale for the decision. Remember, 'If it isn't written down it didn't happen!'

It is inherent in the idea of seeking consent that it may be refused. If professionals consider it justifiable to override the refusal in the interests of the welfare of the child then they can and must do so. This decision must be proportionate to the harm that may be caused by proceeding without consent.

Where it is believed that the aims of the local authority to safeguard and promote the welfare of children might be compromised if agencies were to seek consent, the disclosing agency must consider and record the grounds to override the consent issue.

Adults

An at-risk adult who is the focus of a safeguarding enquiry needs to be made aware at the earliest opportunity of the need to share information, and to give their consent. This of course may not always be possible. Where it is not possible for the person to consent to the sharing of information, after full consideration of the Mental Capacity Act (2005)[16], a best interests decision will need to be made. Family and friends may be involved in this consideration but cannot consent unless they have the requisite legal standing. See Chapter 5: Safeguarding vulnerable adults for more information.

Adult refusal to consent to share information

It is not possible in this short chapter to cover all the circumstances where a person may withhold consent to share information. A common example, however, is where the alleged victim of financial abuse withholds consent to share information with the police out of loyalty to a family member who is the perpetrator. In these circumstances the professional receiving the information or investigating the abuse can inform the police if they believe a crime has been committed.

If consent is not obtained to share information in an adult safeguarding matter, there are several considerations to be made about sharing information without it. Sharing information without consent can be legitimate where there is an overriding public interest, as identified earlier in relation to children. An example might be an abuser targeting older people in a particular locality where the victims do not want to take action, but others might also be at risk.

There is also the notion of 'legitimate purpose' in sharing information without consent, which can include issues such as preventing serious harm to an adult at risk or providing urgent medical treatment. Information can also be shared without consent where the vital interests of the individual are affected.
Professionals who have concerns that an adult is at risk should consult their local authority adult safeguarding team and look to local or national procedures for guidance. The issues are rarely clear cut and the rights of the individual must always be respected.

---

16 As amended by the Mental Capacity (amendment) Act (2019) and code of practice.

Necessity, proportionality and relevance

Once a professional has considered the legality of sharing a person's personal information and decided about the matter of consent, they need to consider three further tests before they share any personal information with another professional or organisation. Some professionals find it useful to remember this as the 'NP&R test'. It is vital all three tests are considered, not either/or.

- N – Necessity: The amount and type of information shared should only be that necessary to achieve the lawful aim.

- P – Proportionality: Information is always to be considered in terms of its proportionality in each set of circumstances, but it must always be remembered that the right to life is paramount.

- R – Relevance: Only relevant information should be shared. This should be decided on a case-by-case basis.

Finally, it is also useful to consider two very simple questions before sharing information with another professional or organisation: does the person or organisation 'need-to-know' the information, or is it really a case of it being nice for them to know?

In summary: the seven golden rules

HM government has published updated guidance, *Information Sharing: Guidance for practitioners and managers 2018*, in which they identify the 'seven golden rules of information sharing':

1. Remember that the General Data Protection Regulation (GDPR) and human rights law are not barriers to justified information sharing, but provide a framework to ensure that personal information about living individuals is shared appropriately.

2. Be open and honest with the individual (and/or their family where appropriate) from the outset about why, what, how and with whom information will or could be shared, and seek their agreement, unless it is unsafe or inappropriate to do so.

3. Seek advice from other practitioners or your information governance lead if you are in any doubt about sharing the information concerned, without disclosing the identity of the individual where possible.

4. Where possible, share information with consent, and where possible respect the wishes of those who do not consent to having their information shared. Under the GDPR and Data Protection Act (2018) you may share information without consent if, in your judgement, there is a lawful basis to do so, such as where safety may be at risk. You will need to base your judgement on the facts of the case. When you are sharing or requesting personal information from someone, be clear of the basis upon which you are doing so. Where you do not have consent, be mindful that an individual might not expect information to be shared.

5. Consider safety and well-being: base your information-sharing decisions on considerations of the safety and well-being of the individual and others who may be affected by their actions.

6. Necessary, proportionate, relevant, adequate, accurate, timely and secure: ensure that the information you share is necessary for the purpose for which you are sharing it, is shared only with those individuals who need to have it, is accurate and up-to-date, is shared in a timely fashion, and is shared securely.

7. Keep a record of your decision and the reasons for it – whether it is to share information or not. If you decide to share, then record what you have shared, with whom and for what purpose.

Key learning

- Local authorities have the legal duty to safeguard children and co-ordinate the safeguarding of vulnerable adults.

- The police, a Clinical Commissioning Group for an area and the local authority are designated as Safeguarding Partners by law.

- Safeguarding Partners and all relevant agencies have a duty to work together to safeguard and promote the welfare of children.

- Duty to work together or co-operate includes sharing information.

- Sharing of information between agencies creates a more holistic knowledge picture of individuals and families.

- Better decisions leading to more appropriate and proportionate interventions are made when based on a partnership-based, holistic knowledge picture.

- Information should be shared with the consent of the individual or someone legally allowed to consent on their behalf, such as the parent of a child or an advocate for a vulnerable adult.

- A child 16 years or over can consent to their information being shared.

- Information can be shared without consent under certain circumstances to prevent or stop significant harm to an individual.

- Necessity, proportionality and relevance (NP&R) should be considered when information is to be shared in relation to a given concern.

- Professionals always consider the seven golden rules for information sharing.

Remember: 'if it isn't written down it didn't happen'

Multi-Agency Safeguarding Hubs (MASH)

For many years, organisations that are or may become involved in safeguarding vulnerable people have found sharing information problematic to achieve. On many occasions they have failed to communicate effectively when required to do so, both within single organisations and across multiple organisations or partnerships. As a result, children and vulnerable adults have died or suffered significant harm. Many Serious Case Reviews have evidenced failings in these two key areas of practice and recommended changes, but the same failings in communication continue to occur and the same recommendations are made.

Academic research over many years has identified the need for change, but also just how difficult it is for public sector bodies to work closely together to deliver the necessary improvements. Cameron and Lart (2003) stated that, 'professionals should ensure that future joint working initiatives address the issues already known to promote and inhibit their success'.

Cleaver *et al* (2009) stated, 'Effective collaborative working is the cornerstone of a successful children's safeguarding system'. Research and professional knowledge would suggest that there are two key ingredients to effective information sharing and communication, in addition to good knowledge of the law and procedure:

- confidence
- trust between the professionals who represent the different organisations who hold the information.

Some organisations, such as law enforcement, have additional legal obligations to consider. They need to protect not just the data but also, on many occasions, the sources of their information.

There is no single accepted model for information sharing and decision making in place across the country for protecting vulnerable people. Local authorities and their safeguarding partners approach the issue in many and varied ways. In some instances, organisations have come together and professionals from the different agencies work in a single location, and in others the communication and sharing of information takes place in a virtual way covered by information sharing agreements (ISA) and Service Level Agreements.

In 2010, a new model known as the MASH model was conceived and developed. MASH stands for Multi Agency Safeguarding Hub, and these have been implemented in many places. Some look very different to the original design but all are attempting to share information more effectively and work in an integrated partnership manner. Essentially, a MASH is a secure partnership office where representatives of agencies who hold information concerning vulnerable individuals and families work together in an integrated way to share information when necessary on a case-by-case basis. Professionals within the MASH use the partnership's collective knowledge to risk assess concerns and make decisions concerning any level of intervention that may be appropriate. A MASH takes place in the real world, not virtual.

MASH is not a replacement for MAPPA meetings (see Chapter 8). MAPPA allows agencies to come together to formulate a course of action in relation to the management of an individual who poses a risk to the community, while MASH is concerned with the identification and safeguarding of potential victims. MARAC meetings are where plans are discussed to support and mitigate risks relating to domestic abuse victims.

MASH can have a significant role in identifying the risks to children who may be connected to both domestic abuse cases and MAPPA individuals who are subsequently discussed at a MAPPA or a MARAC. MASH can ensure any interventions for the children can be underway before the MAPPA or MARAC meets.

The word 'safeguarding' was deliberately used within the name of the model in line with its widest meaning:

- The action of keeping safe and secure (noun).

- That keeps safe, protects; that acts as a safeguard (adj).

- To keep secure from danger or attack; to guard, protect, defend; to make safe.

- To protect against something undesirable with an appropriate measure (verb).

(Taken from Oxford Dictionary online (2019)).

Need, harm and risk are not always immediately apparent to a professional or member of the public – one professional may see only a slight indicator of a problem, but when added to information identified by another agency or agencies over a period of time, a clearer picture may emerge. This repetitive reporting of concerns is known as the 'drip drip' effect, and MASH was designed to identify it.

The core MASH model and vision was intended to cover the whole spectrum of harm, from early help prevention and diversion through to statutory intervention. MASH was not designed to just deal with cases of child abuse. They have been identified as best practice in numerous governments and cross-party parliamentary reviews. The Review of Child Protection by Professor Munro (2011) identified the concept, albeit new at the time, and Ofsted have described it as a good model for information sharing. Munro also strongly supported the provision of an Early Offer of Help for children and families whose cases do not meet the statutory threshold. MASH was designed to identify the cases suitable for this Early Help provision as early as possible.

MASH is a consent-based model where consent can be overridden in certain circumstances as described earlier in this chapter. The MASH model is designed to remove once and for all the inhibitors to effective sharing of information and communication between partners. The model is built on the premise that partner organisations need to be co-located and not virtual entities, and they were designed to deliver three clear outcomes in relation to both children and vulnerable adults:

1. Early identification and understanding of need, harm and risk. All available information is seen to ensure that need, harm and risk are identified as early as possible. Better informed decisions ensuring earlier, proportionate and necessary prevention, diversion and interventions for children and families.

2. Victim identification and intervention. Pooled knowledge from safeguarding partners to identify hidden need, harm and risk. Hidden victims are identified through third-party reporting.

3. Harm identification and its reduction for individuals, families and communities. MASH is a safe haven for information where the full partnership information picture is seen and can inform activity to reduce and prevent harm and risk.

This allows analytic capability on two levels:

■ Dynamic analysis of information on a day-to-day basis to identify need, harm and risk to individuals, families and communities which is hidden to one or more safeguarding partners.

■ Analysis products to aid integrated partnerships to better understand their strategic harm picture and inform commissioning intentions.

Not all local authorities have moved to the full, true MASH model, but many use similar processes and collaborations to allow their safeguarding partners to share information.

Five core elements

In order achieve the intended outcomes, together with the confidence and trust needed to deliver them, the MASH model needs to operate in a certain way and with a few clear rules. These can be referred to as the 'five core elements'.

These are:

1. All notifications relating to safeguarding and promoting the welfare of children are to go through the hub. Co-ordination to Early Help for a single agency, multi agency and a targeted approach, driving prevention, diversion and intervention.

2. Co-location of professionals from core agencies (see below) to research, interpret and determine what is necessary, proportionate and relevant to share.

3. The hub is fire walled, keeping MASH activity confidential and separate from operational activity and providing a confidential record system of activity to support this.

4. An agreed process for analysing and assessing risk, based on the fullest information picture available, and dissemination of a suitable information product to the most appropriate agency for necessary action.

5. A process to identify victims and emerging harm through research and analysis.

It is widely accepted that the following core partners and agencies are required to be co-located in the MASH to achieve best effect, but this is certainly not an exhaustive list:

- Children's Social Care

- Police

- Health

- Education

- Probation

- Housing

- Youth Offending Service

Basic rules of MASH model

There are essential rules concerning the sharing of information within a MASH that should be agreed within a specific MASH partnership information sharing agreement (ISA).

These are:

- The local authority decision maker should, if it is necessary, see all information and intelligence which is available within any partner organisation, both confidential and non-confidential (sensitive or non-sensitive), to ensure they can make the best possible decisions. (Remember not all decisions are by their nature difficult and requiring of further information from an agency other than the referrer or local authority)

- Any professional within the MASH may, at the request of the local authority assisting in the decision-making of a case, see the information if it is relevant to their involvement, for example a health professional.

- All information shared with the local authority should be stored as part of the audit trail of a decision within a database that cannot be accessed outside the MASH.

- The 'need to know' principle should operate within the MASH. Professionals within the hub who do not have a 'need to know' the information should not see it. There is never an argument to suggest it is 'nice to know'. There needs to be a lawful purpose and all good practice guidance supports this.

- The MASH should operate in a sterile environment that supports this 'need to know' principle. Professionals from whatever organisation should not work within the MASH or have access to it if they are not involved within the business it is conducting. A MASH enables excellent communication between partner agencies concerning the intelligent assessment of need, harm and risk to individuals and families. These conversations are always personal and can be very sensitive. They do not need to be overheard by anyone who does not 'need to know'.

- An originating partner who shares information with the local authority always retains the right to decide whether it stays within the hub or is passed to practitioners who may subsequently use it within their case management files.

- If a partner refuses to allow information to be shared outside the hub after a decision has been made, this must be respected and not disregarded. It can of course be challenged, but the owning organisation must always make the final decision. This enables organisations such as the police, who have a duty of care to the sources of some information, to fulfil their legal obligations to the individuals who have provided it. There are occasions where a person's well-being may be compromised if information becomes known to others.

- It is helpful to consider information as being 'revealed' within the MASH, and 'shared' when it is allowed to leave.

- If confidential (sensitive) information is revealed to the decision maker but not sanctioned for release from the hub, the existence of it and its owner must be signposted to the professionals who will be receiving the particular case. They are then able to discuss with the data owner in a controlled manner and again comply with the 'need to know' principle. The data owner may of course not share the content if they do not feel it necessary or proportionate.

How a MASH works

The model delivers partnership-informed analysis to all issues of need, harm and risk to a child or children (or adult who may be at risk) as opposed to focusing solely on statutory thresholds and social work case allocation. The model espouses a needs analysis led decision-making model without borders i.e. working with needs rather than thresholds, although recognising the importance of statutory responsibilities.

It works within the regulatory framework but ensures that the statutory responsibilities do not affect or restrain the needs analysis or the identification of need. It is a need-driven journey to providing support, intervention or diversion. The driver becomes the early identification of opportunities to intervene at the appropriate level and to divert from statutory service provision. It identifies the cases for diversion and intervention earlier and more effectively. This provides greater opportunities for services to succeed. Cases are signposted (stepped down) appropriately and long before approaching a crisis point. The model delivers a seamless pathway for the child and recognises the need to hear and see children.

Professionals work within the MASH model and represent the statutory agencies as identified in the Children Act (2004)[17] and the Care Act (2014). In some hubs they are joined by representatives from third sector bodies who may be delivering services in a particular area. The three statutory organisations of local authority, health and the police, as the safeguarding partners, are key to the working of the model and should be embedded within the hub having direct access to as many of their own databases as possible to enable immediate research and information gathering. Representatives covering other sectors such as education, housing, probation and the third sector are also best located within the hub but are found as virtual partners in many models.

It must be acknowledged that not all information is available through databases, and when necessary a representative of an organisation within the MASH may need to 'reach out' and locate information and knowledge through personal enquiries within their own professional sector. They gather and add all relevant information to the case.

All contacts and referrals to the local authority from across a safeguarding partnership area from a professional or a member of the public will arrive at the MASH and be risk assessed in line with a locally agreed partnership risk assessment. In other words, they will be screened against the local levels of need document.

In essence the outcome is the same. Concerns are immediately considered and if a decision is clearly able to be made based on the presenting information, then it

17 As amended by the Social Work Act (2017).

is made, and the appropriate action taken. This can be an immediate escalation to safeguard a child or signposting to a universal service. As stated earlier, decisions are not necessarily difficult because of the severity or otherwise of the concern. The main driver should always be the intent not to cause delay for any child.

Any case that clearly requires a child or adult at risk to be safeguarded is immediately actioned to the relevant team or teams outside the MASH. Information may still be shared within the hub on these urgent cases in support of the operational staff who will be carrying out the work, but it must not hold up any action to safeguard and protect.

Adult cases are considered in a similar manner but may vary in respect of individual models. Not all MASH models across the country have integrated the adult processes, although this is achievable.

Once assessed or screened, a decision will be made by the local authority as to whether further information is required from any partner and, if so, this is requested through the staff embedded within the MASH or those supporting in a virtual way. On occasions, information may be requested from all partners, and on others it may be only one or a few, depending on the circumstances of the case.

These cases are often referred to as 'unclear' (on presenting information). It is these cases where additional information is required to support decision making. This gathering of additional information is very often subject to a locally agreed timescale which is of course appropriate to ensure that there is no delay for children, and to comply with the *Working Together 2018* requirement of making a decision within a day. Further information is then sought and forwarded to the local authority decision maker within the locally agreed timescale, which is based on the need as described within the levels of need.

The MASH model is designed to allow the police within the hub to risk assess their own notifications before they forward them to the local authority decision maker in the MASH. They should also have direct (limited) access to the local authority children's case records to establish if the child or children are already open to social work. If they are, then the notification should be forwarded to the relevant social work team without delay.

The police generate a substantial volume of contacts within most local authority areas and hold information within their data sets, which is very useful in the initial understanding of need, harm and risk. Police notify a local authority of their involvement with children and families. Police notify their concerns to a local authority and do not make referrals. As such they do not require consent.

Many police forces record every contact with a child. This generates many records where a child or children have no additional needs. It is appropriate, however, for the police to record professional contact with children even if they decide there is no requirement for notification to the local authority as they have no concerns and are satisfied the child has no additional needs. The police will file these cases and not forward them to the local authority but their existence is noted on the particular IT audit system that each MASH needs. They are then visible to the other members of the MASH should another contact be received by the hub for the same individual or family. This ensures that even very low-level need, harm and risk is not hidden and can be viewed together with other concerns if or when they occur. It also ensures that a local authority is not swamped with very low-level matters for which no service is required.

Once all the information that has been requested on a case has been returned, the local authority decision maker within the hub can make a decision based on a more complete picture of an individual or family. The decision, or in some models a recommendation, is then forwarded to the appropriate service outside the hub for action, intervention or support proportionate to the need, harm and risk.

MASH was designed, as has been stated, to assess all levels of harm. It therefore follows that cases leaving the MASH need to move to an appropriate service if one is required. MASH models that fully exploit these opportunities will be connected to an Early Offer of Help, Troubled Families teams and other specialist services such as partnership Child Sexual Exploitation teams.

These pathways also allow for cases to return to the MASH if necessary through a 'step up, step down' procedure should risk escalate or reduce. It is very much a local decision as to which services utilise the MASH as the gateway for assessing need, harm and risk.

Researching information and intelligence

Professionals charged with identifying information and intelligence that is relevant to any given case face a challenge in terms of determining which information is relevant and which is not. All organisations hold vast quantities of data, which makes the task of research potentially like looking for a needle in a haystack, even with highly efficient search engines and software. The experience and skills of the professional carrying out this important role play a huge part in their ability to identify the appropriate type of information, but they can be aided by set research criteria highlighting potential areas of need, harm and risk, which may successfully contribute to informing the picture around any given concern.

Social workers within MASH settings have to analyse the wealth (or dearth) of their own and partnership information and provide a clear initial assessment of it, which should underpin their recommendation to a manager. This initial analysis of a concern is paramount in order to gain an early understanding of need, harm and risk.

Key learning

- MASH was developed to enable agencies to be able to share information and make better decisions in relation to children and vulnerable adults.

- MASH is a consent-based model, where consent may be over-ridden if lawful to do so.

- Statutory agencies and others work together in an integrated way.

- MASH is not a virtual entity, although some agencies may work with it in a virtual way.

- It is a secure and safe location and was designed to deliver three key outcomes:

  - early identification and understanding of need, harm and risk
  - victim identification and intervention
  - harm identification and its reduction for individuals, families and communities.

- There are five core elements of a MASH that enable it to function correctly and deliver the three key outcomes.

- MASH does not replace meetings such as MAPPA, MARAC or strategy meetings.

- Safeguarding means to protect from harm or damage. MASH was developed to cover all levels of harm, not just the most severe. MASH can identify cases for both statutory and early intervention.

Further reading

Department of Health (2013) *Information: To share or not to share? The information governance review* [online]. London: TSO. Available at: www.gov.uk/government/uploads/system/uploads/attachment_data/file/192572/2900774_InfoGovernance_accv2.pdf (accessed September 2019).

General Medical Council (2018) *Protecting children and young people: The responsibilities of all doctors* [online]. Available at: www.gmc-uk.org/ethical-guidance/ethical-guidance-for-doctors/protecting-children-and-young-people (accessed September 2019).

HM Government (2018) *Information Sharing: Advice for practitioners providing safeguarding services to children, young people, parents and carers*. London TSO.

Home Office (2014) *Multi-Agency Working and Information Sharing Project: Final report* [online]. London: TSO. Available at: www.gov.uk/government/uploads/system/uploads/attachment_data/file/338875/MASH.pdf (accessed September 2019).

Munro E (2011) *The Munro Review of Child Protection: Final report – a child-centred system* [online]. London: Department for Education. Available at: www.gov.uk/government/publications/munro-review-of-child-protection-final-report-a-child-centred-system (accessed September 2019).

Local Government Association (ISOS Partnership) (2019). *Key enablers of developing an effective partnership-based early help offer: final report*. Available at https://static1.squarespace.com/static/5ce55a5ad4c5c500016855ee/t/5d1cdabd4e65e f00014b3ff0/1562172100381/Early+help+report+final+for+publication+14.03.19.pdf (accessed September 2019).

The legislation relevant to this chapter is:

The Care Act (2014)

The Children Act (1989)

The Children Act 2004 (as amended by the Social Work Act 2017)

The Data Protection Act (2018) (together with the General Data Processing Regulation (GDPR) 2016/679)

The Mental Capacity Act (2005) as amended by the Mental Capacity (amendment) Act 2019

The Human Rights Act (1998)

References

Cameron A & Lart R (2003) Factors promoting and obstacles hindering joint working: a systematic review of the research evidence. *Journal of Integrated Care* **11** (2) 9–17.

Cleaver *et al* (2009) *Safeguarding children: A shared responsibility*. Wiley Blackwell.

Department for Education (2018) *Working Together to Safeguard Children: A guide to inter-agency working to safeguard and promote the welfare of children* [online]. London: DfE. Available at: www.gov.uk/government/publications/working-together-to-safeguard-children (accessed September 2019).

Department of Health (2000a) *No Secrets: Guidance on developing and implementing multi-agency policies and procedures to protect vulnerable adults from abuse* [online]. London: DH. Available at: www.gov.uk/government/publications/no-secrets-guidance-on-protecting-vulnerable-adults-in-care (accessed September 2019).

Department of Health (2000b) *The Framework for Assessment of Children in Need and their Families* [online]. London: DH.

HM Government (2018) *Information Sharing: Guidance for practitioners and managers* [online]. London: TSO. Available at: www.gov.uk/government/uploads/system/uploads/attachment_data/file/277834/information_sharing_guidance_for_practitioners_and_managers.pdf (accessed September 2019).

HM Government (2015) *Information Sharing: Advice for practitioners providing safeguarding services to children, young people, parents and carers*. London TSO.

Munro E (2011) *The Munro Review of Child Protection: Final report – a child-centred system* [online]. London: Department for Education. Available at: www.gov.uk/government/publications/munro-review-of-child-protection-final-report-a-child-centred-system (accessed September 2019).

Oxford Dictionary (2019) Safeguard [online]. Available at: www.oed.com/view/Entry/169677?rskey=40fNEi&result=1#eid (accessed September 2019).

Chapter 10: Suicide in adults and children

By Russell Wate

Chapter overview

- Introduction.

- Prevalence and suicide prevention profile.

- Relationship between self-harm and suicide.

- Suicide prevention strategies.

- Applied Suicide Intervention Skills Training (ASIST).

- Support organisations.

- Suicide and domestic abuse.

- Suicide by children and young people.

- Young person specific support groups.

Introduction

Suicide has a devastating impact on families, communities and those professionals who have worked with individuals to safeguard them from harming themselves. Papyrus, a support group charity, states that the grief in the aftermath of suicide is often intense and it is said there is often a lack of 'closure', as people and professionals look for 'answers' and try to find reasons the person took their life. Sometimes, people may feel responsible in some way for the person's death, for example if a student took their life and were bullied at school.

Suicide in the UK is defined as, *'deaths given an underlying cause of intentional self-harm for persons aged 10 years and over, and deaths where the intent was undetermined for those aged 15 years and over'*.

To record a verdict of suicide, coroners used to have to come to a verdict that was 'beyond reasonable doubt' (criminal standard of proof) that the person intended to end their life. Where this can't be proved, coroners may record an open verdict, or find the death to have been caused by accident or misadventure. For this reason, the Office National Statistics includes in its suicide statistics those deaths of 'undetermined intent'. However, in July 2018 the High Court made a ruling that the suicide standard of proof should be changed to the balance of probabilities, rather than beyond reasonable doubt. The family in this case have appealed this judgement, but it is currently used and will alter data collection going forward.

In 2012, the government published the *Cross-Government National Suicide Prevention Strategy*, which was updated in 2017 to strengthen delivery of its key areas for action, including expanding the scope of the strategy to include addressing self-harm as an issue in its own right. The National Suicide Prevention Strategy is implemented by partners across government, working individually and collectively to address suicide prevention within their areas of responsibility, and to ensure all partners remain committed to implementing the strategy's aims to reduce suicides everywhere. Most if not all areas have in place a suicide strategy, with a zero suicide ambition.

There is a government minister responsible for overseeing this area of work – the Minister for Mental Health, Inequalities and Suicide Prevention.

Prevalence and suicide prevention profile

Thirteen people die every day in England by taking their own life through suicide. The Office of National Statistics in their dataset (2018) *Suicides in the UK* state that, in 2017, 5,821 people took their own lives through suicide. Of these by far the largest majority were males, making up 4,382 of that overall figure. This proportion of males – up three-quarters of suicides – has been mostly consistent since the mid-1990s. The number of people taking their life by suicide is, however, the lowest figure since the ONS started collecting data in 1981. This downward trend has been particularly seen in the last two years. However, this is not the case in children and young people, in particular the 15-19 years age group, which is rising year on year.

Methods of suicide over the last decade show that the most common methods of suicide were hanging/strangulation, followed by self-poisoning (overdose) and multiple injuries – mainly jumping from a height or being struck by a train. There are also new and emerging challenges to tackle – areas such as gambling addiction and online safety and the impact of social media on the mental health of young people.

Public Health England have published a suicide prevention profile and within this they highlight related risk factors that professionals should be aware of when working with people who have these vulnerabilities:

- Depression.
- Severe mental health issues.
- Substance misuse – drugs (crack cocaine and opiates).
- Substance misuse – alcohol.
- Long-term health problems and disability.
- Self-reported well-being that is characterised by:
  - low satisfaction
  - low happiness
  - low worthwhile
  - high anxiety.
- The prisoner population.
- Those in contact with the Youth Justice system.
- Children leaving care.
- Domestic abuse.
- Marital breakdown (in particular males who have separated)
- Adult social care users who do not have as much social contact as they would like.
- Adult carers who do not have as much social contact as they would like.
- Older people living alone.
- People living alone.
- Unemployment.
- Homelessness.
- Long term claimants of jobseekers' allowance.

The relationship between self-harm and suicide

The relationship between self-harm and suicide is complicated. Although people who self-harm are significantly more likely to die by suicide or to harm themselves using more serious methods than the general population who do not self-harm, people may have many motivations for self-harm and are not always intent on dying (Klonsey et al, 2014).

Self-harm should always be taken seriously, as it will inevitably reflect an attempt to manage a high level of psychological distress. It is therefore important to work with the person to understand their motivations and to not assume the motivations for self-harm are the same every time.

Health Education England (HEE) and the National Collaborating Centre for Mental Health (NCCMH) have launched a series of self-harm and suicide prevention frameworks. Within these, three parallel competence frameworks have been developed: one for those working with adults and older adults, one for those working with children and young people, and one for those offering support in the community to the wider public. The last is aimed at professionals who will not usually have training in mental health. It will be relevant to individuals carrying out public health initiatives, employers, providers of education and other public services, such as transport or police.

The main areas of the competencies cover:

- Working collaboratively with the adult, child or young person, their family and carers.
- Person-centred rather than protocol-centred.
- Sharing information.
- Managing transitions between services.

Other areas include training, knowledge of self-harm, postvention (which is support for people bereaved by suicide, and support for people in organisations affected by suicide.)

Further information is available at: www.hee.nhs.uk/our-work/mental-health/self-harm-suicide-prevention-frameworks (accessed September 2019).

Suicide prevention strategies

The National Suicide Prevention Strategy for England has included work to reduce the risk of suicide in high-risk groups. These include young and middle-aged men, people in the care of mental health services, people from the LBGT community, and those in the criminal justice system.

Applied Suicide Intervention Skills Training (ASIST)

This programme has been developed by the charity Livingworks. Their view and vision for their work is that:

'We believe that suicide is preventable and everyone has a role to play. Some participants in our workshops are highly trained mental health professionals, while others have no previous experience. All of them learn the skills to save a life.

'Saving lives from suicide is possible because most people with thoughts of suicide don't want to die – what they want is to escape from the pain in their lives. We know that most people thinking about suicide would choose life and try to work through their difficulties if only they could get help from someone with the right knowledge and skills.'

Further information is available at: www.livingworks.net/asist/ (accessed September 2019).

Livingworks run a two-day interactive workshop in suicide first aid. ASIST teaches participants to recognise when someone may have thoughts of suicide and work with them to create a plan that will support their immediate safety. Although ASIST is widely used by healthcare providers, participants don't need any formal training to attend the workshop – anyone 16 or older can learn and use the ASIST model.

Since its development in 1983, ASIST has received regular updates to reflect improvements in knowledge and practice, and over 1 million people have taken the workshop. Studies show that the ASIST method helps reduce suicidal feelings in those at risk and is a cost-effective way to help address the problem of suicide. A 2013 study that monitored over 1,500 suicidal callers to crisis lines found that callers who spoke with ASIST-trained counsellors were 74% less likely to be suicidal after the call, compared to callers who spoke with counsellors trained in methods other than ASIST. Callers were also less overwhelmed, less depressed, and more hopeful after speaking with ASIST-trained counsellors.

Preventing suicide campaigns

There are campaigns both nationally and locally to target prevention of suicide. One of these is the highly regarded STOP Suicide campaign – an award-winning campaign that reaches across Cambridgeshire and Peterborough. It started life in 2014 as one of four different NHS England-funded pilot campaigns and is now continuing via other funding streams. The campaign is being led by the charities

Cambridgeshire, Peterborough and South Lincolnshire Mind (CPSL Mind) and Lifecraft, supported by local NHS and Public Health teams. The message of the campaign is that 'suicide is everybody's business'.

It seeks to alert communities across Cambridgeshire and Peterborough to the warning signs of suicidal behaviour and reassure them that an open and honest approach to suicide is the best way to prevent it. The campaign also aims to challenge the stigma and myths around suicide and the high-profile media campaign will be crucial to achieving this. Overall, the campaign hopes to achieve a suicide-safer community.

Further information is available at: www.stopsuicidepledge.org/ (accessed September 2019).

Support organisations

The Samaritans is a unique charity dedicated to reducing the feelings of isolation and disconnection that can lead to suicide. They state that:

'Every six seconds, a we respond to a call for help. Every year, we answer more than 5 million calls for help by phone, email, SMS, letter, face to face at one of our local branches and through our Welsh language service. We're here 24/7, before, during and after a crisis.

Whether it's an 'are you ok?' at just the right moment, or the midnight support of a trained volunteer; whether it's better training in the workplace or campaigning for more investment in national and local suicide prevention – we're here. Our charity works to make sure there's always someone there, for anyone who needs someone. Every life lost to suicide is a tragedy, and Samaritans' vision is that fewer people die by suicide.'

The Samaritans are part of The National Suicide Prevention Alliance (NSPA), which is a cross-sector, England-wide coalition working to reduce suicide. Ahead of the World Suicide Prevention Day on 10 September 2017, Samaritans shared the story of someone who considered suicide – Kristian.

Case study: Kristian's story

Kristian had lost both his parents by the time he was 12, leaving his grandparents to bring him up.

'I shut away my grief and didn't deal with it,' he said. 'As I got older, it particularly affected my ability to form close relationships.'

In his 20s, Kristian was working as a teacher, and circumstances combined to make him feel very lonely and isolated. 'Everyone around me seemed to be settling down with their partners, buying houses, and it just wasn't happening for me,' he said. He was being bullied at work, which intensified his feelings of unhappiness.

'I started waking up at night and crying, and I had a lot of bad thoughts. I knew two people who had taken their own lives, and they had said they felt helpless, and I felt like that too.'

'I also had problems dealing with the comedown from drinking alcohol, and on one particular day I went to the gym the morning after, but couldn't really do anything, so I ended up at the beach nearby. I was about the only person there apart from some surfers a quarter of a mile away. The tide was a long way out. I was crying, I felt I had had enough and thought no one could help me.'

'I started walking in to the waves, but when I had got quite a way in that made it real, and I started to panic that I couldn't do it. I got myself out and something in my head went: 'Call Samaritans'. I sat in my car, soaking wet and spoke to this man for 40 minutes. It probably saved my life.'

The Samaritans say that, 'Many people struggle to cope at one point or another of their lives. Experiencing a range of emotions during these times is common'.

The following signs that someone may not be okay are important for professionals to be aware of:

- Feeling restless and agitated.
- Feeling tearful.
- Not wanting to talk to or be with people.
- Not wanting to do things you usually enjoy.
- Using alcohol or drugs to cope with feelings.
- Finding it hard to cope with everyday things.
- Not replying to messages or being distant.

You might not always be able to spot these signs, and these emotions show up differently in everyone.

Situations for professionals to look out for are:

- Relationship and family problems.

- Loss, including loss of a friend or a family member through bereavement.

- Financial worries.

- Job-related stress.

- College or study-related stress.

- Loneliness and isolation.

- Depression.

- Painful and/or disabling physical illness.

- Heavy use of or dependency on alcohol or other drugs.

- Thoughts of suicide.

Again, these may not apply to everyone who is struggling, but they can be useful to look out for.

What can a professional do? Talk to them about their feelings. Encourage them to contact the Samaritans. They can call on 116 123, email jo@samaritans.org, visit one of the branches in person or send a letter. The professional can contact Samaritans, on their behalf. If they call or email, the Samaritans will reach out to them. They won't tell them you asked them to do that unless you want them to. If you think they are in immediate danger, you should call an ambulance on 999.

Further information is available at: www.samaritans.org/.

Suicide and domestic abuse

The Home Office in 2016 included suicide for the first time in their updated guidance on the conducting of Domestic Homicide reviews. It states:

'Where a victim took their own life (suicide) and the circumstances give rise to concern, for example it emerges that there was coercive controlling behaviour in the relationship, a review should be undertaken, even if a suspect is not charged with an offence or they are tried and acquitted. Reviews are not about who is culpable.'

For those professionals who work in criminal justice agencies, it is worth considering further the research described in the report *Domestic Abuse and Suicide: Exploring the links with Refuge's client base and work force* by Ruth Aitken and Vanessa E Munro on behalf Warwick Law school and Refuge. It states: *'The suicide of Gurjit Dhaliwal, who took her own life after enduring years of physical and psychological abuse, was the impetus for this research. Dismayed at the apparent inability of the legal system to punish perpetrators who drive their victims to suicide, and by its failure to recognise the psychological injury which precedes it as a legitimate offence, we were moved to act'.*

This report also highlights certain information that local areas need to include, if they don't already, the risk factor of domestic abuse in suicide:

'Domestic abuse is a high-risk situation, whether this refers to the immediate risk of serious, physical harm from the perpetrator, or to the longer-term risk to the victim's psychological well-being, to their life chances in terms of lost opportunities and potential, or significant damage to 'the self'. Domestic abuse is also a risk to life, either through homicide or suicide of the victim. Although domestic abuse is mentioned as a risk factor within the national suicide strategy, neither suicide nor suicidality are mentioned within the Government's most recent violence against women and girls (VAWG) or domestic abuse strategy. It seems clear that any meaningful integration of policy or practice across both spheres is lacking.'

Suicide by children and young people

It is widely stated that the biggest killer of young people in the UK is suicide. It is believed that over 200 school children take their life by suicide every year.

The impact of children dying through suicide is devastating not only to their families, but also to their friends, peers and schools. Schools in particular have to deal with a combined grief that at times impacts the whole school community, including those schools where siblings attend. They need to put in place strategies and plans for if this did happen in their school.

In April 2015, the National Confidential Inquiry into Suicide and Safety in Mental Health (NCISH) established the UK's first national study combining multiple sources of information to examine the factors related to suicide by children and young people aged 10-19 years. In total, there were 316 deaths by suicide in England and Wales in the two-year time period that the enquiry looked at. This is not an exact figure for the number of children that died by taking their own life, in the main due to how coroners in some areas classified the deaths. However, the number is as accurate as interpretation and the data collection will allow.

The most common method of suicide was hanging/strangulation, followed by jumping/multiple injuries, i.e. jumping or lying in front of a train or other vehicle, jumping from a height or other multiple injuries. There were 66 deaths by self-poisoning (overdose).

In the first of two reports from this study, 10 issues that are common to many suicides by children and young people were highlighted that should help target prevention:

- family factors such as mental illness

- abuse and neglect

- bereavement and experience of suicide

- bullying

- suicide-related internet use

- academic pressures, especially related to exams

- social isolation or withdrawal

- physical health conditions that may have a social impact

- alcohol and illicit drugs

- mental ill health, self-harm and suicidal ideas.

Key messages from the research by Manchester University

- Suicide in young people is rarely caused by one thing; it usually follows a combination of previous vulnerability and recent events.

- The stresses we have identified before suicide are common in young people; most come through them without serious harm.

- Important themes for suicide prevention are support for or management of family factors (e.g. mental illness, physical illness, or substance misuse), childhood abuse, bullying, physical health, social isolation, mental ill-health and alcohol or drug misuse.

- Specific actions are needed on groups we have highlighted: (1) support for young people who are bereaved, especially by suicide (2) greater priority for mental health in colleges and universities (3) housing and mental health care for looked after children (4) mental health support for LGBT young people. →

- Further efforts are needed to remove information on suicide methods from the internet, and to encourage online safety, especially for under 20s.

- Suicide prevention in children and young people is a role shared by front-line agencies; they need to improve access, collaboration and risk management skills. A later, more flexible transition to adult services would be more consistent with our finding of antecedents across the age range.

- Services that respond to self-harm are key to suicide prevention in children and young people, and should work with services for alcohol and drug misuse, factors that are linked to subsequent suicide.

In 2016, the Department for Education published *Pathways to harm, pathways to protection*, a triennial analysis of serious case reviews, 2011 to 2014. In this publication they devoted a section of a chapter to adolescent suicide. They made the following observations that it is important for professionals to be aware of:

'*Although the majority of adolescents navigate the transition to adulthood successfully, they mostly do so in a supportive environment which is conducive to building resilience.*'

'*Adolescent suicide is influenced by the intersection of biological, psycho-social, environmental and cultural factors. Suicide has an associative but non-causal link with self-harm, and those who deliberately self-harm has a risk of suicide some 30 times greater than the general population (Cooper et al, 2005).*'

'*ChildLine studies and other research have found that young people often self-harm instead of talking to others about their feelings and as a way to distract themselves from suicidal thoughts (NSPCC, 2014; McLean et al, 2008).*'

'*The isolation and exclusion that so many of the young people experienced was likely to result in reduced or even absent supportive networks, leaving them with few people to confide in about their feelings and thoughts.*'

Learning points (from this study)

- These adolescents' vulnerabilities were compounded by the cumulative effect of abuse and neglect and the challenges of adolescent development.

- Loss and rejection in early life can influence psychological well-being in adolescence and lead to behavioural and mental health issues, and it is therefore important to have knowledge of their early life experiences.

- Self-harm and/or suicide attempts preceded all but one of the suicides and should be taken seriously whenever they occur.

- The best chance of adolescents responding to relationship-based practice is when it is consistent, holistic and available over a long period of time, on their own terms if possible.

- Behaviour should be viewed as symptomatic of other underlying problems and difficulties. The cause of the behaviour should be explored and addressed through multi-agency support.

- The importance of a trusted adult should not be underestimated.

Rachel's case study, shared with us here by Sally Giddings, a safeguarding improvement officer, is a true story. It has been written with kind permission from Rachel's father in order for agencies to learn what went wrong and to explore how to improve safeguarding practice with a view to Rachel's experience never happening to any young person again.

Case study: Rachel's story

Rachel is a 17-year-old girl who lives with her father and brother. She has a very close relationship with them. Her home address is situated on a county border and her health provision therefore comes under a different county to the one in which she lives. Rachel attends college and has good relationships with her tutors, one in particularly who she often confides in about how she feels. She also has a part time job at the local pub, which she enjoys and is a sociable young person having many friends. Her father described Rachel, prior to Christmas 2017, as being her normal 'effervescent self'.

In January 2018 Rachel's father noticed that she seemed 'distant'. Rachel's father made web searches onto Mumsnet to try and find out more about his daughter's behaviour and whether this was 'normal teenage angst'. As her father was still worried, he persuaded Rachel to see the doctor, as a routine appointment. Rachel was reluctant but went to see the GP. →

At the GP surgery, Rachel explained that she feels depressed but cannot fully explain the reasons why. The GP suggested that Rachel could make a self-referral to a locally based tier two provision for mental health. As soon as they got home Rachel and her father made the referral to this provision online. After not hearing for a quite a while they both tried again making a referral to the second local tier two provision on their website.

Rachel says that she uses drink and drugs (cannabis) to help her to sleep and occasionally has used cocaine, though will not tell her father about this. She worries about general things in life but is able to speak to her dad about it.

The tier two organisation worker contacted her by phone and ascertained that she takes cannabis to sleep and drinks, but only socially. The worker asked if Rachel would attend a drugs group but Rachel refused. The worker suggested that she go to the inclusion service (a local adult substance misuse agency) for help with her substance misuse and wrote a letter to Rachel closing her case. Around the same time the second tier two service tried unsuccessfully to contact Rachel. Her father acknowledged that Rachel felt 'disappointed' that the tier two organisation would not help her.

Rachel's father described Rachel as being a healthy eater, but by February she had stopped eating and was not drinking as much water. Rachel seemed to become more 'fatigued' and as a result her father called the GP to ask for her to have some blood tests to rule out anything untoward.

By February, Rachel's mood had deteriorated and at times she had taken to her bed. Her father was extremely worried and took a 'very reluctant' Rachel back to the doctors and Rachel saw a second GP. Her father explained what had been happening and he was asked to leave the room so the GP could speak to Rachel alone. Some time later Rachel came out with a piece of paper with CAMH's number written on it. After seeing Rachel, the GP sent an 'Urgent referral' letter regarding Rachel being in 'low mood, severe fatigue' and having 'suicidal thoughts'. Both Rachel and her father tried to contact the CAMH telephone number and left messages and details of how to contact Rachel. Unfortunately, no one from CAMH responded.

Rachel's college made a referral to a Child and Adolescent Substance Use Service for support with her drug use. Her father recalled that the college were extremely supportive of Rachel, and to help her they had asked her to work with them on a project – this was a cover story so her friends did not know that Rachel was seeking help from the college. At the start of March, the CASUS worker phoned Rachel and had a discussion around her drug use.

Her father rang the GP about some blood tests and asked why CAMH had not seen Rachel, to which the GP explained that CAMH have huge waiting lists. Rachel's father asked if he should look at private counselling for Rachel, however the ➔

GP advised not to go down this route. Rachel's father informed Rachel that her blood tests were fine and in response Rachel appeared disappointed and said to her father, 'how are we going to know what's wrong then?'

During the second week of March, Rachel had been experiencing headaches and was at home in bed. Late on the Thursday evening, a work day, her boyfriend came around to Rachel's house as he had received a text message from Rachel and he was worried about her. Rachel's father checked Rachel's bedroom and called her place of work but Rachel had called in sick. Rachel's father and boyfriend found Rachel's body in the back garden and called an ambulance.

Rachel's inquest took place during January 2019 and the coroner ruled that there was evidence that Rachel had planned to take her own life and stated that 'there was no intention of agencies to mislead or demoralise [Rachel] – this was the consequences of misinformation and structural difficulties.'

Young person specific support groups

As already mentioned earlier in this chapter, the Samaritans are a key support group in relation to suicide. In terms of children and young people, another key organisation and charity for professionals to be aware of is Papyrus. They are a national charity dedicated to the prevention of suicide in young people. They are active members of the National Suicide Prevention Strategy Advisory Group in England. The beliefs that guide their thinking are:

- PREVENTION: Many young suicides are preventable.

- PASSION: Those who are touched personally by a young suicide have a unique contribution to make to our work.

- HOPE: No young person should have to suffer alone with thoughts or feelings of hopelessness and nobody should have to go through the heartbreak of losing a young person to suicide.

- LEARNING: There are always lessons to be learned from listening to young people at risk of suicide, those who give them support and those who have lost a young person to suicide.

A key piece of work they do is providing confidential helpline support and advice to young people struggling with thoughts of suicide and anyone worried about a young person. The helpline number is HOPELINEUK 0800 068 41 41. This number is for professionals to call for advice as well.

They also run training throughout the UK with the objective of equipping both professionals and volunteers with the skills to prevent suicide in young people. They are a leading supplier of the ASIST training mentioned earlier in this chapter.

Further information is available from their website: https://papyrus-uk.org/

References

Aitken R and Munro V (2018) *Domestic Abuse and Suicide: Exploring the links with Refuge's client base and work force* [online]. Refuge and Warwick Law School. Available at: www.refuge.org.uk/wp-content/uploads/2018/07/domestic-abuse-suicide-refuge-warwick-july2018.pdf (accessed September 2019).

Hartley K (2018) *Joint Cambridgeshire and Peterborough Suicide Prevention Strategy 2017-2020*. Public Health Cambridgeshire and Peterborough.

Home Office (2016) *Multi-agency Statutory Guidance for the Conduct of Domestic Homicide Reviews*. HM Government.

HM Government (2019) *Cross-Government Suicide Prevention Workplan*. HM Government.

HM Government (2019) *Preventing Suicide in England: Fourth progress report of the cross-government outcomes strategy to save lives*. HM Government

Klonsky ED, Victor SE & Saffer BY (2014) Non suicidal self-injury: what we know, and what we need to know. *Canadian Journal of Psychiatry*. **59** 565–8.

National Collaborating Centre for Mental Health October (2018) *Self-harm and Suicide Prevention Competence Framework: Adults and older adults*. Health Education England.

Office of National Statistics (2017) *Who is most at risk of suicide? Analysis and explanation of the contributory risks of suicide*. ONS

Office of National Statistics (2018) *Suicides in the UK: 2017 registrations*. ONS.

Public Health England (2019) *Suicide Prevention: Resources and guidance*. Public Health England.

Sidebotham P, Brandon M, Bailey S, Belderson P, Dodsworth J, Garstang J, Harrison E, Retxer A and Sorenson P (2016) *Pathways to Harm Pathways to Protection: Triennial analysis of Serious Case Reviews 2011 – 2014*. University of Warwick and University of East Anglia. Department for Education.

University of Manchester (2016) *Suicide by Children and Young People in England. National confidential inquiry into suicide and homicide by people with mental illness* (NCISH). Manchester.

University of Manchester (2017) *Suicide by Children and Young People. National Confidential inquiry into suicide and homicide by people with mental illness* (NCISH). Manchester.

Chapter 11: Channel: Safeguarding individuals vulnerable to radicalisation

By Paul Rollinson and Dr Amy McKee (edited by Russell Wate)

Chapter overview

- Background.
- Overview of radicalisation.
- What is Channel.
- Multi-agency safeguarding response.
- Support packages: education, mentoring and diversion.

Introduction

In 2017 the UK suffered five terrorist attacks that led to the deaths of 36 innocent people and injured hundreds more. Furthermore, between 2017 and 2018 the police and MI5 disrupted a further 12 Islamist and four extreme right-wing terror plots (HM Government, 2018). However, the threat of terrorism towards the UK is not a new phenomenon.

Throughout the latter half of the 20th century, terrorists have been responsible for repeated attacks on UK interests, both at home and overseas. In the 30-year period between 1969 and 1998, Irish-related terrorism claimed the lives of 3,500 people from the UK alone (HM Government, 2009). Then, following the September 11th attacks in the US, there was a dramatic shift in focus to the threat posed by extremist Islamist groups who wrongly use religion to justify violence as they seek to inflict mass casualty attacks in the UK and across western Europe (HM Government, 2006a).

What is new, though, is the threat from home-grown radicalised terrorists. In 2006, the former Director General of the Security Service declared that there is an increasing threat from radicalised individuals because:

'*...more and more people are moving from passive sympathy towards active terrorism through being radicalised or indoctrinated by friends, families, in organised training events here and overseas, by images on television, through chat rooms and websites on the internet.*' (Manningham-Buller, 2006)

This threat from radicalised British citizens has now been realised in several high-profile events such as the attacks on July 7th 2005, when four British citizens carried out near simultaneous suicide bombings in London, killing 56 people and injuring over 700 (Intelligence and Security Committee, 2006), to the more recent suicide bomb attack at a music concert committed by Manchester-born Salman Abedi in 2017, which resulted in the deaths of 22 innocent people and injuring over 500 more (Greater Manchester Police, 2017).

In recognition of the threat now posed by radicalised, home-grown individuals, significant emphasis is placed on the 'Prevent' strand of the government's counter terrorism strategy, CONTEST, which aims to stop people becoming terrorists or supporting terrorism. In support of this aim, the government introduced the Counter Terrorism and Security Act (2015), which placed a statutory duty on specified authorities to have 'due regard to the need to prevent people from being drawn into terrorism' (HM Government, 2015).

One of the key initiatives devised as part of the government's Prevent strategy is to focus on the underlying causes of extremism and prevent radicalisation among vulnerable individuals. As part of this Prevent strategy there has now been a national roll-out of the government's Channel project, a holistic safeguarding strategy that seeks to identify individuals at risk of radicalisation and reduce their vulnerability through multi-agency support and community-based interventions (HM Government, 2010).

Overview of radicalisation

It is important to understand the causes of terrorism in order to establish what may be done to reduce the risk of radicalisation, and it is important to distinguish the difference between the concepts of recruitment and radicalisation, as they are not mutually exclusive. Although essentially related, the difference lies in that recruitment involves practical steps towards inclusion in a specific group that advocates political violence, whereas radicalisation represents the underlying processes that changes an individual's general attitude towards the use of violence for political aims (Jensen, 2006).

In this context, radicalisation is understood to be *'a process of personal development whereby an individual adopts ever more extreme political or political-religious ideas and goals, becoming convinced that the attainment of these goals justifies extreme methods.'* (Ongering, 2007).

Dominant vulnerability factors include a lack of identity, social isolation and alienation from mainstream values, which can all lead vulnerable individuals to question their identity. When such an individual begins to ask what it means to be British in a multi-cultural Britain, or to be a Muslim in Britain, they often find conflicting messages from within their family, friends and the media, leading them to start looking elsewhere for answers. It is then that they become at risk of radicalisation as they potentially become exposed to violent and extreme narratives. When this happens, new people or groups to which they are exposed will often give the individual a new focus and feeling of self-importance, increasing their self-esteem as they become part of something with a renewed sense of purpose and belonging (Post, 1990).

Another factor commonly cited as a cause of terrorism is that of religion – the high-profile terrorist attacks on the West, such as 9/11 and 7/7, perpetrated by violent Muslim extremists under the pretext of a religious ideology, reinforced this view. However, the British Security Service acknowledges that religion can actually be a protective factor against radicalisation. It is often the misinterpretation of religious narratives that can serve to radicalise vulnerable individuals. However, when the correct meaning and interpretations are understood, religion can act as a counter-narrative to previously held beliefs. In addition to this, the social and community structured nature of religious practices can serve to protect against other vulnerabilities, such as isolation, lack of peer support and low self-esteem. Therefore, religion in itself should not be considered a root cause of terrorism.

Finally, an important concept to consider is that terrorists are, in essence, normal. A comparison of both political and non-political murders in Ireland identified that the politically motivated murders were committed by individuals who came from more secure and settled environments and that the occurrence of 'psychological disturbance' was significantly lower than in the non-political murders carried out by common criminals. It has also been recognised that the majority of the terrorists who carried out the September 11th attacks were college educated and from middle class families. The so-called leader of the 7/7 bombers, Mohammed Sidique Khan, for example, was a married father of one who held a respectable job as a teaching assistant (BBC, 2001), and Salman Abedi was like most other young boys with whom he attended school and college (BBC, 2017). In fact, normality is often seen as a necessary trait among recruits as they are more reliable and less likely to attract unnecessary attention.

Given that so many people experience the same underlying risk factors that can lead to radicalisation, the fact that so few ultimately engage in terrorism can only be attributed to individual differences. It is this that makes every case unique and so difficult to establish a preventative panacea. However, the introduction of the government's Channel Project, which utilises collaborative working between the police and local authorities to identify and support individuals at risk of radicalisation, is the first step towards such a preventative paradigm.

Key learning points

- Radicalisation is process of personal development.
- Vulnerable individuals are 'normal'.
- Religion alone is not a risk factor, and can be used to support against radicalisation.
- Key vulnerabilities include:
  - presence of grievances
  - feelings of humiliation
  - lack of personal identity
  - isolation
  - low self-esteem.

What is Channel?

Channel is a local authority chaired, multi-agency early intervention strategy aimed at safeguarding vulnerable individuals from being drawn into terrorism. It uses existing collaboration between local authorities, statutory partners, the police and local communities to identify individuals at risk of being drawn into violent extremism, to assess the nature and extent of that risk, and to develop an appropriate support plan to safeguard that vulnerable individual (HM Government, 2015).

It is important to recognise that Channel does not focus solely on one form of extremism; instead it is concerned with all types of violent extremism including international and domestic extremism, as well as single issue extremists such as animal rights activists and environmental extremists.

It is also important to recognise that Channel is not about identifying those who pose an immediate risk to themselves or the public. Instead it is about the early identification of vulnerability. Those individuals who are identified as posing a current and credible threat should be referred directly to the police. However, where individuals are identified to be vulnerable to the process of radicalisation, a multi-agency approach should be adopted to safeguard them.

The Channel programme now provides national coverage across all policing areas of England and Wales, although delivery varies slightly from area to area, reflecting local demand and working practices. Each policing area has a specially trained police officer who acts as Channel Police Practitioner responsible for co-ordinating Channel cases. In some areas this role may be carried out by an officer as part of their wider responsibilities, in which case they may be referred to as a Channel SPOC (Single Point of Contact) or Prevent Officer (HM Government, 2015).

In its recent guidance, the government recognised the key role that safeguarding has to play in reducing the risk of radicalisation. It considers violent extremism as another form of exploitation, comparable to sexual exploitation, for example, and highlights the responsibility that multi-agency practitioners have in safeguarding those exposed to it (HM Government, 2015). This approach also recognises, therefore, that the risk factors associated with radicalisation (low self-esteem, isolation, lack of identity, grievances etc) are all synonymous with the risk factors associated with other high-risk activities that are already widely considered to be safeguarding issues, again such as sexual exploitation.

The safeguarding approach that Channel has adopted is therefore essential as the agencies working with Channel have existing safeguarding strategies in place for supporting individuals at risk. Through collaborative work with Channel, these existing strategies have been drawn upon to develop an understanding of who is at risk of radicalisation into violent extremism, and how to support and protect them against it.

The Channel assessment

Once an individual is identified as potentially at risk of radicalisation, the Channel SPOC responsible for that region carries out a vulnerability assessment, focusing on three factors specific to this agenda:

- Are they engaged with a group, cause or ideology?

- Do they intend to cause harm?

- Do they have the capability to cause harm?

Each dimension is considered independently from the others, for example it is possible to be engaged without intending to cause harm and also possible to intend to cause harm without being particularly engaged (HM Government, 2015).

Not all of the individuals identified will be assessed as being vulnerable to violent extremism. Where a referred individual demonstrates vulnerability not related to terrorism, the Channel Police Practitioner will signpost these cases to other more appropriate support services. This ensures that only cases where there is a genuine vulnerability to being drawn into terrorism are managed through the Channel process. For those cases where the individual is assessed as vulnerable to the process of radicalisation, the case will be referred to a Channel panel in order that a multi-agency safeguarding approach can be adopted as outlined in Chapter 9.

Between 2017 and 2018 there were 7,318 national referrals to Channel. Of these, 18% were identified as vulnerable to being drawn into terrorism and received support from Channel panels, 40% were signposted to other support services after being identified as vulnerable but not to terrorism, and 42% of referrals required no further action (Home Office, 2018).

Key learning points

- Vulnerability factors are synonymous with other high-risk safeguarding agendas.

- Channel SPOC conducts vulnerability assessments.

- Those at immediate risk of harm to self or others should be referred immediately to the police.

Channel Panels: a multi-agency safeguarding response

Recognising that the vulnerabilities around violent extremism are synonymous with those associated to other forms of exploitation, the Channel process uses a panel of professionals from a range of safeguarding bodies to co-ordinate a multi-agency response to safeguard vulnerable individuals against being drawn into terrorism. Just as mainstream safeguarding structures provide multi-agency support to individuals vulnerable to sexual exploitation, drug abuse, domestic violence or gang membership.

Chaired by the responsible local authority, this multi-agency response aims to bring together appropriate professionals from relevant disciplines to share information and develop an appropriately tailored support package, based on an assessment of the individual's vulnerability. Where other statutory safeguarding frameworks exist to manage wider vulnerabilities, the lead professional working with the vulnerable individual is required to attend the Channel panel, which aims to ensure specific support is in place to manage the risk of radicalisation.

A key point here is the tailoring of specific agencies to meet the needs of the vulnerable individual. This process begins with an initial Channel panel meeting of key professionals from various agencies looking holistically at the case in question, which reflects existing safeguarding guidance aimed at supporting any child or vulnerable adult from significant harm. Such a meeting provides a forum in which information can be shared and an agreement reached as to what support is required to safeguard the individual (HM Government, 2006b).

Participation in Channel is voluntary and all individuals who receive support through the Channel process are made aware that they are receiving support to reduce their vulnerability to being drawn into terrorism. For cases that relate to a child, the parent or guardian are asked to provide consent on their behalf (HM Government, 2015).

Support packages: education, mentoring and diversion

As previously discussed, there is no easy way to identify which individuals will become involved in violent extremism. Instead of looking to establish a specific 'profile' to identify those at risk, the Channel process is a preventative strategy that focuses on understanding the factors that make a person vulnerable to engaging with violent extremism. Such an approach recognises that the key to reducing these vulnerabilities already exists and does not require something significantly different specifically to achieve this. Experience has shown that mainstream safeguarding mechanisms can be used to holistically address the individual's vulnerabilities, with specific focus on education, mentoring and diversion.

Education is a significant area in which support can be provided to Channel referrals. One of the main types of support provided by educational establishments is their ability to provide a safe space to openly discuss and counter extremist views and perceived grievances, which play a key role in the radicalisation process. When considering this type of educational support, the support does not have to be specifically targeted towards the Channel referral but can be delivered to a much wider audience as part of classroom discussions and lesson plans, which is important when trying not to alienate or embarrass. Schools have for years delivered lesson plans around difficult subjects such as sex and drugs, and more recently they have started to address issues such as guns and gangs. Issues of radicalisation and violent extremism can also be discussed in a safe learning environment when tailored to the specific audience.

Schools therefore have an important role in providing a space where individuals can safely discuss such topics, which reflects recent guidance concerning the need for schools to assist in preventing violent extremism by helping their students 'develop the skills needed to evaluate effectively and discuss potentially controversial issues' (DCSF, 2008).

While Channel does not focus specifically on Islamic extremism, a significant barrier to the effectiveness of providing education in this context is often a lack of professional knowledge and understanding of Islam. So, while limited knowledge may suffice to engage in basic conversation, there have been instances where Channel referrals require specific input on their religion to counter extreme and violent beliefs. In these cases, the lead professional may consider help from within their local communities, and seek the support of local religious mentors who could hold regular sessions to discuss and challenge any inappropriate beliefs through the provision of counter narratives.

The wider use of mentoring should also be used as another common intervention to support Channel referrals. Such mentoring involves identifying a suitable mentor who can discuss the cause for concern with the subject, exploring the ideological and motivational factors causing movement towards, or engagement in, violent extremism, facilitating discussion and providing them with a point of contact should they wish to disengage with their current behaviour. This latter point is essential as it provides the subject with an exit strategy, so when they need it they know where to turn. However, it is important to recognise that this mentor should be appropriately identified so that they are able to connect at a local level with the referral. They need to be able to understand and relate to the environment and lifestyle in which the referral has been exposed, otherwise their support is likely to be rejected.

Another form of both mentoring and educational support that is commonly provided to Channel referrals is helping individuals to understand the consequences of their actions; something that those vulnerable to violent extremism often fail to comprehend. To address this issue, support may be provided by individuals that have since disengaged with similar extremist activities, who can put into context what they went through, why they went through it, and ultimately why and how they disengaged.

The provision of safe learning environments, educational or religious support and mentoring all aim to help the individuals formulate rational choices based on balanced messages. This is particularly relevant in the process of radicalisation where individuals are provided with a single narrative. This narrow, selective view of events prejudices mainstream views and promotes an extremist narrative to the point where rational choices are then made on partial and biased beliefs.

A third approach is the use of diversionary tactics, which work by building new peer groups and social networks, improving an individual's self-esteem and providing a new sense of purpose and belonging in a social environment. A consequence of this social engagement and group interaction is that it allows for personally held beliefs to be naturally challenged by peers, without any requirement for focusing on such topics. Diversionary activities also provide another important benefit in that they reduce the chance someone has of coming into contact with extremists. Engagement must start somewhere, and by removing or limiting this opportunity and replacing it with a positive outcome reduces the potential for engagement in violent extremism.

For most of the referrals of school age, educational establishments are able to provide diversionary support through their own school activities. However, for adult referrals, where extra-curricular activities are not a viable option, diversionary tactics can still be employed by providing other voluntary services, including the Prince's Trust, Duke of Edinburgh schemes and local community activity groups.

While experience has shown that tailored support around these three key areas can have a significant impact in reducing an individual's vulnerability to radicalisation, it is important that a holistic approach is taken to address the needs of the individual and their family.

Case study 1: Khalid

Khalid is a 17-year-old British Muslim who was reported to Channel after his family had noticed a change in his behaviour over a period of several months, ultimately resulting in Khalid being sectioned under the Mental Health Act (1983).

Khalid had recently started becoming more withdrawn from his family, he stopped going to work, started smoking cannabis and began spending lots of time on the internet in his bedroom. He started telling his parents that they were not following their religion as they should be and started to become much more controlling in his behaviour over them. Following a fall out with a neighbour, Khalid threw a rucksack at him and shouted 'Allah hu Akbar' as he ran away; shortly after this he was stopped in the street threatening to blow people up and he was subsequently 'sectioned' by local police officers.

A Channel panel was convened and chaired by the local authority safeguarding lead. The panel was made up of practitioners from the mental health team, domestic abuse team, MASH (multi-agency support team), local authority employment support services, local neighbourhood police team, the drug and alcohol team and his GP.

A tailored support plan was devised that sought to address and support his vulnerabilities.

■ The mental health practitioner provided a formulation around his mental health needs resulting in a diagnosis of drug-induced psychosis.

■ The drug and alcohol team provided a tailored support plan around his drug misuse.

■ The GP referred Khalid for anger management support and counselling.

■ A domestic advocate provided support to Khalid and his parents around domestic abuse.

■ The local authority employment and support team worked with Khalid to secure him a new job.

■ The local neighbourhood police officer obtained the support of the local Imam who provided Khalid with support and mentoring around his religion.

As a result, Khalid's behaviour and health improved. He disengaged from his drug misuse, he became gainfully employed, he re-engaged with the local mosque and his relationship with his family improved significantly. Consequently, he became less isolated and withdrawn and disengaged from spending long periods of time on the internet on his own, which his family believed was the root cause of his changing behaviour.

Case study 2: James

James was a 50-year-old white British male who was unemployed and had recently started attending EDL demonstrations resulting in several arrests for minor public order offences. James had also been reported to the Local Authority Housing team for allegedly making racist comments to a neighbouring Somali family. While at the address the Local Housing Officer identified a number of extreme right-wing items in his house, including swastikas, posters of Hitler and books related to the Nazi movement.

During a follow-up visit by the local neighbourhood team in response to the Housing Officer's report it was established that James had not been able to find a job since he left the Royal Navy and that he had been encouraged to attend EDL demonstrations after meeting some online friends through internet chat sites. James explained that his interest in Hitler was more historical but admitted that since engaging in on-line chat forums his views had become more extreme. James also reported suffering from anxiety and depression but disclosed that he had not sought help from his GP.

A Channel panel was convened and chaired by the Local Authority safeguarding lead. The panel was made up of practitioners from the Local Authority Housing team, Local Authority Supported Employment team, local neighbourhood police team, the Prevent officer and his GP.

- The GP provided support and medication for James' anxiety and depression.
- The GP referred James to the local Community Mental Health team who subsequently diagnosed him with bi-polar disorder, for which a support plan was devised.
- The Supported Employment team helped James secure meaningful employment and referred him to NOVA, a support group for veterans who have been arrested.
- The local police team invited James to speak with the Imam at the local Mosque to expose him to other cultures and religions.
- The Supported Employment team later recruited James to provide inputs to other out-of-work military veterans.

As a result of supporting his needs and vulnerabilities, James disengaged from the internet chat groups and stopped attending EDL demonstrations. He received the necessary support and counselling to manage his health issues and secured employment that reduced his isolation. James disclosed that the most impactful support he received was visiting the mosque and meeting people from other cultures and religions, which enabled him to challenge his own views and perceptions of others.

Conclusion

This chapter has discussed how the vulnerabilities associated with radicalisation are synonymous with those found in individuals exploited into other forms of high-risk activity. It is therefore important to recognise that there is a complex interplay between the vulnerabilities surrounding an individual, the environment and the influences that are present in a person's life, and that, dependent on their particular environment, a person may engage with any number of high-risk activities depending on who the influencer is.

As a consequence of embedding violent extremism within a safeguarding model, existing safeguarding frameworks that already exist to support against other forms of exploitation are ideally placed to protect against the processes of radicalisation and engagement in violent extremism. A knock-on effect of treating violent extremism through safeguarding frameworks is that it automatically lends itself to delivering support through existing mainstream intervention activities.

One of the difficulties that Channel faces is in quantifying the success of such preventative work. As Channel specifically focuses on vulnerability rather than an identified threat, it is not possible to predict that engagement in violent extremism is a certainty. In fact, as only a small percentage of individuals ever go on to engage in such activity, the probability is very small. Nevertheless, addressing these vulnerabilities at the earliest opportunity aims to provide the individual with the necessary resilience to reject extremist narratives and prevent future engagement in violent extremism.

Further reading

CONTEST: The United Kingdom's Strategy for Countering Terrorism. Available at: www.gov.uk/government/publications/counter-terrorism-strategy-contest-2018 (accessed September 2019).

HM Government: Revised Prevent Duty Guidance: for England and Wales. Available at: www.gov.uk/government/publications/prevent-duty-guidance (accessed September 2019).

HM Government: Channel Duty Guidance Protecting vulnerable people from being drawn into terrorism. Available at: www.gov.uk/government/publications/channel-guidance (accessed September 2019).

References

BBC (2001, March 2) *Profile: Mohammed Sidique Khan*. Retrieved from BBC News: www.bbc.com/news/uk-12621381 (Accessed September 2019).

BBC (2017, June 12) *Manchester attack: Who was Salman Abedi?* Retrieved from BBC News: www.bbc.co.uk/news/uk-40019135 (September 2019).

DCSF (2008) *Learning Together to be Safe: A toolkit to help schools contribute to the prevention of violent extremism* [online]. Nottingham: DCSF Publications. Available at: http://dera.ioe.ac.uk/8396/1/DCSF-Learning%20Together_bkmk.pdf (accessed September 2019).

Greater Manchester Police (2017). *Manchester Arena Attack Investigation Update*. Retrieved from Greater Manchester Police: www.gmp.police.uk/live/nhoodv3.nsf/TriageWebsitePages/A527CC1AE4C06DD2802581CB008006E6

HM Government (2006a) *Countering International Terrorism: The United Kingdom's strategy*. Norwich: The Stationery Office.

HM Government (2006b) *Working Together to Safeguard Children: A guide to inter-agency working to safeguard and promote the welfare of children*. Norwich: The Stationery Office.

HM Government (2010) *Pursue Prevent Protect Prepare: The United Kingdom's strategy for countering international terrorism* [online]. London: Home Office. Available at: www.gov.uk/government/uploads/system/uploads/attachment_data/file/228907/7833.pdf (accessed September 2019).

HM Government (2012) *Channel: Protecting vulnerable people from being drawn into terrorism* [online]. London: Home Office. Available at: www.gov.uk/government/uploads/system/uploads/attachment_data/file/118194/channel-guidance.pdf (accessed September 2019).

HM Government (2015) *Channel Duty Guidance: Protecting vulnerable people from being drawn into terrorism*. London.

HM Government (2015) *Revised Prevent Duty Guidance: for England and Wales*. London.

HM Government (2018) *CONTEST: The United Kingdom's Strategy for Countering Terrorism*. London.

Home Office (2018) *Individuals referred to and supported through the Prevent Programme, April 2017 to March 2018*. London: Home Office.

Intelligence and Security Committee (2006) *Report into the London Terrorist Attacks on 7 July 2005*. London.

Jensen MT (2006) *An Overview and Analysis of Jihadi Activity in Denmark 1990-2006*. Copenhagen: Danish Institute for International Studies.

Manningham-Buller E (2006) *The International Terrorist Threat to the UK* [online]. London: The Security Service. Available at: www.mi5.gov.uk/home/about-us/who-we-are/staff-and-management/director-general/speeches-by-the-director-general/the-international-terrorist-threat-to-the-uk.html (accessed September 2019).

Ongering L (2007) *Home-Grown Terrorism and Radicalisation in the Netherlands: Experiences, explanations and approaches* [online]. Available at: www.investigativeproject.org/documents/testimony/292.pdf (accessed September 2019).

Post JM (1990) Terrorist psycho-logic: terrorist behaviour as a product of psychological *forces. In: W Reich (Ed)* Origins of Terrorism: Psychologies, ideologies, theologies, states of mind (pp25–40). Cambridge: Cambridge University Press.